Sample Determination

201
Q&A

SAP Certified Application Associate
PLM-QM

ALSO BY BILLIE G. NORDMEYER

CALIBRATION INSPECTIONS
201 Q&A
SAP CERTIFIED APPLICATION ASSOCIATE – PLM-QM

CATALOGS & INSPECTION METHODS
201 Q&A
SAP CERTIFIED APPLICATION ASSOCIATE – PLM-QM

DEFECTS RECORDING
201 Q&A
SAP CERTIFIED APPLICATION ASSOCIATE – PLM-QM

DYNAMIC MODIFICATION
201 Q&A
SAP CERTIFIED APPLICATION ASSOCIATE – PLM-QM

INSPECTION LOT COMPLETION
201 Q&A
SAP CERTIFIED APPLICATION ASSOCIATE – PLM-QM

QUALITY COSTS
201 Q&A
SAP CERTIFIED APPLICATION ASSOCIATE – PLM-QM

STABILITY STUDIES
201 Q&A
SAP CERTIFIED APPLICATION ASSOCIATE – PLM-QM

TEST EQUIPMENT MANAGEMENT
201 Q&A
SAP CERTIFIED APPLICATION ASSOCIATE – PLM-QM

Sample Determination 201 Q&A

SAP Certified Application Associate PLM-QM

Billie G. Nordmeyer, MBA, MA

Library of Congress Cataloging in Publication Data has been applied for.

ISBN 13: 9781503120686
ISBN 10: 1503120686

Trademarks

Terms that are referred to in this book, which are known trademarks or service marks, are capitalized. The trademarks are the property of their owners. The inclusion in the book of any term that is a known trademark should not be thought to affect the validity of the trademark. The author of this book is not associated with any product or vendor mentioned in this book.

SAP EC is neither the author nor the publisher of this book, or affiliated with the author or publisher of this book in any way. Nor is SAP EC responsible for the content of the book. The book's content reflects the views of the author and not that of SAP EC. Any omissions or inaccuracies that might be present in this book, which do not correctly depict SAP EC or its products, are purely accidental, without maleficent intent.

Warning and Disclaimer

The author and publisher of this book have taken every precaution to ensure the content of the book is accurate and complete. Neither the author nor the publisher, however, assume any responsibility for inaccurate or inadequate information or for errors, inconsistencies or omissions in this book. Nor do the author or publisher assume any liability or responsibility to any person or entity for any damages or losses that result from the use of information published in this book. Neither the author nor the publisher guarantees that the use of the book will ensure that a candidate will pass any exam.

About the Author

Billie G. Nordmeyer, MBA, MA is an SAP consultant, trainer and published author. She has held Senior Consultant and Business Development Manager of SAP Practice positions with a "Big 4" consulting firm, three "Fortune 100" firms and six "Fortune Most Admired Companies." Nordmeyer has consulted with Fortune 100 and Fortune 500 enterprises and supported clients in the aerospace, oil and gas, software, retail, pharmaceutical and manufacturing industries. Nordmeyer holds a BSBA in accounting, an MBA in finance and an MA in international management.

CONTENTS

INTRODUCTION

A technical certification is a valuable achievement in part because employers consider it confirmation that a job candidate is a well-qualified professional. Accordingly, if your goal is a position with a consulting firm, a major firm in industry or a leading not-for-profit organization, SAP certification training will help you get there. SAP training aimed at enhancing your understanding of particular concepts so you might sit for a standardized exam and obtain a professional credential is available both online and at bricks-and mortar institutions. But some training programs fail to accomplish the key objective...namely, prepare a candidate to achieve a passing grade on a certification exam.

In an exam setting, you must identify correct answers to questions that may bear little resemblance to the way major concepts are presented in the day-to-day operation of SAP applications. Consequently, while in your professional life you may play a key role in support of SAP software and solutions, to do well on the exam, you'll need training that provides a global view of interrelated functions and activities. But some training programs fail to provide a certification candidate either the information needed to perform well during a testing process or the means necessary to identify his training needs.

You should also be aware that SAP certification exams assume that, as a certification candidate, you're knowledgeable about definitions and master data, as well as the application of a fairly extensive set of transactions and customizing functions. For example, during the testing process, you may be expected to recognize specific attributes of major transactions and customizing functions, definitions of key system elements, the interrelationship among all of these factors, or other characteristics of the system to which you may not be exposed on a daily basis. Your training program, however, may fail to provide a sufficient number of questions and explanations for you to learn or confirm your knowledge of even the most perfunctory concepts addressed by the certification exam.

What's more, when sitting for the certification exam and the answer to each question is one of several different -- and often complex -- alternatives, you want to be assured ahead of time that you can make the right choice. Reviewing documentation or working through a relatively small number of practice test questions, however, may not provide you with the practical skills needed to apply your knowledge in a multiple-choice testing environment.

Hence this book series for the SAP Certified Application Consultant PLM-QM exam that allows you to enhance and test your knowledge using hundreds of multiple-choice questions well before you take the actual exam. The 201 Q&A SAP Certified Application Consultant PLM-QM book series is composed of individual books, each of which addresses one module, scenario or master data that may be covered in the certification exam. In turn, each study guide, such as Calibration Inspections, provides both a short and detailed answer for each of the 201 questions included in the book. These explanations allow you to grasp the bigger picture, connect new information with prior knowledge and use this knowledge to increase your score on the actual exam.

In the case that you want to review and analyze your knowledge pertaining to only one topic, you can purchase the one book that addresses that topic. If instead, you want to review a number of topics the exam may address, you can purchase some or all of the books in the series. In either case, using the 201 practice exam questions provided in each book, you can analyze your training needs in regards to one function, scenario or master data and then focus your study on the specific areas where you need to enhance your knowledge. In either case, I wish you the best of luck on the exam!

CHAPTER I

QUESTIONS

QUESTIONS

Q-1:   You want to calculate a sample size in part on the basis of the inspection lot size. What is required to do so? Select all that apply.

A. Define sampling scheme

B. Assign sampling scheme to sampling procedure

C. Define dynamic modification rule

D. Assign dynamic modification procedure to task list characteristic

Short Answer: 109
Answer & Explanation: 130

Q-2:   You want to calculate a sample size on the basis of specifications that are documented in inspection characteristics. What is needed to do so?

A. Enter sampling procedure in the material master record inspection setup

B. Assign sampling procedure to the inspection characteristic

C. Assign sampling procedure to an inspection plan header

Short Answer: 109
Answer & Explanation: 131

Q-3:   Which of the following is a valid description of a sampling procedure? Select all that apply.

A. Rules that control the calculation of a sample size

B. Rules that control the number of inspection points to be created for each characteristic

C. Rules that govern the valuation of inspection characteristics during the results recording process

D. Rules that determine if a sample size for a characteristic is dynamically modified

Short Answer: 109
Answer & Explanation: 131

Q-4:   A control chart is used in a sampling procedure. What attributes of the chart are controlled by the control chart type? Select all that apply.

A. The characteristic values referenced in the control chart

B. The characteristics to which the control chart applies

C. The control variables referenced in the control chart

D. The algorithm used to calculate the chart's control limits

Short Answer: 109
Answer & Explanation: 132

Q-5: What statement is correct regarding an inspection with inspection points?

A. The inspection point type is defined in a sampling procedure

B. The number of inspection points created during an inspection is determined by the inspection point type defined in a task list

C. Valid inspection point types for a master recipe are "free inspection points" and "inspection points for plant maintenance"

Short Answer: 109
Answer & Explanation: 133

Q-6: A customer decides to valuate individual samples prior to valuating a characteristic. What sampling procedure control will enable them to do so? Select all that apply.

A. Independent multiple sampling control indicator

B. Valuation rule for independent multiple samples

C. Inspection points control indicator

D. Number of independent multiple samples

E. Lot size

Short Answer: 109
Answer & Explanation: 134

Q-7:   Why is the definition of a function module required in a valuation rule if dependent multiple samples are processed during a quality inspection?

A. Automatic valuation of dependent multiple samples

B. Manual valuation of dependent multiple samples if automatic valuation cannot be performed

C. Default valuation of dependent multiple samples

Short Answer: 109
Answer & Explanation: 135

Q-8:   What would you use to define inspection severities for a sampling scheme?

A. Valuation parameter

B. Acceptability constant

C. K-factor

D. Sampling plan table

Short Answer: 110
Answer & Explanation: 136

Q-9:   Which of the following elements are included in the structure of a sampling procedure? Select all that apply.

A. Sampling type

B. Valuation mode

C. Sampling plan

D. Sampling scheme

E. Inspection points

Short Answer: 110
Answer & Explanation: 138

Q-10:   The selection of the "no stage change" control indicator in a sampling procedure has what effect? Select all that apply.

A. A dynamic modification procedure is used to determine both the inspection scope and sample size

B. A dynamic modification procedure is not used to determine either the inspection scope or the sample size

C. The inspection severity that influences the calculation of the sample size for a characteristic is determined by the sampling procedure

D. The inspection severity that influences the sample size is determined by the sampling type

Short Answer: 110
Answer & Explanation: 139

Q-11: An inspection plan will not be used to conduct a quality inspection. What restriction pertains to the sampling procedure that will be used for the inspection? Select all that apply.

A. Valuation mode with no valuation parameters is selected

B. Valuation mode with valuation parameters is selected

C. Sampling scheme is assigned to the sampling procedure

D. Dynamic modification is not used to determine inspection scope

Short Answer: 110
Answer & Explanation: 140

Q-12: A valuation rule for independent multiple samples is used. What requirement is met by doing so?

A. Record inspection results for multiple individual samples prior to valuating characteristic

B. Inspection results are not recorded for each individual sample

C. Inspection results are recorded for each individual sample

D. Inspection results are recorded for characteristic rather than individual sample

Short Answer: 110
Answer & Explanation: 141

Q-13:   What is a prerequisite that enables double sampling inspections and multiple sampling inspections to be processed? Select all that apply.

A. Define function module for valuation of dependent multiple samples in valuation rule for dependent multiple samples

B. Specify less than 100 percent inspection

C. Define inspection points in task list

Short Answer: 110
Answer & Explanation: 142

Q-14:   A customer requires a sampling scheme for a variable inspection. The related sampling plan will consist of which of the following? Select all that apply.

A. Sample size

B. Acceptance number

C. K-factor

D. Rejection number

Short Answer: 110
Answer & Explanation: 143

Q-15: Which of the following is a true statement regarding a sampling scheme? Select all that apply.

A. Determines sample size on the basis of inspection lot size, inspection severity, or inspection severity and acceptable quality level

B. Requires the creation of sampling plans consisting of sample size, acceptance number c and rejection number d

C. Created only for attributive inspections and variable inspections

Short Answer: 110
Answer & Explanation: 145

Q-16: What setting is required for the system to determine a sample size on the basis of a quality level if a task list is not used for an inspection?

A. System retrieves the dynamic modification criteria from a sampling type

B. System retrieves the dynamic modification criteria from the inspection lot origin

C. System retrieves the dynamic modification criteria from the material master record inspection setup

Short Answer: 110
Answer & Explanation: 146

Q-17:   What is the significance of a sampling type to a sampling procedure?

A. Determines the formula used to calculate a sample size

B. Determines the rules used by the system to determine if a characteristic is accepted or rejected

C. Determines if a sampling procedure will be defined in a task list or a material master record

Short Answer: 111
Answer & Explanation: 147

Q-18:   A sampling procedure can be used to plan what types of samples? Select all that apply.

A. Single samples

B. Independent multiple samples

C. Dependent multiple samples

D. All of the above

E. None of the above

Short Answer: 111
Answer & Explanation: 148

Q-19:   What criteria influence the acceptance or rejection of characteristics when independent samples are used in a quality inspection?

A. Valuation rule that combines the valuations for individual samples

B. Valuation rule that valuates each individual sample separately

Short Answer: 111
Answer & Explanation: 149

Q-20:   What setting is required to valuate individual samples prior to the valuation of a characteristic?

A. Valuation mode with valuation rule for independent multiple samples

B. Independent multiple samples control indicator in the sampling procedure

C. Inspection points control indicator in sampling procedure

D. 100% inspection sampling type defined in sampling procedure

Short Answer: 111
Answer & Explanation: 150

Q-21:   A sampling procedure can be assigned to which of the following? Select all that apply.

A. Task list characteristic

B. Task list header

C. Inspection type in material master record

D. Task list operation

Short Answer: 111
Answer & Explanation: 151

Q-22:   Which of the following is an example of a
standard sampling procedure valuation mode? Select all that
apply.

A. Attributive inspection per nonconforming units

B. Attributive inspection per s-method

C. Variable inspection per nonconforming units

D. Variable inspection per s-method

E. No valuation parameters

Short Answer: 111
Answer & Explanation: 152

Q-23:   What method is used to assign a sampling
procedure to a characteristic if an inspection plan is not
used for a quality inspection?

A. Sampling procedure is specified in the inspection setup for a material master record inspection type

B. Sampling procedure is specified in the master inspection characteristic

C. Sampling procedure is assigned to a characteristic using the Customizing application

Short Answer: 111
Answer & Explanation: 154

Q-24:   A sampling procedure is created. However, independent multiple samples are referenced rather than single samples. What could be the issue?

A. Control indicator for independent multiple samples is set in sampling procedure

B. Control indicator for single samples is not deselected in sampling procedure

C. Control indicator for independent multiple samples is set in material master record and sampling procedure cancels each out

Short Answer: 111
Answer & Explanation: 155

Q-25:   What are the main activities that are performed in order to process a dependent multiple sample inspection? Select all that apply.

A. Set the dependent multiple samples control indicator in the sampling procedure

B. Define the number of dependent multiple samples in a sampling scheme

C. Define the valuation rule for dependent multiple samples for sampling procedure

Short Answer: 111
Answer & Explanation: 156

Q-26:   In what instance is a sampling scheme used in the sample determination process? Select all that apply.

A. Determine the number of physical samples to be inspected on the basis of an inspection lot size or the number of containers in an inspection lot

B. Define a normal, reduced, or tightened inspection

C. Specify the valuation parameter for the inspection type for which sampling scheme is used

D. Define the sample size on the basis of the sampling type

Short Answer: 112
Answer & Explanation: 157

Q-27:   What is the purpose of the blocking indicator in a sampling scheme header?

A. Prevents the assignment of the sampling scheme to an inspection characteristic

B. Prevents the assignment of the sampling scheme to the task list header

C. Prevents the assignment of the sampling scheme to a sampling procedure

Short Answer: 112
Answer & Explanation: 158

Q-28:   Attributive inspection on the basis of nonconforming units is an example of which of the following?

A. Usage indicator is defined in sampling procedure

B. Valuation mode defined in sampling procedure

C. Sampling type is defined in sampling procedure

Short Answer: 112
Answer & Explanation: 159

Q-29:   Which of the following is evaluated in an attributive inspection? Select all that apply.

A. Number of defects in a sample as compared to the acceptance number for each characteristic

B. Number of nonconforming units in a sample as compared to the acceptance number for each characteristic

C. Number of defects in a sample as compared to the rejection number for each characteristic

D. Number of nonconforming units in a sample as compared to the rejection number for each characteristic

Short Answer: 112
Answer & Explanation: 161

Q-30:   If the sampling procedure is defined for a characteristic in an inspection plan, which of the following is a standard sampling type used to determine the rules that govern the selection of a sample? Select all that apply.

A. 100 percent inspection

B. Variable sample

C. Sampling scheme

D. Percentage sample

E. Skip

Short Answer: 112
Answer & Explanation: 162

Q-31:   The customer wants to calculate the size of a sample on the basis of an inspection lot size as well as prior inspection results. What must exist to do so?

A. Dynamic modification rule stored in inspection plan and sampling procedure

B. Dynamic modification rule stored in inspection plan and sampling scheme

C. Dynamic modification rule stored in inspection plan and sampling plan

D. Allowed relationship maintained for sampling procedure and dynamic modification rule

Short Answer: 112
Answer & Explanation: 163

Q-32:   What method can be used to determine a sample size if an inspection is conducted without an inspection plan or material specification? Select all that apply.

A. "100%" inspection control indicator in material master record inspection setup

B. "Fixed percent" control indicator in material master record inspection setup

C. "Sampling procedure" control indicator in material master record inspection setup

D. "Variable percent" control indicator in material master record inspection setup

E. "Sampling plan" control indicator in material master record inspection setup

Short Answer: 112
Answer & Explanation: 164

Q-33:   The customer wants to record inspection results for a number of individual samples, valuate each sample separately and then valuate a characteristic on the basis of the recorded results for the multiple independent samples. How is the requirement met?

A. Define the single sample valuation type in the valuation mode using a valuation rule

B. Define the number of samples

C. Define the multiple samples valuation type in the valuation mode using a valuation rule

Short Answer: 113
Answer & Explanation: 165

Q-34:   What option can be used to valuate inspection results for double sampling inspections?

A. Automatic acceptance of samples

B. Manual acceptance of samples

C. Automatic rejection of samples

D. Manual rejection of samples

Short Answer: 113
Answer & Explanation: 166

Q-35:   You are processing multiple sampling inspections.
The number of defects in a sample is greater than the
acceptance number but less than the rejection number. As
a result, dependent multiple samples were not automatically
valuated by the system. How should the samples be
valuated?

A. Manual procedure used to valuate the sample

B. Select a different sampling scheme as a basis of
    valuating the samples

C. Change the sampling type to force the valuation of the
    samples

Short Answer: 113
Answer & Explanation: 167

Q-36:   A sampling scheme without valuation parameters
can be created for which of the following? Select all that
apply.

A. Sampling procedure for sample calculation for
    inspection without a task list

B. Sampling procedure for sample calculation for inspection without a sampling plan

C. Sampling procedure for a sample calculation for an inspection without a sampling table

D. Sampling scheme in sample-drawing procedure

Short Answer: 113
Answer & Explanation: 169

Q-37: A valuation parameter for the sampling type for which a sampling scheme is used is found where?

A. Sampling scheme

B. Sampling type

C. Sampling procedure

Short Answer: 113
Answer & Explanation: 170

Q-38: During sample determination for an inspection lot, the inspection severity is determined on what basis?

A. Dynamic modification level

B. Quality level

C. Valuation rule

D. Dynamic modification rule

Short Answer: 113
Answer & Explanation: 172

Q-39:   The rules that determine if a characteristic or sample is accepted or rejected for its intended purpose are defined where?

A. Valuation mode defined in a material master

B. Valuation mode defined in a sampling scheme

C. Valuation mode defined in a sampling procedure

D. Valuation mode defined in a sampling plan

Short Answer: 113
Answer & Explanation: 172

Q-40:   The customer wants a certain percentage of the inspection lot to be automatically selected as the sample. However, a task list will not be used to inspect the material. What is required to accomplish this objective?

A. Percentage sample control indicator in the inspection lot header

B. Percentage sample control indicator in the characteristic

C. Percentage sample control indicator in the dynamic modification rule

D. Percentage sample control indicator in the material master record inspection setting for inspection type

Short Answer: 113
Answer & Explanation: 173

Q-41: In what circumstance does the sampling procedure structure require the entry of a control chart type?

A. Requirement for a fixed sample with valuation on the basis of action limits

B. Requirement for a 100% sample with valuation on the basis of action limits

C. Requirement for a percentage sample with valuation on the basis of action limits

Short Answer: 113
Answer & Explanation: 174

Q-42: What is the purpose of the valuation rule in a sampling procedure?

A. Define inspection type in the valuation mode

B. Define the valuation type in the valuation mode

C. Define sampling type in the valuation mode

Short Answer: 113
Answer & Explanation: 175

Q-43: The customer wants to accept or reject a characteristic during a quality inspection on the basis of the actual number of defects in a sample as compared to a predefined acceptable number of defects in a sample. What setting is required to do so?

A. Variable inspection according to s-method valuation mode defined in the sampling procedure

B. Variable inspection on the basis of nonconforming units valuation mode defined in the sampling procedure

D. Attributive inspection according to s-method valuation mode defined in the sampling procedure

E. Attributive inspection on the basis of nonconforming units valuation mode defined in the sampling procedure

Short Answer: 113
Answer & Explanation: 176

Q-44:   The current inspection severity to be used in a sampling scheme is influenced by which of the following? Select all that apply.

A. Quality level

B. Dynamic modification rule

C. Sampling plan

Short Answer: 114
Answer & Explanation: 178

Q-45: The customer wants to ensure that the dynamic modification of the inspection scope does not play a role in the sample determination process. What setting is required to accommodate the requirement?

A. Special control indicator in the sampling procedure

B. Special control indicator in the sampling plan

C. Special control indicator in the sampling scheme

Short Answer: 114
Answer & Explanation: 179

Q-46: A sampling scheme sampling table may apply to which of the following?

A. AQL

B. Inspection severity

C. Inspection severity and AQL

Short Answer: 114
Answer & Explanation: 179

Q-47: What component can be used to both evaluate samples on the basis of inspection characteristic values and implement statistical process control by means of a control chart.

A. Sample Determination

B. SPC

C. Quality Management

Short Answer: 114
Answer & Explanation: 181

Q-48:   Which of the following is defined in a sampling procedure? Select all that apply.

A. Sampling type

B. Inspection type

C. Valuation mode

D. Valuation rule

Short Answer: 114
Answer & Explanation: 182

Q-49:   The customer wants to prevent the execution of the dynamic modification procedure that would otherwise impact the calculation of the sample size. How is the requirement met?

A. Deselect the sampling type in the sampling procedure

B. Select the special control indicator in the sampling procedure

C. Deselect the usage control indicator in the sampling procedure

D. Select the valuation mode in the sampling procedure

Short Answer: 114
Answer & Explanation: 183

Q-50:   What setting in a sampling procedure is required to use multiple independent samples in an inspection?

A. Usage control indicator

B. Valuation rule

C. Sampling scheme sampling type

Short Answer: 114
Answer & Explanation: 183

Q-51:   Why is a sampling table used in a sampling scheme?

A. Relates the allowable number or percentage of nonconforming units to an inspection severity and inspection lot quantity

B. Relates inspection lot quantity to inspection severity and to accepted number of units or percentage of accepted units

C. Relates inspection lot quantity to normal, reduced, or tightened inspection and accepted number of units or percentage of accepted units

Short Answer: 114

Answer & Explanation: 185

Q-52:   Identify an entry in a sampling scheme header.
Select all that apply.

A. Text

B. Valuation mode

C. Sampling table variable

D. Inspection severity

E. AQL value

Short Answer: 114
Answer & Explanation: 186

Q-53:   A sampling plan requires the entry of an
acceptability constant. Why?

A. Defines the maximum number of nonconforming units
    that leads to the acceptance of the sample

B. Defines the minimum quality score that leads to the
    acceptance of the sample

C. Defines the minimum number of conforming units that
    leads to the rejection of the sample

Short Answer: 114
Answer & Explanation: 187

Q-54:   The customer has decided that a sampling scheme should be used to calculate the sample size. What setting is required to accomplish this objective?

A. Sampling type in sampling procedure

B. Valuation mode in sampling procedure

C. Inspection point type in sampling procedure

D. Special indicator in sampling procedure

Short Answer: 114
Answer & Explanation: 189

Q-55:   The customer wants to use control charts in the quality inspection process. How is this requirement met?

A. Control chart type in the sampling procedure

B. Control chart type in the sampling plan

C. Control chart type in the sampling scheme

Short Answer: 114
Answer & Explanation: 189

Q-56:   What determines if a sampling scheme is a required entry in a sampling procedure?

A. Sampling type

B. Control chart type

C. Inspection type

Short Answer: 114
Answer & Explanation: 190

Q-57:   Identify an option that can be used to valuate the inspection results of dependent multiple samples. Select all that apply.

A. Immediate acceptance of the sample

B. Immediate rejection of the sample

C. No valuation of samples

D. All of the above

E. None of the above

Short Answer: 115
Answer & Explanation: 191

Q-58:   Which of the following is a valid definition of the AQL value that is specified in a sampling plan table? Select all that apply.

A. Minimum number of accepted units per 100 units that ensures acceptance of the inspection lot during quality inspection

B. Maximum number of defects per 100 units that does not preclude acceptance of the inspection lot during quality inspection

C. Maximum percentage of defects per 100 units that does not preclude acceptance of the inspection lot during quality inspection

D. Minimum number of defects per 100 units that precludes the acceptance of an inspection lot during a quality inspection

Short Answer: 115
Answer & Explanation: 192

Q-59:   Identify a prerequisite to the creation of a sampling procedure.   Select all that apply.

A. Sampling type

B. Valuation mode

C. Control chart type

D. Quality level

E. Sampling procedure

Short Answer: 115
Answer & Explanation: 194

Q-60:   What is included in a sampling plan that specifies the maximum number of defects in a sample that leads to the acceptance of an inspection lot for an attributive inspection?

A. Acceptance number c

B. Acceptability constant

C. Rejection number d

Short Answer: 115
Answer & Explanation: 195

Q-61: At what level in a task list is a sampling procedure normally defined? Select all that apply.

A. Task list header level

B. Task list operation level

C. Task list characteristic level

Short Answer: 115
Answer & Explanation: 196

Q-62: Which of the following is considered to be a special condition that can be defined for a sampling procedure? Select all that apply.

A. Valuation mode

B. Sampling scheme

C. Control chart type

D. Inspection points

E. Sampling type

Short Answer: 115
Answer & Explanation: 196

Q-63: Which of the following is a parameter of a sampling scheme used by the system to determine the sample size if a fixed sample and an attributive inspection valuation mode is required? Select all that apply.

A. Sample size

B. K-factor

C. Acceptance number

D. Inspection frequency

Short Answer: 115
Answer & Explanation: 197

Q-64: What controls the valuation of a sample on the basis of action limits?

A. Control chart type in the sampling procedure

B. Sampling type in the sampling procedure

C. Inspection type in the material master record

Short Answer: 115
Answer & Explanation: 198

Q-65: Why is the dependent multiple samples control indicator selected in a sampling procedure?

A. Enables the valuation of an inspection lot following the valuation of a number of individual samples

B. Enables the valuation of a characteristic following the valuation of a number of individual characteristics

C. Enables the valuation of a characteristic following the valuation of a number of dependent multiple samples

D. Enables the valuation of an inspection lot after the valuation of a number of individual characteristics

Short Answer: 115
Answer & Explanation: 199

Q-66:   Which of the following is used in a sampling scheme to represent the maximum number of defects per 100 units that does not preclude the acceptance of the inspection lot?

A. Inspection severity

B. Valuation parameter

C. AQL value

D. K-factor

Short Answer: 115
Answer & Explanation: 200

Q-67:   A sampling scheme can be used for which of the following?

A. Independent multiple samples

B. Dependent multiple samples

C. Single samples

Short Answer: 115
Answer & Explanation: 202

Q-68:   The customer requires a sample size equal to100 percent inspection. How is this requirement defined?

A. Sampling procedure

B. Sampling type

C. Sampling scheme

D. Valuation mode

Short Answer: 115
Answer & Explanation: 203

Q-69:   Where is the Acceptability Constant for a variable inspection defined?

A. Sampling scheme

B. Sampling plan

C. Sampling procedure

Short Answer: 116

Answer & Explanation: 204

Q-70:   What setting establishes the maximum number of samples to which a sampling plan applies?

A. Sample size

B. Acceptability Constant

C. Lot size

Short Answer: 116
Answer & Explanation: 205

Q-71:   A control chart type can be defined in which of the following?

A. Sampling scheme

B. Sampling plan

C. Sampling procedure

Short Answer: 116
Answer & Explanation: 206

Q-72:   Which of the following represents the significance of the valuation mode to the sample determination process? Select all that apply.

A. A parameter used to determine the sample size

B. A criterion used to determine the sampling scheme

C. A parameter used to define the rules for the acceptance or rejection of characteristic or sample during a quality inspection

D. A criterion used to select the sampling plan

Short Answer: 116
Answer & Explanation: 207

Q-73:   Which of the following is an attribute of a sampling procedure for which dependent multiple samples are defined? Select all that apply.

A. Inspection points are defined in the task list

B. A sampling type with a sampling scheme is defined

C. A valuation mode for a variable inspection is defined

D. Function module defined to valuate dependent multiple samples in valuation mode

E. Dependent multiple samples control indicator set with Create Sampling Procedure transaction

Short Answer: 116
Answer & Explanation: 208

Q-74:   The user wants to determine the sample size on the basis of the lot size and inspection severity, or lot size, inspection severity and acceptable quality level of the material inspected. How is this objective accomplished?

A. Sampling procedure

B. Sampling plan

C. Dynamic modification rule

D. Sampling scheme

Short Answer: 116
Answer & Explanation: 210

Q-75:   Which of the following is defined at the header level in a sampling scheme? Select all that apply.

A. Quality level

B. Valuation mode

C. Sampling table description

D. Sampling plan

Short Answer: 116
Answer & Explanation: 210

Q-76:   A sampling plan defined for a variable inspection contains what elements? Select all that apply.

A. Sample size

B. Acceptance number

C. K-factor

D. Rejection number

Short Answer: 116
Answer & Explanation: 212

Q-77:   The customer wants to use inspection points in a quality inspection. Where is the control indicator set that determines the number of inspection points to be created for an inspection lot?

A. Sampling procedure

B. Inspection lot header

C. Sampling scheme

D. Sampling plan

Short Answer: 116
Answer & Explanation: 213

Q-78:   The sampling type and valuation mode are combined at what level in the sampling procedure structure?

A. Inspection lot

B. Inspection characteristic

C. Inspection operation

Short Answer: 116
Answer & Explanation: 214

Q-79:   Which of the following influences the sample determination process? Select all that apply.

A. Sampling plan

B. Sampling procedure

C. Dynamic modification rule

D. Task list or material specification

E. Material type

Short Answer: 116
Answer & Explanation: 215

Q-80:   A sampling scheme is assigned to which of the following?

A. Sampling procedure

B. Inspection characteristic

C. Inspection operation

D. Material master record

Short Answer: 116
Answer & Explanation: 216

Q-81:   A customer wants to use control charts to valuate characteristics during the conduct a quality inspection.
What setting is required to do so? Select all that apply.

A. Control limits

B. Special control indicator in sampling procedure

C. Control chart variables

D. 100% inspection control indicator in the material master record

E. Characteristics

Short Answer: 116
Answer & Explanation: 217

Q-82:   Each sampling procedure requires the entry of a valuation mode. Which valuation mode is used for a qualitative inspection?

A. Attributive inspection on the basis of nonconforming units

B. Attributive inspection according to s-method

C. SPC inspection

D. Inspection without valuation parameters

Short Answer: 117
Answer & Explanation: 218

Q-83:   What criteria influences the ability to process a dependent multiple sampling inspection? Select all that apply.

A. Inspection points in a task list

B. Sampling type with sampling scheme

C. Attributive inspection valuation mode

D. Function module defined for sampling type in the valuation rule

E. Dependent multiple samples control indicator

Short Answer: 117
Answer & Explanation: 219

Q-84:   Which of the following is used to define the criteria that determines if and on what basis a sample is accepted or rejected? Select all that apply.

A. Sampling scheme

B. Sampling procedure

C. Sampling plan

Short Answer: 117
Answer & Explanation: 220

Q-85:   A current inspection severity that is used in a sampling scheme is influenced by what? Select all that apply.

A. Quality level

B. Dynamic modification rule

C. Valuation mode

Short Answer: 117
Answer & Explanation: 221

Q-86:   What statement is true regarding a sampling plan?

A. Structure includes acceptability constant for an attributive inspection

B. Structure includes rejection number d for an attributive inspection

C. Structure includes an acceptance number c for an attributive inspection

Short Answer: 117
Answer & Explanation: 222

Q-87:   How would you define the minimum number of defects in a sample that leads to the rejection of the sample following a quality inspection?

A. Acceptance number c

B. Acceptability constant

C. Rejection number d

Short Answer: 117
Answer & Explanation: 223

Q-88:   Valuation mode, sampling type, and multiple samples are examples of controls that are set in the structure of which of the following?

A. Sampling procedure

B. Sampling scheme

C. Sampling plan

D. Material master record

Short Answer: 117
Answer & Explanation: 225

Q-89:   What is a difference between one control chart type that is defined in a sampling procedure and another? Select all that apply.

A. Characteristics

B. Control variables

C. Calculation of control limits

E. Special control indicators

F. Usage indicators

Short Answer: 117
Answer & Explanation: 226

Q-90: What element is used to define a valuation rule for dependent multiple samples that are required for the conduct of a quality inspection?

A. Valuation mode in sampling procedure

B. Dependent multiple samples control indicator in sampling procedure

C. Sampling type in sampling procedure

Short Answer: 117
Answer & Explanation: 227

Q-91: Which of the following is the purpose of the inspection severity in a sampling scheme? Select all that apply.

A. Selection of normal, reduced or tightened inspection

B. Means of adjusting the inspection effort to reflect the current quality of material as measured by inspection results

C. Means of adjusting the probability of acceptance of a material during quality inspection

D. Means of specifying the maximum number of nonconforming units that are permitted for the acceptance of the inspection lot

Short Answer: 117
Answer & Explanation: 228

Q-92:   What requirement is met by entering the lot size, sample size and k-factor in a sampling table?

A. Create a sampling scheme for an attributive inspection

B. Create a sampling scheme for a variable inspection

C. Create a sampling scheme without valuation parameters

Short Answer: 117
Answer & Explanation: 229

Q-93:   What is the difference between the acceptability constant that is defined for a variable inspection and the acceptance number c that is defined for an attributive inspection?

A. An acceptability constant determines the minimum quality score that leads to the acceptance of a sample and an acceptance number c determines the maximum number of defects that leads to the acceptance of a sample

B. An acceptance number c determines the minimum number of nonconforming units that leads to the rejection of a sample and an acceptability constant determines the minimum quality score that leads to the acceptance of a sample

C. An acceptability constant determines the maximum quality score that leads to the rejection of a sample and an acceptance number c determines the maximum number of defects that leads to the acceptance of a sample

Short Answer: 118
Answer & Explanation: 230

Q-94:   The system does not incorporate the use of control chart data in the quality inspection process. What should be considered to correct this issue?

A. De-selection of the special indicator in the sampling procedure

B. Entry of the control chart type in sampling procedure

C. Selection of the usage indicator in the sampling procedure

D. Selection of the fixed sample sampling type

E. Selection of the valuation on basis of action limits valuation mode

Short Answer: 118
Answer & Explanation: 232

Q-95:   Each sampling procedure requires that a valuation mode be defined. Which valuation mode is used for a quantitative inspection?

A. Variable inspection on the basis of nonconforming units

B. Variable inspection according to s-method

C. SPC inspection

Short Answer: 118
Answer & Explanation: 233

Q-96:   What option can be used to process dependent multiple samples?

A. Dependent multiple samples control indicator in sampling procedure

B. Dependent multiple samples control indicator in sampling plan

C. Dependent multiple samples control indicator in sampling scheme

Short Answer: 118
Answer & Explanation: 234

Q-97:   Normal, reduced, and tightened are examples of which of the following?

A. Valuation parameter

B. Inspection severity

C. AQL value

D. K-factor

Short Answer: 118
Answer & Explanation: 235

Q-98:   What is controlled by the attributive inspection valuation parameters in a sampling procedure? Select all that apply.

A. Sample size

B. K-factor

C. Acceptance number

D. Rejection number

Short Answer: 118
Answer & Explanation: 236

Q-99:   What function can be used to create a sampling scheme? Select all that apply.

A. Create sampling scheme function

B. Copy sampling scheme function

C. Reference sampling scheme function

Short Answer: 118
Answer & Explanation: 237

Q-100:   Which of the following is a true statement regarding a sampling scheme sampling plan? Select all that apply.

A. The sample size defines the upper limit to which the sampling plan applies

B. The acceptability constant is the minimum quality score that leads to an acceptance of a sample

C. The acceptance number c is minimum number of conforming units in a sample that leads to an acceptance of a sample

D. The rejection number d is the minimum number of nonconforming units in a sample that leads to the rejection of a sample

Short Answer: 118
Answer & Explanation: 238

Q-101:   Which of the following must be available in order to conduct a variable inspection according to s-method?

A. Sampling type in sampling procedure

B. Valuation mode in sampling procedure

C. Sampling type in sampling scheme

D. Valuation mode in sampling scheme

Short Answer: 118

Answer & Explanation: 240

Q-102: What element of the sample determination process can be used to prevent the dynamic modification of a sample size?

A. No stage change control indicator in the sampling procedure

B. No stage change control indicator in the sampling plan

C. No stage change control indicator in the sampling scheme

Short Answer: 119
Answer & Explanation: 241

Q-103: "Attributive inspection on the basis of nonconforming units" is an example of what?

A. Valuation mode that determines the rules for the acceptance or rejection of a characteristic or sample

B. Valuation rule that determines the rules for the acceptance or rejection of a characteristic or sample

C. Valuation type that determines the rules for the acceptance or rejection of a characteristic or sample

D. Valuation procedure that determines the rules for the acceptance or rejection of a characteristic or sample

Short Answer: 119

Answer & Explanation: 242

Q-104:   What criteria is used to define dependent multiple samples in a sampling procedure? Select all that apply.

A. Task list inspection points

B. Sampling type with a sampling scheme

C. Valuation mode for a variable inspection

D. Function module for the valuation of dependent multiple samples is defined in the valuation rule for dependent multiple samples

E. Dependent multiple samples control indicator in sampling plan

Short Answer: 119
Answer & Explanation: 243

Q-105:   Identify an "additional function" that is used in relation to a where-used list for a sampling procedure. Select all that apply.

A. Replace sampling procedure in task list

B. Display sampling plan

C. Display master inspection characteristic

D. Display inspection type

E. Display material master record

Short Answer: 119
Answer & Explanation: 244

Q-106:   An inspection severity in a sampling table of a sampling scheme reflects which of the following?

A. The probability of acceptance of the inspection lot and the anticipated inspection effort based on an existing quality level

B. The maximum fraction of nonconforming units per 100 units that is permitted for an inspection lot to be accepted

C. The basis of the acceptance or rejection of a characteristic

D. The number of physical samples per the lot size

Short Answer: 119
Answer & Explanation: 245

Q-107:   Each sampling scheme requires the definition of an inspection severity. Why?

A. A means to select the appropriate sampling plan in a sampling scheme

B. A means to adjust the requirements of an individual inspection on the basis of the current quality level of the material that is inspected.

C. A means to adjust the requirements of an individual inspection on the basis of the current quality level of the material that is inspected that in turn infers the probability of an 'accepted' valuation of the inspection lot

D. A means to select an appropriate AQL value

Short Answer: 119
Answer & Explanation: 246

Q-108: What is the purpose of a sampling plan?

A. Document lot size, sample size, and acceptability constant or acceptance number used to determine if a sample is accepted or rejected

B. Determine the sample size on the basis of lot size, inspection severity or inspection severity and the actual quality level

C. Define the rules that determine the calculation of the sample size and the valuation of inspection results for a characteristic

Short Answer: 119
Answer & Explanation: 247

Q-109: "Percentage sample" and "variable inspection according to s-method" are examples of what?

A. Sampling scheme parameters

B. Sampling procedure parameters

C. Sampling plan parameters

Short Answer: 119
Answer & Explanation: 248

Q-110:   Which of the following is needed to ensure that individual characteristics are not dynamically modified?

A. Special control indicator in the sampling procedure

B. Usage control indicator in the sampling procedure

C. Sampling type in the sampling procedure

Short Answer: 119
Answer & Explanation: 250

Q-111:   Each sampling procedure requires a valuation mode. Which of the following is a standard valuation mode used for qualitative inspection characteristics?

A. Variable inspection according to s-method

B. Valuation according to control chart limits

C. Valuation based on inspection point results

Short Answer: 119
Answer & Explanation: 250

Q-112: Identify an entry in a where-used list for a sampling procedure. Select all that apply.

A. Sampling type

B. Number of times used

C. Material master

D. Operation number

E. Dynamic modification criteria

Short Answer: 120
Answer & Explanation: 252

Q-113: To adjust the probability of acceptance of an inspection lot, as well as the effort employed to inspect a material, the system uses which of the following?

A. Inspection severity defined in a sampling table in a sampling procedure

B. Inspection severity defined in a sampling table in a sampling scheme

C. Inspection severity defined in a sampling table in a sampling plan

Short Answer: 120
Answer & Explanation: 252

Q-114: In what way does a quality level lead to a sampling plan in a sampling scheme?

A. The quality level and dynamic modification rule determine an inspection severity and the inspection severity leads to the sampling plan in the sampling scheme

B. An inspection severity and dynamic modification rule determine a quality level and the quality level leads to the sampling plan in the sampling scheme

C. A quality level and an inspection severity determine the dynamic modification rule and the dynamic modification rule leads to the sampling plan in the sampling scheme

Short Answer: 120
Answer & Explanation: 254

Q-115: Identify a type of inspection for which a sampling scheme is created.

A. Attributive inspection

B. Variable inspection

C. Inspection without valuation parameters

Short Answer: 120
Answer & Explanation: 255

Q-116: Which of the following is an element of a sampling plan for a variable inspection used to define the lowest quality score that allows the acceptance of a sample?

A. Acceptability constant

B. Acceptance number

C. Acceptance constant

D. Acceptability number

Short Answer: 120
Answer & Explanation: 257

Q-117: How would you define the rules that determine the way the system calculates a sample size and valuates an inspection characteristic during the inspection process?

A. Sampling scheme

B. Sampling procedure

C. Sampling plan

D. Material master record inspection type

Short Answer: 120
Answer & Explanation: 258

Q-118: How would you determine the particular characteristics to be referenced in a control chart that is used in a sampling procedure, as well as the manner in which control chart control limits are calculated?

A. Special control indicator in sampling procedure

B. Control chart type in sampling procedure

C. Control chart control variables in sampling scheme

Short Answer: 120
Answer & Explanation: 259

Q-119:   The data displayed in the where-used list for a sampling procedure includes which of the following?

A. Dynamic modification rule

B. Material number

C. Inspection characteristic

Short Answer: 120
Answer & Explanation: 260

Q-120:   The inspection severity that is defined in a sampling scheme is closely associated with which of the following?

A. The maximum percentage of nonconforming units per 100 units permitted for an inspection lot to be accepted

B. Inspection scope

C. AQL value

D. The maximum number of nonconforming units per 100 units permitted for an inspection lot to be accepted

Short Answer: 120
Answer & Explanation: 260

Q-121: An AQL value is defined in a sampling scheme. Why? Select all that apply.

A. Define the minimum number of conforming units permitted per 100 units for the lot to be accepted

B. Define the maximum number of defects permitted per 100 units for the lot to be accepted

C. Define the minimum number of defects permitted per 100 units for the lot to be rejected

D. Define the maximum fraction of nonconforming units permitted per 100 units for the lot to be accepted

Short Answer: 120
Answer & Explanation: 262

Q-122: A sampling plan table is found in what sample determination element?

A. Sampling procedure

B. Sampling scheme

C. Valuation parameter

Short Answer: 120
Answer & Explanation: 263

Q-123:   The valuation mode in a sampling procedure is used for what purpose? Select all that apply.

A. Defines rules that determine the acceptance or rejection of a characteristic or sample during a quality inspection

B. Prevents a sampling procedure from being referenced in a task list

C. Defines the method used to calculate a sample size

D. Determines the number of inspection points to be created for each inspection lot

Short Answer: 121
Answer & Explanation: 265

Q-124:   You want to prevent the dynamic modification of characteristics in an inspection plan. How does the system determine that the inspection severity used to calculate a sample size for these characteristics should originate with the sampling procedure?

A. Usage indicator in the sampling procedure

B. Special indicator in the sampling procedure

C. Valuation mode in the sampling procedure

Short Answer: 121
Answer & Explanation: 265

Q-125: The rejection of a sample on the basis of the number of defects did not occur as expected. What may need to be changed in the sampling procedure?

A. Valuation model

B. Sampling type

C. Usage indicator

Short Answer: 121
Answer & Explanation: 266

Q-126: Which of the following data elements appears in a where-used list for a sampling procedure? Select all that apply.

A. Key date

B. Number of times the sampling procedure is referenced in the material master record inspection set-up

C. Valuation model

D. Master inspection characteristic

E. Inspection point

Short Answer: 121
Answer & Explanation: 267

Q-127: The customer wants to calculate a sample size on the basis of the inspection lot quantity. How can you accomplish this goal?

A. Sampling scheme

B. Sampling procedure

C. Sampling plan

Short Answer: 121
Answer & Explanation: 268

Q-128: The customer requires a sampling scheme for an attributive inspection. The structure of the related sampling table will consist of which of the following elements? Select all that apply.

A. Sample size

B. K-factor

C. Acceptance number d

D. Rejection number d

Short Answer: 121
Answer & Explanation: 269

Q-129: The actual quality level and inspection severity are elements found in which of the following?

A. Sampling scheme

B. Sampling procedure

C. Sampling plan table

Short Answer: 121
Answer & Explanation: 271

Q-130:   Each sampling procedure requires a sampling type
to_____?

A. Specify the rules used to calculate a sample size

B. Determine rules for acceptance or rejection of a
   characteristic

C. Determine if a sampling procedure is or is not
   referenced in a task list

D. Determine if independent or dependent samples are
   planned for the inspection

Short Answer: 121
Answer & Explanation: 272

Q-131:   What should be considered when a control chart
type is selected for a sampling procedure? Select all that
apply.

A. Inspection type

B. Inspection characteristics referenced in the control chart

D. Control variables referenced in the control chart

E. Algorithm used to calculate control limits

F. Dynamic modification control limits

Short Answer: 121
Answer & Explanation: 273

Q-132:   You want to reject a sample if the number of nonconforming units is greater than a predefined number. What will allow you to do so?

A. Attributive inspection

B. Variable inspection

Short Answer: 121
Answer & Explanation: 274

Q-133:   What is used to determine if a sampling procedure is successfully replaced in a task list?

A. Display replacement mode

B. Display replacement log

C. Display sampling procedure function

Short Answer: 121
Answer & Explanation: 275

Q-134:   What element is required to create a sampling plan for an attributive inspection? Select all that apply.

A. Valuation parameter

B. Inspection severities

C. Lot number

D. Acceptance number c

E. Sample size

Short Answer: 121
Answer & Explanation: 276

Q-135:   How is a rejection number determined for an attributive inspection sample that is calculated on the basis of a lot size and inspection severity?

A. Sampling scheme

B. Sampling procedure

C. Sampling plan

Short Answer: 121
Answer & Explanation: 277

Q-136:   Which of the following determines the lowest quality score in the sample that leads to the acceptance of the sample?

A. Acceptance constant in sampling plan

B. Acceptance number c in sampling plan

C. Rejection number d in sampling plan

Short Answer: 122
Answer & Explanation: 279

Q-137: The customer wants to define a new method to be used to calculate a sample size for an inspection with a task list. What Customizing setting is required to do so?

A. Sampling type

B. Inspection type

C. Valuation mode

Short Answer: 122
Answer & Explanation: 280

Q-138: Which of the following is an element in the structure of a sampling plan?

A. Valuation rule

B. Sampling type

C. Control chart variable

Short Answer: 122
Answer & Explanation: 281

Q-139: What entry in a sampling procedure is required if inspection results for more than one sample are to be

recorded for a characteristic as a collective valuation?
Select all that apply.

A. Valuation mode with valuation parameters

B. Multiple samples control indicator

C. Inspection points

Short Answer: 122
Answer & Explanation: 282

Q-140:   Identify a valuation parameter for which a
sampling scheme can be created. Select all that apply.

A. Attributive inspection

B. Variable inspection

C. No valuation parameter

Short Answer: 122
Answer & Explanation: 283

 Q-141: Which of the following is included in the structure
of a sampling plan for an attributive inspection? Select all
that apply.

A. Sample size

B. AQL value

C. Acceptance number

D. K-factor

Short Answer: 122
Answer & Explanation: 284

Q-142:   What does the sample determination process use to specify that an attributive inspection on the basis of nonconforming units will be used to determine if a characteristic is accepted or rejected?

A. Valuation mode defined for inspection type

B. Sampling type defined for inspection type

C. Valuation mode defined for sampling procedure

D. Inspection type defined for sampling procedure

Short Answer: 122
Answer & Explanation: 286

Q-143:   Which of the following is a sampling procedure parameter that influences the creation of samples for a quality inspection? Select all that apply.

A. Sampling type

B. Valuation rule

C. Inspection points

D. Dynamic modification criteria

Short Answer: 122
Answer & Explanation: 287

Q-144:   The sampling type and the valuation mode are
combined on what level in order to define the rules that
determine the sample size when an inspection plan is used
to conduct an inspection?

A. Inspection type level

B. Inspection lot level

C. Inspection characteristic level

D. Inspection operation level

Short Answer: 122
Answer & Explanation: 288

Q-145:   Sample determination was not executed when an
inspection lot was created for an inspection without an
inspection plan. What could be the issue?

A. Sampling procedure was not assigned to the inspection
    characteristic

B. Sampling type was not entered in the material master
    record inspection setup

C. Allowed relationship was not maintained for sampling
    procedure and dynamic modification rule

Short Answer: 122

Answer & Explanation: 289

Q-146: What setting is required to reject a sample if its measured value is greater than the specification limit defined for the characteristic

A. Variable inspection sampling type in sampling procedure

B. Variable inspection valuation mode in sampling procedure

C. Variable inspection sampling scheme in sampling procedure

Short Answer: 122
Answer & Explanation: 290

Q-147: In order to determine a sample size on the basis of lot size, inspection severity or inspection severity and AQL, a _____ is used.

A. Sampling procedure

B. Sampling plan

C. Sampling scheme

Short Answer: 122
Answer & Explanation: 291

Q-148: Which of the following can be used to determine the number of samples in a population that will be inspected if a sampling scheme is used for a qualitative inspection? Select all that apply.

A. Inspection lot size

B. K-factor

C. Acceptance number c

D. AQL

Short Answer: 122
Answer & Explanation: 293

 Q-149: The number of inspection points to be created for an inspection lot is defined where?

A. Inspection type

B. Inspection lot

C. Inspection characteristic

D. Sampling procedure

Short Answer: 122
Answer & Explanation: 294

Q-150:   You want to create a sampling scheme for a variable inspection. The sampling plan will consist of which of the following?

A. Sample size, acceptance number and rejection number

B. Sample size and k-factor

C. Sample size

Short Answer: 122
Answer & Explanation: 295

Q-151: Each sampling procedure requires a valuation mode to determine if a characteristic or sample is accepted or rejected. How is the valuation mode defined?

A. Create Sampling Procedure transaction

B. Customizing application

C. Basic Data function

Short Answer: 123
Answer & Explanation: 296

Q-152: A change in inspection severity in a sampling plan will lead to what? Select all that apply.

A. Change in inspection scope

B. Change in probability of acceptance

C. Change in maximum percent of nonconforming units per 100 units that leads to the acceptance of the inspection lot

D. Change in sample size and k-factor

Short Answer: 123
Answer & Explanation: 297

Q-153: Why is a k-factor used in a sampling plan?

A. Define the minimum quality score that leads to an acceptance of the sample for an attributive inspection

B. Define the minimum quality score that leads to an acceptance of the sample for a variable inspection

C. Define the maximum quality score that leads to the rejection of the sample for an attributive inspection

D. Define the maximum quality score that leads to the rejection of the sample for a variable inspection

Short Answer: 123
Answer & Explanation: 298

Q-154: What is controlled by the usage control indicator in a sampling procedure?

A. Prevents the reference of a sampling procedure by a task list

B. Prevents the reference of a sampling scheme by a sampling procedure

C. Prevents the reference of a dynamic modification rule by a sampling procedure

Short Answer: 123
Answer & Explanation: 299

Q-155:   An inspection plan will be used to conduct a
quality inspection. You want to enable the dynamic
modification of an inspection scope and use a sampling
scheme to determine the sample size. Which of the
following is a setting that is required to meet this
requirement? Select all that apply.

A. Assign sampling procedure to the inspection
    characteristic

B. Maintain allowed relationship for sampling procedure
    and dynamic modification rule

C. Maintain the rule for sample determination for the
    inspection type in the material master record inspection
    setup

D. Inspection point identifier in sampling procedure

Short Answer: 123
Answer & Explanation: 300

Q-156:   Which of the following can be used to determine
the number of nonconforming units in a sample? Select all
that apply.

A. Qualitative inspection characteristic

B. Quantitative inspection characteristic

85

C. Variable inspection

D. Attributive inspection

Short Answer: 123
Answer & Explanation: 302

Q-157: Which of the following can be defined in a sampling plan for an attributive inspection? Select all that apply.

A. Inspection lot size

B. Sample size

C. Acceptability constant for variable inspection

D. Acceptance number

E. K-factor

Short Answer: 123
Answer & Explanation: 303

Q-158: Which of the following parameters that control the sample determination process can be defined in a sampling procedure? Select all that apply.

A. Dynamic modification rules

B. Inspection points

C. Valuation mode

D. Control chart limits

E. Sampling type

Short Answer: 123
Answer & Explanation: 305

Q-159:   You want to use the automatic sample determination process. However, you want to inspect without an inspection plan. What setting is required to do so?

A. Assign sampling procedure to the inspection characteristic

B. Maintain allowed relationship for sampling procedure and dynamic modification rule

C. Maintain the inspection type in the material master record inspection setup

Short Answer: 123
Answer & Explanation: 306

Q-160:   What setting is required to enable a 100 percent inspection if an inspection plan is not used for the inspection?

A. Assign a sampling procedure to the inspection characteristic

B. Maintain an allowed relationship for sampling procedure and dynamic modification rule

C. Maintain the 100 percent inspection type in the material master record inspection setup

Short Answer: 123
Answer & Explanation: 307

Q-161:   Which of the following is a valuation mode defined in a sampling procedure to valuate a qualitative inspection characteristic?

A. Variable inspection according to s-method

B. Attributive inspection on the basis of nonconforming units

C. Variable inspection on the basis of nonconforming units

D. Attributive inspection according to s-method

Short Answer: 123
Answer & Explanation: 308

Q-162: What is the purpose of the usage control indicator in a sampling procedure?

A. Prevent reference of characteristic in control chart type

B. Prevent reference of sampling procedure in task list

C. Prevent reference of sampling type in material master record

Q-163: What is used to control a sample determination procedure if neither an inspection plan nor a material specification is used in the quality inspection?

A. Usage control indicator in sampling plan

B. Sampling type in the material master record

C. Multiple samples control indicator in sampling procedure

Short Answer: 124
Answer & Explanation: 310

Q-164: A sampling procedure is used. What requirement is met by doing so? Select all that apply.

A. Define sampling type that controls the calculation of a sample size

B. Define a valuation mode that governs the acceptance or rejection of a characteristic

C. Define the AQL for each inspection severity

D. Define inspection severity for quality level

Short Answer: 124
Answer & Explanation: 311

Q-165:   What entry is required to use a control chart to valuate a sample?

A. Control chart type in a sampling procedure

B. Control chart type in a task list header

C. Control chart type in a task list characteristic

Short Answer: 124
Answer & Explanation: 312

Q-166: Which of the following is a function of an attributive inspection? Select all that apply.

A. Determine the number of defects or nonconforming units in a sample

B. Accept characteristic if the number of defects is less than a predefined number of defects

C. Define specification limit for quantitative characteristic

D.   Accept characteristic if measured value is more than the qualitative specification limit

Short Answer: 124
Answer & Explanation: 313

Q-167:   What is an AQL value?

A. Identifier for normal, reduced or tightened inspection

B. The maximum number of permitted defects per 100 units that allows an acceptance valuation of an inspection lot

C. The minimum percent of permitted defects per 100 units that allows a rejection valuation of an inspection lot

D. Number of physical samples per lot size

Short Answer: 124
Answer & Explanation: 314

Q-168: What is controlled by an acceptability constant in a sampling plan?

A. The minimum quality score that results in the acceptance of the sample for a variable inspection

B. The maximum number of defects per sample that results in the acceptance of the sample for a variable inspection

C. The maximum quality score that results in the acceptance of the sample for a variable inspection

D. The minimum number of defects per sample that results in the acceptance of the sample for a variable inspection

Short Answer: 124
Answer & Explanation: 315

Q-169:   On what level are the sampling type and valuation mode most frequently combined for the sample determination process?

A. Inspection type

B. Inspection lot

C. Inspection characteristic

Short Answer: 124
Answer & Explanation: 317

Q-170:   Inspection points are not considered as expected in a sampling procedure for the inspection of physical samples. What change is required to address this issue?

A. Select the "Inspection points for sample management" control indicator in the sampling scheme

B. Select the "Inspection points for sample management" control indicator in the sampling type

C. Select the "Inspection points for sample management control indicator in the sampling procedure

Short Answer: 124
Answer & Explanation: 317

Q-171:   What element in a sampling procedure is required to valuate a sample on the basis of action limits?

A. Acceptability constant

B. Control chart type

C. Rejection number d

Short Answer: 124
Answer & Explanation: 318

Q-172:   Which of the following is a valid inspection point type for a sampling procedure that is used for an inspection conducted with a master recipe? Select all that apply.

A. Without inspection points

B. Free inspection points

C. Inspection points for sample management

Short Answer: 125
Answer & Explanation: 319

Q-173:   AQL values and inspection severities are elements of what structure?

A. Sampling scheme

B. Sampling plan table

C. Sampling procedure

Short Answer: 125
Answer & Explanation: 320

Q-174: Which of the following is an example of a data element in a sampling plan for an attributive inspection? Select all that apply.

A. Acceptance constant

B. Acceptance number c

C. Rejection number d

Short Answer: 125
Answer & Explanation: 321

Q-175: In what way is a sampling procedure used to specify how a sample size will be determined?

A. Define sampling procedure at characteristic level of task list

B. Define sampling procedure at inspection operation level of task list

C. Define sampling procedure at header level of task list

Short Answer: 125
Answer & Explanation: 323

Q-176: The dynamic modification of the inspection scope is required. Which of the following is needed to implement this requirement?

A. Allowed relationship between a sampling procedure and the dynamic modification rule

94

B. Allowed relationship between a sampling plan and the dynamic modification rule

C. Allowed relationship between a sampling type and the dynamic modification rule

Short Answer: 125
Answer & Explanation: 324

Q-177:   What is a requirement to create inspection points for an inspection lot when a routing is used to conduct the inspection?   Select all that apply.

A. "Without inspection points" control indicator in the sampling plan

B. "Free inspection points" control indicator in the sampling procedure

C. "Inspection points for sample management" control indicator in sampling procedure

Short Answer: 125
Answer & Explanation: 325

Q-178:   What element is required for a sampling scheme that is defined for a valuation mode without valuation parameters?

A. Sample size

B. Acceptance number

C. Rejection number

D. K-factor

Short Answer: 125
Answer & Explanation: 326

Q-179:   Why is the usage indicator an element of a
sampling procedure?

A. Determines if the sampling procedure is used for a
    variable inspection or an attributive inspection

B. Prevents the reference of the sampling procedure in a
    task list

C. Determines if the sampling procedure is used for a
    particular sampling type

Short Answer: 125
Answer & Explanation: 327

Q-180:   You want to determine samples for an
inspection for which an inspection plan is used. Which of
the following is an alternative that can be used for the
sample determination procedure?

A. Define sampling procedure in Customizing

B. Create allowed relationship between sampling
    procedure and dynamic modification rule

C. Assign sampling procedure to inspection characteristic

Short Answer: 125
Answer & Explanation: 328

Q-181:   How is a sampling procedure determined if either an inspection plan or a material specification is used to conduct the inspection? Select all that apply.

A. Sampling procedure is defined in material master record

B. Sampling procedure is assigned to inspection characteristic

C. Sampling procedure is defined using the Customizing application

Short Answer: 125
Answer & Explanation: 329

Q-182:   In what circumstance can an inspection point be created for each item of equipment in an inspection lot?

A. "Plant maintenance" inspection point type

B. "Free inspection points" inspection point type

C. "Sample management" inspection point type

Short Answer: 125
Answer & Explanation: 330

Q-183:   Types of samples that can be planned using a sampling procedure include which of the following? Select all that apply.

A. Dependent multiple samples

B. Independent multiple samples

C. Single samples

Short Answer: 126
Answer & Explanation: 331

Q-184:   You want to inspect physical samples. How does the system determine that inspection points should be created?

A. Free inspection points control indicator

B. Without inspection points control indicator

C. Sample management inspection points control indicator

Short Answer: 126
Answer & Explanation: 332

Q-185:   Which of the following is used to control the inspection of independent multiple samples?

A. Independent multiple samples control indicator in the sampling plan

B. Independent multiple samples control indicator in the sampling procedure

C. Independent multiple samples control indicator in the task list characteristic

Short Answer: 126
Answer & Explanation: 333

Q-186: How do you enable inspection points when an inspection plan is used for an inspection? Select all that apply.

A. Without inspection points inspection point type

B. Inspection points for plant maintenance inspection point type

C. Free inspection points inspection point type

Short Answer: 126
Answer & Explanation: 334

Q-187: What determines that dynamic modification does not pertain to a characteristic and that the inspection severity will be determined solely by a sampling procedure?

A. "No stage change" control indicator in the sampling procedure

B. "No stage change" control indicator in the sampling plan

C. "No stage change" control indicator in the sampling scheme

Short Answer: 126
Answer & Explanation: 335

Q-188:   Which of the following can be specified as an inspection point type in a sampling procedure when a maintenance task list is used for an inspection?

A. "Without inspection points" inspection point type

B. "Free inspection points" inspection point type

C. "Plant maintenance inspection points" inspection point type

Short Answer: 126
Answer & Explanation: 336

Q-189:   A sample is created.   However the sample appears to have been calculated on the basis of the lot size and inspection severity rather than lot size, inspection severity and the AQL. What could be the origin of this error?

A. The sampling plan table is defined on the basis of the inspection lot quantity and an inspection severity excluding the actual quality level

B. The sampling scheme is defined on the basis of the inspection lot quantity and inspection severity excluding the actual quality level

C. The sampling procedure is defined on the basis of the inspection lot quantity and inspection severity excluding the actual quality level

Short Answer: 126
Answer & Explanation: 337

Q-190:   The variables in a control chart that are used to valuate a sample are dependent on what?

A. Control chart type

B. Sampling type

C. Sampling procedure

Short Answer: 126
Answer & Explanation: 338

Q-191:   Which of the following is a standard inspection point type for a routing? Select all that apply.

A. Without inspection points

B. Free inspection points

C. Inspection points for sample management

D. Inspection points for plant maintenance

Short Answer: 126
Answer & Explanation: 339

Q-192: Which of the following is a description of a sampling scheme? Select all that apply.

A. A collection of sampling plans

B. Specification that determines if a sample size is of a fixed size, 100 percent of the sample or a percentage of the sample

C. Specification that defines the minimum quality score which leads to the acceptance or rejection of a sample

D. Specification that enables the determination of a sample size on the basis of an inspection lot size, inspection severity or combination of inspection severity and acceptable quality level

Short Answer: 126
Answer & Explanation: 340

Q-193:   The customer does not want characteristics to be dynamically modified. What setting is required to meet the requirement?

A. Special control indicator in sampling procedure

B. Special control indicator in inspection characteristic

C. Special control indicator in task list header

Short Answer: 126
Answer & Explanation: 342

Q-194: What inspection point type is used for sample determination without an inspection plan?

A. Without inspection points

B. Free inspection points

C. Inspection points for sample management

Short Answer: 127
Answer & Explanation: 342

Q-195: Which of the following is a purpose of a sampling scheme? Select all that apply.

A. Determine a sample size on the basis of a lot size and inspection severity

B. Determine the number of materials per inspection lot size

C. Determine the number of physical samples per the number of containers in an inspection lot

D. Determine the rules for the acceptance or rejection a characteristic or sample

Short Answer: 127
Answer & Explanation: 344

Q-196: What data element appears in a sampling plan without valuation parameters?

A. Sample size

B. Acceptance number

C. Rejection number

D. k-factor

Short Answer: 127
Answer & Explanation: 345

Q-197:   A valuation mode for an attributive sample and a sampling type with a sampling scheme are prerequisites for which of the following?

A. Single samples

B. Dependent multiple samples

C. Independent multiple samples

Short Answer: 127
Answer & Explanation: 346

Q-198:   Which of the following is a valuation mode defined in a sampling procedure?

A. Variable inspection according to s-method

B. Fixed sample

C. Sampling scheme

D. Attributive inspection on the basis of nonconforming units

E. Percentage sample

Short Answer: 127
Answer & Explanation: 348

Q-199:   What is a required entry in a sampling procedure to process independent multiple samples? Select all that apply.

A. Inspection points control indicator is set in the task list

B. "100%" inspection control indicator is not set for the sampling procedure

C. The "no parameters" valuation mode is set for the sampling procedure

Short Answer: 127
Answer & Explanation: 349

Q-200:   If samples are used to evaluate the material in an inspection lot, how does the user ensure that the inspection lot size and inspection severity are considered in the sample determination process?

A. Sampling procedure

B. Sampling scheme

C. Sampling plan

D. Material master record

Short Answer: 127
Answer & Explanation: 350

Q-201:   Which of the following is included in the structure
of a sampling plan for a variable inspection?

A. Sample size

B. Sample size and k-factor

C. Sample size, acceptance number c and rejection number
d

Short Answer: 127
Answer & Explanation: 352

CHAPTER II

SHORT ANSWERS

SHORT ANSWERS

Q-1: A. Define sampling scheme and B. Assign sampling scheme to sampling procedure

Q-2: B. Assign sampling procedure to the inspection characteristic

Q-3: A. Rules that control the calculation of a sample size, C. Rules that govern the valuation of inspection characteristics during the results recording process and D. Rules that determine if a sample size for a characteristic is dynamically modified

Q-4: B. The characteristics to which the control chart applies, C. The control variables referenced in the control chart and D. The algorithm used to calculate the chart's control limits

Q-5: A. The inspection point type is defined in a sampling procedure

Q-6: A. Independent multiple sampling control indicator, B. Valuation rule for independent multiple samples and D. Number of independent multiple samples

Q-7: A. Automatic valuation of dependent multiple samples

Q-8:   D. Sampling plan table

Q-9:   A. Sampling type, B. Valuation mode and E. Inspection points

Q-10:   B. A dynamic modification procedure is not used to determine either the inspection scope or the sample size and C. The inspection severity that influences the calculation of the sample size for a characteristic is determined by the sampling procedure

Q-11:   A. Valuation mode with no valuation parameters is selected and C. Sampling scheme is assigned to the sampling procedure

Q-12:   A. Record inspection results for multiple individual samples prior to valuating characteristic and C. Inspection results are recorded for each individual sample

Q-13:   Define function module for valuation of dependent multiple samples in valuation rule for dependent multiple samples

Q-14:   A. Sample size and C. K-factor

Q-15:   A. Determines sample size on the basis of inspection lot size, inspection severity, or inspection severity and acceptable quality level

Q-16:   B. System retrieves the dynamic modification criteria from the inspection lot origin

Q-17:   A. Determines the formula used to calculate a sample size

Q-18:   D. All of the above

Q-19:   A. Valuation rule that combines the valuations for individual samples

Q-20:   A. Valuation mode with valuation rule for independent multiple samples and B. Independent multiple samples control indicator in the sampling procedure

Q-21:   A. Task list characteristic and C. Inspection type in material master record

Q-22:   A. Attributive inspection per nonconforming units, D. Variable inspection per s-method and E. No valuation parameters

Q-23:   A. Sampling procedure is specified in the inspection setup for a material master record inspection type

Q-24:   A. Control indicator for independent multiple samples is set in sampling procedure

Q-25:   A. Set dependent multiple samples control indicator in the sampling procedure and C. Define the valuation rule for dependent multiple samples for sampling procedure

Q-26: A. Determine the number of physical samples to be inspected on the basis of an inspection lot size or the number of containers in an inspection lot and C. Specify the valuation parameter for the inspection type for which the sampling scheme is used

Q-27: C. Prevents the assignment of the sampling scheme to a sampling procedure

Q-28: B. Valuation mode defined in sampling procedure

Q-29: B. Number of nonconforming units in a sample as compared to the acceptance number for each characteristic and D. Number of nonconforming units in a sample as compared to the rejection number for each characteristic

Q-30: A. 100 percent inspection, C. Sampling scheme and D. Percentage sample

Q-31: A. Dynamic modification rule stored in inspection plan and sampling procedure and D. Allowed relationship maintained for a sampling procedure and dynamic modification rule

Q-32: A. "100%" inspection control indicator in material master record inspection setup, B. "Fixed percent" control indicator in material master record inspection setup and C. "Sampling procedure" control indicator in material master record inspection setup

Q-33:   B. Define the number of samples and C. Define the multiple samples valuation type in the valuation mode using a valuation rule

Q-34:   A. Automatic acceptance of samples, C. Automatic rejection of samples and D. Manual rejection of samples

Q-35:   A. Manual procedure used to valuate the sample

Q-36:   A. Sampling procedure for sample calculation for inspection without a task list and D. Sampling scheme in sample-drawing procedure

Q-37:   A. Sampling plan

Q-38:   B. Quality level and D. Dynamic modification rule

Q-39:   C. Valuation mode defined in a sampling procedure

Q-40:   D. Percentage sample control indicator in the material master record inspection setting for inspection type

Q-41:   A. Requirement for fixed sample with valuation on the basis of action limits

Q-42:   B. Define the valuation type in the valuation mode

Q-43:   D. Attributive inspection on the basis of nonconforming units valuation mode defined in the sampling procedure

Q-44:   A. Quality level and B. Dynamic modification rule

Q-45:   A. Special control indicator in the sampling procedure

Q-46:   B. Inspection severity and C. Inspection severity and AQL

Q-47:   A. Sample Determination

Q-48:   A. Sampling type and C. Valuation mode

Q-49:   B. Select the special control indicator in the sampling procedure

Q-50:   B. Valuation rule

Q-51:   A. Relates the allowable number or percentage of nonconforming units to an inspection severity and inspection lot quantity

Q-52:   A. Text, B. Valuation mode and C. Sampling table variable

Q-53:   B. Defines the minimum quality score that leads to the acceptance of the sample

Q-54:   A. Sampling type in sampling procedure

Q-55:   A. Control chart type in the sampling procedure

Q-56:   A. Sampling type

Q-57:   D. All of the above

Q-58:   B. Maximum number of defects per 100 units that does not preclude acceptance of the inspection lot during quality inspection and C. Maximum percentage of defects per 100 units that does not preclude acceptance of the inspection lot during quality inspection

Q-59:   A. Sampling type, B. Valuation mode and D. Quality level

Q-60:   A. Acceptance number c

Q-61:   C. Task list characteristic level

Q-62:   A. Valuation mode and C. Control chart type

Q-63:   A. Sample size and C. Acceptance number

Q-64:   A. Control chart type in the sampling procedure

Q-65:   C. Enables the valuation of a characteristic following the valuation of a number of dependent multiple samples

Q-66:   C. AQL value

Q-67:   A. Independent multiple samples, B. Dependent multiple samples and C. Single samples

Q-68:   B. Sampling type

Q-69:   B. Sampling plan

Q-70:   C. Lot size

Q-71:   C. Sampling procedure

Q-72:   C. A parameter used to define the rules for the acceptance or rejection of a characteristic or sample during a quality inspection

Q-73:   B. A sampling type with a sampling scheme is defined and D. Function module defined to valuate dependent multiple samples in valuation mode

Q-74:   D. Sampling scheme

Q-75:   B. Valuation mode and C. Sampling table description

Q-76:   A. Sample size and C. K-factor

Q-77:   A. Sampling procedure

Q-78:   B. Inspection characteristic

Q-79:   A. Sampling plan, B. Sampling procedure and C. Dynamic modification rule

Q-80:   A. Sampling procedure

Q-81:   A. Control limits, C. Control chart variables and E. Characteristics

Q-82: A. Attributive inspection on the basis of nonconforming units

Q-83: B. Sampling type with sampling scheme, C. Attributive inspection valuation mode and E. Dependent multiple samples control indicator

Q-84: C. Sampling plan

Q-85: A. Quality level and B. Dynamic modification rule

Q-86: C. Structure includes an acceptance number c for an attributive inspection

Q-87: C. Rejection number d

Q-88: A. Sampling procedure

Q-89: A. Characteristics, B. Control variables and C. Calculation of control limits

Q-90: B. Dependent multiple samples control indicator in sampling procedure

Q-91: A. Selection of normal, reduced or tightened inspection, B. Means of adjusting the inspection effort to reflect the current quality of material as measured by inspection results and C. Means of adjusting the probability of acceptance of a material during quality inspection

Q-92: B. Create a sampling scheme for variable inspection

Q-93:   A. An acceptability constant determines the minimum quality score that leads to the acceptance of a sample and an acceptance number c determines the maximum number of defects that leads to the acceptance of a sample

Q-94:   B. Entry of the control chart type in the sampling procedure, D. Selection of the fixed sample sampling type and E. Selection of the valuation on basis of action limits valuation mode

Q-95:   B. Variable inspection according to s-method

Q-96:   A. Dependent multiple samples control indicator in sampling procedure

Q-97:   B. Inspection severity

Q-98:   A. Sample size, C. Acceptance number and D. Rejection number

Q-99:   A. Create sampling scheme function and B. Copy sampling scheme function

Q-100:   B. The acceptability constant is the minimum quality score that leads to an acceptance of a sample and D. The rejection number d is the minimum number of nonconforming units in a sample that leads to the rejection of a sample

Q-101:   B. Valuation mode in sampling procedure

Q-102:   A. No stage change control indicator in the sampling procedure

Q-103:   A. Valuation mode that determines the rules for the acceptance or rejection of a characteristic or sample

Q-104:   B. Sampling type with a sampling scheme, D. Function module for the valuation of dependent multiple samples is defined in the valuation rule for dependent multiple samples

Q-105:   C. Display master inspection characteristic and D. Display inspection type

Q-106:   The probability of acceptance of the inspection lot and the anticipated inspection effort based on an existing quality level

Q-107:   A. A means to select the appropriate sampling plan in a sampling scheme

Q-108:   A. Document lot size, sample size, and acceptability constant or acceptance number used to determine if a sample is accepted or rejected

Q-109:   C. Sampling procedure parameters

Q-110:   A. Special control indicator in the sampling procedure

Q-111:   Variable inspection according to s-method

Q-112:   B. Number of times used and D. Operation
         number

Q-113:   B. Inspection severity defined in a sampling table
         in a sampling scheme

Q-114:   A. The quality level and dynamic modification rule
         determine an inspection severity and the
         inspection severity leads to the sampling plan in
         the sampling scheme

Q-115:   A. Attributive inspection, B. Variable inspection
         and C. Inspection without valuation parameters

Q-116:   A. Acceptability constant

Q-117:   B. Sampling procedure

Q-118:   B. Control chart type in sampling procedure

Q-119:   A. Dynamic modification rule

Q-120:   B. Inspection scope

Q-121:   B. Define the maximum number of defects
         permitted per 100 units for the lot to be accepted
         and D. Define the maximum fraction of
         nonconforming units permitted per 100 units for
         the lot to be accepted

Q-122:   B. Sampling scheme

Q-123: A. Defines rules that determine the acceptance or rejection of a characteristic or sample during a quality inspection

Q-124: B. Special indicator in the sampling procedure

Q-125: A. Valuation mode

Q-126: A. Key date, B. Number of times the sampling procedure is referenced in the material master record inspection set-up and D. Master inspection characteristic

Q-127: A. Sampling plan

Q-128: A. Sample size and D. Rejection number d

Q-129: C. Sampling plan table

Q-130: A. Specify the rules used to calculate a sample size

Q-131: B. Inspection characteristics referenced in the control chart, C. Control variables referenced in the control chart and D. Algorithm used to calculate control limits

Q-132: A. Attributive inspection

Q-133: B. Display replacement log

Q-134: D. Acceptance number c and E. Sample size

Q-135: C. Sampling plan

Q-136:   A. Acceptance constant in sampling plan

Q-137:   B. Sampling type

Q-138:   B. Sampling type

Q-139:   B. Multiple samples control indicator

Q-140:   A. Attributive inspection, B. Variable inspection
         and C. No valuation parameter

Q-141:   A. Sample size and C. Acceptance number

Q-142:   C. Valuation mode defined for sampling
         procedure

Q-143:   A. Sampling type and C. Inspection points

Q-144:   C. Inspection characteristic level

Q-145:   B. Sampling type was not entered in the material
         master record inspection setup

Q-146:   B. Variable inspection valuation mode in sampling
         procedure

Q-147:   C. Sampling scheme

Q-148:   A. Inspection lot size and D. AQL

Q-149:   D. Sampling procedure

Q-150:   B. Sample size and k-factor

Q-151:   B. Customizing application

Q-152:   A. Change in inspection scope and B. Change in probability of acceptance

Q-153:   B. Define the minimum quality score that leads to an acceptance of the sample for a variable inspection

Q-154:   A. Prevents the reference of a sampling procedure by a task list

Q-155:   A. Assign sampling procedure to the inspection characteristic and B. Maintain allowed relationship for sampling procedure and dynamic modification rule

Q-156:   A. Qualitative inspection characteristic and D. Attributive inspection

Q-157:   B. Sample size and D. Acceptance number

Q-158:   B. Inspection points, C. Valuation mode and E. Sampling type

Q-159:   C. Maintain the inspection type in the material master record inspection setup

Q-160:   C. Maintain the 100 percent inspection type in the material master record inspection setup

Q-161:   B. Attributive inspection on the basis of nonconforming units

Q-162:   B. Prevent reference of sampling procedure in task list

Q-163:   B. Sampling type in the material master record

Q-164:   A. Define sampling type that controls the calculation of a sample size and B. Define a valuation mode that governs the acceptance or rejection of a characteristic

Q-165:   A. Control chart type in a sampling procedure

Q-166:   A. Determine the number of defects or nonconforming units in a sample and B. Accept characteristic if the number of defects is less than a predefined number of defects

Q-167:   B. The maximum number of permitted defects per 100 units that allows an acceptance valuation of an inspection lot

Q-168:   A. The minimum quality score that results in the acceptance of the sample for a variable inspection

Q-169:   C. Inspection characteristic

Q-170:   C. Select the "Inspection points for sample management" control indicator in the sampling procedure

Q-171:   B. Control chart type

Q-172: B. Free inspection points and C. Inspection points for sample management

Q-173: B. Sampling plan table

Q-174: B. Acceptance number c and C. Rejection number d

Q-175: A. Define sampling procedure at characteristic level of task list

Q-176: A. Allowed relationship between a sampling procedure and the dynamic modification rule

Q-177: B. "Free inspection points" control indicator in the sampling procedure and C. "Inspection points for sample management" control indicator in sampling procedure

Q-178: A. Sample size

Q-179: B. Prevents the reference of the sampling procedure in a task list

Q-180: A. Define sampling procedure in Customizing and C. Assign sampling procedure to inspection characteristic

Q-181: B. Sampling procedure is assigned to inspection characteristic and C. Sampling procedure is defined using the Customizing application

Q-182: A. "Plant maintenance" inspection point type

Q-183: A. Dependent multiple samples, B. Independent multiple samples and C. Single samples

Q-184: C. Sample management inspection points control indicator

Q-185: B. Independent multiple samples control indicator in the sampling procedure

Q-186: C. Free inspection points inspection point type

Q-187: A. "No stage change" control indicator in the sampling procedure

Q-188: C. "Plant maintenance inspection points" inspection point type

Q-189: B. The sampling scheme is defined on the basis of the inspection lot quantity and an inspection severity excluding the actual quality level

Q-190: A. Control chart type

Q-191: B. Free inspection points and C. Inspection points for sample management

Q-192: A. A collection of sampling plans and D. Specification that enables the determination of a sample size on the basis of inspection lot size, inspection severity or combination of inspection severity and the actual quality level

Q-193: A. Special control indicator in sampling procedure

Q-194: A. Without inspection points

Q-195: A. Determine a sample size on the basis of a lot size and inspection severity and C. Determine the number of physical samples per the number of containers in an inspection lot

Q-196: A. Sample size

Q-197: B. Dependent multiple samples

Q-198: A. Variable inspection according to s-method and D. Attributive inspection on the basis of nonconforming units

Q-199: B. "100% inspection" control indicator is not set for the sampling procedure and C. The "no parameters" valuation mode is set for the sampling procedure

Q-200: B. Sampling scheme

Q-201: B. Sample size and k-factor

CHAPTER III

ANSWERS & EXPLANATIONS

ANSWERS & EXPLANATIONS

Q-1:   A. Define sampling scheme and B. Assign
sampling scheme to sampling procedure

When it's not possible to inspect each item produced by a
production process, a sample inspection is used to evaluate
the quality of the items in an inspection lot. The sample is
picked at random from the lot and, on the basis of the
information yielded by the sample, a decision is made
regarding the disposition of the lot...namely, the lot is
accepted or rejected for its intended use. A sampling
procedure can be used to select the entities of the sample,
which are subsequently evaluated according to an
inspection plan. Instructions for drawing the sample, such
as the sample's size and the number of samples to be taken,
are documented in a sample drawing procedure that's
assigned to the inspection plan. The sampling type, which is
defined in the sampling procedure, specifies the method to
be used to calculate the sample size. For example, the
sampling type may require that a sample size be equal the
lot size...namely, a 100 percent inspection, a fixed sample
size or a size determined by a sampling scheme. If the
sampling type requires the use of a sampling scheme that's
assigned to the sampling procedure, it will consist of
individual sampling tables, each of which includes two or
more sampling plans that determine a sample size based on
the lot size, inspection severity, inspection severity and
acceptable quality level, AQL, or the number of containers
in an inspection lot. The valuation parameter for which the

sampling scheme is created determines the structure of the sampling plan. For instance, the structure of a sampling plan created for an attributive inspection valuation mode will consist of a sample size, acceptance number c, or the maximum number of nonconforming units in a sample that is accepted and a rejection number d, or the least number of nonconforming units in a sample that is rejected. In turn, a sampling plan for a variable inspection will consist of a sample size and k-factor, or acceptability constant that defines the minimum quality score that leads to the acceptance of a sample following a quality inspection. A sampling plan with no valuation parameters will consist only of a sample size.

Q-2:   B. Assign sampling procedure to the inspection characteristic

Sampling procedures, sampling schemes and dynamic modification rules are the basic data needed to create the samples used in the inspection process. The manner in which a sampling procedure is selected for use in a quality inspection is dependent on whether a task list or material specification is used to conduct the inspection. If an inspection plan is used, the sampling procedure can be directly assigned to an inspection characteristic in the plan using the inspection planning functions or the Customizing application. If an inspection plan is not used to conduct the inspection, the sampling procedure can be specified in the inspection setup for a material master record inspection type.

Q-3:   A. Rules that control the calculation of a sample size, C. Rules that govern the valuation of inspection characteristics during the results recording process and D. Rules that determine if a sample size for a characteristic is dynamically modified

Sampling procedures, sampling schemes and dynamic modification rules are the basic data needed to create the samples used in the inspection process. In particular, a sampling procedure determines how a sample size is calculated, how inspection characteristics are valuated and if a sample size is dynamically modified. The structure of a sampling procedure includes a sampling type, which specifies how a sample size is calculated, and a valuation mode that includes a valuation rule that governs the acceptance or rejection of a characteristic or sample. The structure also includes an inspection points control indicator that determines the number of inspection points that are created for an inspection lot, an inspection point type, as well as a usage control indicator that ensures a particular sampling procedure is not referenced in a task list. The sampling procedure structure also includes a control chart type that governs the characteristics for which a particular control chart can be used, the variables referenced in the chart and the algorithm used to calculate the chart's control limits. Other control indicators in the sampling procedure are the no stage change control indicator that prevents the use of the dynamic modification procedure to determine the inspection scope or sample size and the multiple samples control indicator for independent or dependent multiple samples.

Q-4:   B. The characteristics to which the control chart applies, C. The control variables referenced in the control chart and D. The algorithm used to calculate the chart's control limits

The structure of a sampling procedure includes a sampling type, which specifies how a sample size is calculated, and a valuation mode that includes a valuation rule that governs the acceptance or rejection of a characteristic or sample. The structure also includes an inspection points control indicator that determines the number of inspection points that are created for an inspection lot, an inspection point type, as well as a usage control indicator that ensures a particular sampling procedure is not referenced in a task list. The sampling procedure structure also includes a control chart type that governs the characteristics for which a particular control chart can be used, the variables referenced in the chart and the algorithm used to calculate the chart's control limits. Other control indicators in the sampling procedure are the no stage change control indicator that prevents the use of the dynamic modification procedure to determine the inspection scope or sample size and the multiple samples control indicator for independent or dependent multiple samples.

Q-5:   A. The inspection point type is defined in a sampling procedure

The structure of a sampling procedure includes a sampling type, which specifies how a sample size is calculated, and a valuation mode that includes a valuation rule that governs the acceptance or rejection of a characteristic or sample. The structure also includes an inspection points control indicator that determines the number of inspection points that are created for an inspection lot, ,an inspection point type, as well as a usage control indicator that ensures a particular sampling procedure is not referenced in a task list. The sampling procedure structure also includes a control chart type that governs the characteristics for which a particular control chart can be used, the variables referenced in the chart and the algorithm used to calculate the chart's control limits. Other control indicators in the sampling procedure are the no stage change control indicator that prevents the use of the dynamic modification procedure to determine the inspection scope or sample size and the multiple samples control indicator for independent or dependent multiple samples.

Q-6:   A. Independent multiple sampling control indicator, B. Valuation rule for independent multiple samples and D. Number of independent multiple samples

Sampling procedures, sampling schemes and dynamic modification rules are the basic data needed to create the samples used in the inspection process. In particular, a sampling procedure determines how a sample size is calculated, how inspection characteristics are valuated and if a sample size is dynamically modified. The structure of a sampling procedure includes a sampling type, which specifies how a sample size is calculated, and a valuation mode that includes a valuation rule that governs the acceptance or rejection of a characteristic or sample. The structure also includes an inspection points control indicator that determines the number of inspection points that are created for an inspection lot, an inspection point type, as well as a usage control indicator that ensures a particular sampling procedure is not referenced in a task list. The sampling procedure structure also includes a

control chart type that governs the characteristics for which a particular control chart can be used, the variables referenced in the chart and the algorithm used to calculate the chart's control limits. Other control indicators in the sampling procedure are the no stage change control indicator that prevents the use of the dynamic modification procedure to determine the inspection scope or sample size and the multiple samples control indicator for independent or dependent multiple samples. The multiple samples control indicator in particular controls a customer's ability to valuate multiple individual samples prior to valuating a characteristic. In this case, the customer selects the independent multiple sampling control indicator and the valuation rule for independent multiple samples in the sampling procedure, and specifies the number of independent multiple samples to be valuated.

Q-7:   A. Automatic valuation of dependent multiple samples

Sampling procedures, sampling schemes and dynamic modification rules are the basic data needed to create the samples used in the inspection process. In particular, a sampling procedure determines how a sample size is calculated, how inspection characteristics are valuated and if a sample size is dynamically modified. The structure of a sampling procedure includes a sampling type, which specifies how a sample size is calculated, and a valuation mode that includes a valuation rule that governs the acceptance or rejection of a characteristic or sample. The structure also includes an inspection points control indicator that determines the number of inspection points that are created for an inspection lot, an inspection point

type, as well as a usage control indicator that ensures a particular sampling procedure is not referenced in a task list. The sampling procedure structure also includes a control chart type that governs the characteristics for which a particular control chart can be used, the variables referenced in the chart and the algorithm used to calculate the chart's control limits. Other control indicators in the sampling procedure are the no stage change control indicator that prevents the use of the dynamic modification procedure to determine the inspection scope or sample size and the multiple samples control indicator for independent or dependent multiple samples. The processing of double sampling inspections and multiple sampling inspections is enabled by the dependent multiple samples function control indicator that's set in the sampling procedure. A valuation rule, which is defined for the function is defined for the valuation mode in the sampling procedure, valuates a characteristic after the dependent multiple samples are valuated. In addition, a function module is defined in the valuation rule so dependent multiple samples can be processed during an inspection. The use of dependent multiple samples requires a sampling type with a sampling scheme, the attributive inspection valuation mode and the definition of a function module for valuating dependent multiple samples in the dependent multiples samples valuation rule.

Q-8:   D. Sampling plan table

When it's not possible to inspect each item produced by a production process, a sample inspection is used to evaluate the quality of the items in an inspection lot. The sample is picked at random from the lot and, on the basis of the

information yielded by the sample, a decision is made regarding the disposition of the lot…namely, the lot is accepted or rejected for its intended use. A sampling procedure can be used to select the entities of the sample, which are subsequently evaluated according to an inspection plan. Instructions for drawing the sample, such as the sample's size and the number of samples to be taken, are documented in a sample drawing procedure that's assigned to the inspection plan. The sampling type, which is defined in the sampling procedure, specifies the method to be used to calculate the sample size. For example, the sampling type may require that a sample size be equal the lot size…namely, 100 percent inspection, a fixed sample size or a size determined by a sampling scheme. If the sampling type requires the use of a sampling scheme That's assigned to the sampling procedure, it will consist of individual sampling tables, each of which includes two or more sampling plans that determine a sample size based on the lot size, inspection severity, inspection severity and acceptable quality level, AQL, or the number of containers in an inspection lot. The valuation parameter for which the sampling scheme is created determines the structure of the sampling plan. For instance, the structure of a sampling plan created for an attributive inspection valuation mode will consist of a sample size, acceptance number c, or the maximum number of nonconforming units in a sample that is accepted and a rejection number d, or the least number of nonconforming units in a sample that is rejected. In turn, a sampling plan for a variable inspection will consist of a sample size and k-factor, or acceptability constant that defines the minimum quality score that leads to the acceptance of a sample following a quality inspection. A

sampling plan with no valuation parameters will consist only of a sample size.

Q-9:   A. Sampling type, B. Valuation mode and E. Inspection points

Sampling procedures, sampling schemes and dynamic modification rules are the basic data needed to create the samples used in the inspection process. In particular, a sampling procedure determines how a sample size is calculated, how inspection characteristics are valuated and if a sample size is dynamically modified. The structure of a sampling procedure includes a sampling type, which specifies how a sample size is calculated, and a valuation mode that includes a valuation rule that governs the acceptance or rejection of a characteristic or sample. The structure also includes an inspection points control indicator that determines the number of inspection points that are created for an inspection lot, an inspection point type, as well as a usage control indicator that ensures a particular sampling procedure is not referenced in a task list. The sampling procedure structure also includes a control chart type that governs the characteristics for which a particular control chart can be used, the variables referenced in the chart and the algorithm used to calculate the chart's control limits. Other control indicators in the sampling procedure are the no stage change control indicator that prevents the use of the dynamic modification procedure to determine the inspection scope or sample size, which means the sampling procedure determines the inspection severity that influences the sample size. The sampling procedure also contains the multiple samples control indicator for independent or dependent multiple samples.

Q-10:   B. A dynamic modification procedure is not used to determine either the inspection scope or the sample size and C. The inspection severity that influences the calculation of the sample size for a characteristic determined by the sampling procedure

Sampling procedures, sampling schemes and dynamic modification rules are the basic data needed to create the samples used in the inspection process. In particular, a sampling procedure determines how a sample size is calculated, how inspection characteristics are valuated and if a sample size is dynamically modified. The structure of a sampling procedure includes a sampling type, which specifies how a sample size is calculated, and a valuation mode that includes a valuation rule that governs the acceptance or rejection of a characteristic or sample. The structure also includes an inspection points control indicator that determines the number of inspection points that are created for an inspection lot, an inspection point type, as well as a usage control indicator that ensures a particular sampling procedure is not referenced in a task list. The sampling procedure structure also includes a control chart type that governs the characteristics for which a particular control chart can be used, the variables referenced in the chart and the algorithm used to calculate the chart's control limits. Other control indicators in the sampling procedure are the no stage change control indicator that prevents the use of the dynamic modification procedure to determine the inspection scope or sample size, which means the sampling procedure determines the inspection severity that influences the sample size. The sampling procedure also contains the multiple samples control indicator for independent or dependent multiple samples.

Q-11:   A. Valuation mode with no valuation parameters is selected and C. Sampling scheme is assigned to the sampling procedure

Sampling procedures, sampling schemes and dynamic modification rules are the basic data needed to create the samples used in the inspection process. In particular, a sampling procedure determines how a sample size is calculated, how inspection characteristics are valuated and if a sample size is dynamically modified. The structure of a sampling procedure includes a sampling type, which specifies how a sample size is calculated, and a valuation mode that includes a valuation rule that governs the acceptance or rejection of a characteristic or sample. The structure also includes an inspection points control indicator that determines the number of inspection points that are created for an inspection lot, an inspection point type, as well as a usage control indicator that ensures a particular sampling procedure is not referenced in a task list. The sampling procedure structure also includes a control chart type that governs the characteristics for which a particular control chart can be used, the variables referenced in the chart and the algorithm used to calculate the chart's control limits. Other control indicators in the sampling procedure are the no stage change control indicator that prevents the use of the dynamic modification procedure to determine the inspection scope or sample size and the multiple samples control indicator for independent or dependent multiple samples. The sampling procedure can be assigned to a task list characteristic if an inspection plan is used for the inspection or the inspection setup for a material master record inspection type if an inspection plan is not used for the inspection. If an inspection plan is not used, a valuation mode without valuation parameters is specified in the sampling procedure and a sampling scheme is assigned to the sampling procedure.

Q-12:   A. Record inspection results for multiple independent samples prior to valuating characteristic and C. Inspection results are recorded for each individual sample

Sampling procedures, sampling schemes and dynamic modification rules are the basic data needed to create the samples used in the inspection process. In particular, a sampling procedure determines how a sample size is calculated, how inspection characteristics are valuated and if a sample size is dynamically modified. The structure of a sampling procedure includes a sampling type, which specifies how a sample size is calculated, and a valuation mode that includes a valuation rule that governs the acceptance or rejection of a characteristic or sample. The structure also includes an inspection points control indicator that determines the number of inspection points that are created for an inspection lot, an inspection point type, as well as a usage control indicator that ensures a particular sampling procedure is not referenced in a task list. The sampling procedure structure also includes a control chart type that governs the characteristics for which a particular control chart can be used, the variables referenced in the chart and the algorithm used to calculate the chart's control limits. Other control indicators in the

sampling procedure are the no stage change control indicator that prevents the use of the dynamic modification procedure to determine the inspection scope or sample size and the multiple samples control indicator for independent or dependent multiple samples. The multiple samples control indicator, in particular, controls a customer's ability to record inspection results for multiple individual samples and to valuate multiple individual samples prior to valuating a characteristic. In this case, the customer selects the independent multiple sampling control indicator and the valuation rule for independent multiple samples in the sampling procedure, and specifies the number of independent multiple samples to be valuated. To valuate independent multiple samples requires a valuation mode without valuation parameters, an inspection type other than the 100 percent inspection and a task list in which the inspection points control indicator is not set.

Q-13:   A. Define function module for valuation of dependent multiple samples in valuation rule for dependent multiple samples

Sampling procedures, sampling schemes and dynamic modification rules are the basic data needed to create the samples used in the inspection process. In particular, a sampling procedure determines how a sample size is calculated, how inspection characteristics are valuated and if a sample size is dynamically modified. The structure of a sampling procedure includes a sampling type, which specifies how a sample size is calculated, and a valuation mode that includes a valuation rule that governs the acceptance or rejection of a characteristic or sample. The structure also includes an inspection points control indicator that determines the number of inspection points that are created for an inspection lot, an inspection point type, as well as a usage control indicator that ensures a particular sampling procedure is not referenced in a task list. The sampling procedure structure also includes a control chart type that governs the characteristics for which a particular control chart can be used, the variables referenced in the chart and the algorithm used to calculate the chart's control limits. Other control indicators in the sampling procedure are the no stage change control indicator that prevents the use of the dynamic modification procedure to determine the inspection scope or sample size and the multiple samples control indicator for independent or dependent multiple samples. The processing of double sampling inspections and multiple sampling inspections is enabled by the dependent multiple samples function control indicator that's set in the sampling procedure. A valuation rule, which is defined for the function is defined for the valuation mode in the sampling procedure, valuates a characteristic after the dependent multiple samples are valuated. The use of dependent multiple samples requires a sampling type with a sampling scheme, the attributive inspection valuation mode and the definition of a function module for valuating dependent multiple samples in the dependent multiples samples valuation rule.

Q-14:   A. Sample size and C. K-factor

When it's not possible to inspect each item produced by a production process, a sample inspection is used to evaluate the quality of the items in an inspection lot. The sample is picked at random from the lot and, on the basis of the information yielded by the sample, a decision is made regarding the disposition of the lot…namely, the lot is accepted or rejected for its intended use. A sampling procedure can be used to select the entities of the sample, which are subsequently evaluated according to an inspection plan. Instructions for drawing the sample, such as the sample's size and the number of samples to be taken, are documented in a sample drawing procedure that's assigned to the inspection plan. The sampling type, which is defined in the sampling procedure, specifies the method to be used to calculate the sample size. For example, the sampling type may require a sample size that's equal the lot size – namely, 100 percent inspection, a fixed sample size or a size determined by a sampling scheme. If the sampling type requires the use of a sampling scheme, it will consist of individual sampling tables, each of which includes two or more sampling plans that determine a sample size based on the lot size, inspection severity, inspection severity and acceptable quality level, AQL, or the number of containers in an inspection lot. The valuation parameter for which the sampling scheme is created determines the structure of the sampling plan. For instance, the structure of a sampling plan created for an attributive inspection valuation mode will consist of a sample size, acceptance number c, or the maximum number of nonconforming units in a sample that is accepted and a rejection number d, or the least number of nonconforming units in a sample that is rejected. In turn, a sampling plan for a variable inspection will consist of a sample size and k-factor, or acceptability constant that defines the minimum quality score that leads to the acceptance of a sample following a quality inspection. A sampling plan with no valuation parameters will consist only of a sample size.

Q-15:   A. Determines sample size on the basis of inspection lot size, inspection severity, or inspection severity and acceptable quality level

When it's not possible to inspect each item produced by a production process, a sample inspection is used to evaluate the quality of the items in an inspection lot. The sample is picked at random from the lot and, on the basis of the information yielded by the sample, a decision is made regarding the disposition of the lot…namely, the lot is accepted or rejected for its intended use. A sampling procedure can be used to select the entities of the sample, which are subsequently evaluated according to an inspection plan. Instructions for drawing the sample, such as the sample's size and the number of samples to be taken, are documented in a sample drawing procedure that's assigned to the inspection plan. The sampling type, which is defined in the sampling procedure, specifies the method to be used to calculate the sample size. For example, the sampling type may require a sample size that's equal the lot size – namely, 100 percent inspection, a fixed sample size or a size determined by a sampling scheme. If the sampling type requires the use of a sampling scheme, it will consist of individual sampling tables, each of which includes two or more sampling plans that determine a sample size based on the lot size, inspection severity, inspection severity and acceptable quality level, AQL, or the number of containers in an inspection lot. The valuation parameter for which the sampling scheme is created determines the structure of the sampling plan. For instance, the structure of a sampling plan created for an attributive inspection valuation mode will consist of a sample size, acceptance number c, or the maximum number of nonconforming units in a sample that is accepted and a rejection number d, or the least number of nonconforming units in a sample that is rejected. In turn, a sampling plan for a variable inspection will consist of a sample size and k-factor, or acceptability constant that defines the minimum quality score that leads to the acceptance of a sample following a quality inspection. A sampling plan with no valuation parameters will consist only of a sample size.

Q-16:   B. System retrieves the dynamic modification criteria from the inspection lot origin

Sampling procedures, sampling schemes and dynamic modification rules are the basic data needed to create the samples used in the inspection process. In particular, a sampling procedure determines how a sample size is calculated, how inspection characteristics are valuated and if a sample size is dynamically modified. The structure of a sampling procedure includes a sampling type, which specifies how a sample size is calculated, and a valuation mode that includes a valuation rule that governs the acceptance or rejection of a characteristic or sample. The structure also includes an inspection points control indicator that determines the number of inspection points that are created for an inspection lot, an inspection point type, as well as a usage control indicator that ensures a particular sampling procedure is not referenced in a task list. The sampling procedure structure also includes a control chart type that governs the characteristics for which a particular control chart can be used, the variables referenced in the chart and the algorithm used to calculate the chart's control limits. Other control indicators in the sampling procedure are the no stage change control

indicator that prevents the use of the dynamic modification procedure to determine the inspection scope or sample size and the multiple samples control indicator for independent or dependent multiple samples. If an inspection plan is used, the sampling procedure can be directly assigned to an inspection characteristic using the inspection planning functions or the Customizing application. If an inspection plan is not used to conduct the inspection, the sampling procedure can be specified in the inspection setup for a material master record inspection type. In the latter case, to determine a sample size on the basis of a quality level, the system retrieves the dynamic modification criteria from the inspection lot origin.

Q-17:   A. Determines the formula used to calculate a sample size

Sampling procedures, sampling schemes and dynamic modification rules are the basic data needed to create the samples used in the inspection process. In particular, a sampling procedure determines how a sample size is calculated, how inspection characteristics are valuated and if a sample size is dynamically modified. The structure of a sampling procedure includes a sampling type, which specifies how a sample size is calculated, and a valuation mode that includes a valuation rule that governs the acceptance or rejection of a characteristic or sample. The structure also includes an inspection points control indicator that determines the number of inspection points that are created for an inspection lot, an inspection point type, as well as a usage control indicator that ensures a particular sampling procedure is not referenced in a task list. The sampling procedure structure also includes a

control chart type that governs the characteristics for which a particular control chart can be used, the variables referenced in the chart and the algorithm used to calculate the chart's control limits. Other control indicators in the sampling procedure are the no stage change control indicator that prevents the use of the dynamic modification procedure to determine the inspection scope or sample size and the multiple samples control indicator for independent or dependent multiple samples.

Q-18:   D. All of the above

Sampling procedures, sampling schemes and dynamic modification rules are the basic data needed to create the samples used in the inspection process. In particular, a sampling procedure determines how a sample size is calculated, how inspection characteristics are valuated and if a sample size is dynamically modified. The structure of a sampling procedure includes a sampling type – single sample, ,independent multiple samples or dependent multiple samples – to specify how a sample size is calculated, and a valuation mode that includes a valuation rule that governs the acceptance or rejection of a characteristic or sample. The structure also includes an inspection points control indicator that determines the number of inspection points that are created for an inspection lot, an inspection point type, as well as a usage control indicator that ensures a particular sampling procedure is not referenced in a task list. The sampling procedure structure also includes a control chart type that governs the characteristics for which a particular control chart can be used, the variables referenced in the chart and the algorithm used to calculate the chart's control limits.

Other control indicators in the sampling procedure are the no stage change control indicator that prevents the use of the dynamic modification procedure to determine the inspection scope or sample size and the multiple samples control indicator to select independent or dependent multiple samples, rather than the standard single samples.

Q-19:   A. Valuation rule that combines the valuations for individual samples

Sampling procedures, sampling schemes and dynamic modification rules are the basic data needed to create the samples used in the inspection process. In particular, a sampling procedure determines how a sample size is calculated, how inspection characteristics are valuated and if a sample size is dynamically modified. The structure of a sampling procedure includes a sampling type, which specifies how a sample size is calculated, and a valuation mode that includes a valuation rule that governs the acceptance or rejection of a characteristic or sample. The structure also includes an inspection points control indicator that determines the number of inspection points that are created for an inspection lot, an inspection point type, as well as a usage control indicator that ensures a particular sampling procedure is not referenced in a task list. The sampling procedure structure also includes a control chart type that governs the characteristics for which a particular control chart can be used, the variables referenced in the chart and the algorithm used to calculate the chart's control limits. Other control indicators in the sampling procedure are the no stage change control indicator that prevents the use of the dynamic modification procedure to determine the inspection scope or sample size

and the multiple samples control indicator for independent or dependent multiple samples. The multiple samples control indicator in particular controls a customer's ability to valuate multiple individual samples prior to valuating a characteristic. In this case, the customer selects the independent multiple sampling control indicator and the valuation rule for independent multiple samples in the sampling procedure, and specifies the number of independent multiple samples to be valuated. To valuate independent multiple samples requires a valuation mode without valuation parameters, an inspection type other than the 100 percent inspection and a task list in which the inspection points control indicator is not set.

Q-20:   A. Valuation mode with valuation rule for independent multiple samples and B. Independent multiple samples control indicator in the sampling procedure

Sampling procedures, sampling schemes and dynamic modification rules are the basic data needed to create the samples used in the inspection process. In particular, a sampling procedure determines how a sample size is calculated, how inspection characteristics are valuated and if a sample size is dynamically modified. The structure of a sampling procedure includes a sampling type, which specifies how a sample size is calculated, and a valuation mode that includes a valuation rule that governs the acceptance or rejection of a characteristic or sample. The structure also includes an inspection points control indicator that determines the number of inspection points that are created for an inspection lot, an inspection point type, as well as a usage control indicator that ensures a particular sampling procedure is not referenced in a task list. The sampling procedure structure also includes a control chart type that governs the characteristics for which a particular control chart can be used, the variables referenced in the chart and the algorithm used to calculate the chart's control limits. Other control indicators in the sampling procedure are the no stage change control indicator that prevents the use of the dynamic modification procedure to determine the inspection scope or sample size and the multiple samples control indicator for independent or dependent multiple samples. The multiple samples control indicator in particular controls a customer's ability to valuate multiple individual samples prior to valuating a characteristic. In this case, the customer selects the independent multiple sampling control indicator and the valuation rule for independent multiple samples in the sampling procedure, and specifies the number of independent multiple samples to be valuated. To valuate independent multiple samples requires a valuation mode without valuation parameters, an inspection type other than the 100 percent inspection and a task list in which the inspection points control indicator is not set.

Q-21:   A. Task list characteristic and C. Inspection type in material master record

Sampling procedures, sampling schemes and dynamic modification rules are the basic data needed to create the samples used in the inspection process. In particular, a sampling procedure determines how a sample size is calculated, how inspection characteristics are valuated and if a sample size is dynamically modified. The structure of a sampling procedure includes a sampling type, which specifies how a sample size is calculated, and a valuation mode that includes a valuation rule that governs the acceptance or rejection of a characteristic or sample. The structure also includes an inspection points control indicator that determines the number of inspection points that are created for an inspection lot, an inspection point type, as well as a usage control indicator that ensures a particular sampling procedure is not referenced in a task list. The sampling procedure structure also includes a control chart type that governs the characteristics for which a particular control chart can be used, the variables referenced in the chart and the algorithm used to calculate the chart's control limits. Other control indicators in the sampling procedure are the no stage change control indicator that prevents the use of the dynamic modification procedure to determine the inspection scope or sample size and the multiple samples control indicator for independent or dependent multiple samples. The sampling procedure can be assigned to a task list characteristic if an inspection plan is used for the inspection. If an inspection plan is not used for the inspection, the sampling procedure can be specified in the inspection setup for a material master record inspection type.

Q-22:   A. Attributive inspection per nonconforming units, D. Variable inspection per s-method and E. No valuation parameters

When it's not possible to inspect each item produced by a production process, a sample inspection is used to evaluate the quality of the items in an inspection lot. The sample is picked at random from the lot and, on the basis of the information yielded by the sample, a decision is made regarding the disposition of the lot…namely, the lot is

accepted or rejected for its intended use. A sampling procedure can be used to select the entities of the sample, which are subsequently evaluated according to an inspection plan. Instructions for drawing the sample, such as the sample's size and the number of samples to be taken, are documented in a sample drawing procedure that's assigned to the inspection plan. The sampling type, which is defined in the sampling procedure, specifies the method to be used to calculate the sample size. For example, the sampling type may require that a sample size be equal the lot size...namely, 100 percent inspection, a fixed sample size or a size determined by a sampling scheme. If the sampling type requires the use of a sampling scheme that's assigned to the sampling procedure, it will consist of individual sampling tables, each of which includes two or more sampling plans that determine a sample size based on the lot size, inspection severity, inspection severity and acceptable quality level, AQL, or the number of containers in an inspection lot. The valuation parameter for which the sampling scheme is created determines the structure of the sampling plan. For instance, the structure of a sampling plan created for an attributive inspection valuation mode will consist of a sample size, acceptance number c, or the maximum number of nonconforming units in a sample that is accepted and a rejection number d, or the least number of nonconforming units in a sample that is rejected. In turn, a sampling plan for a variable inspection will consist of a sample size and k-factor, or acceptability constant that defines the minimum quality score that leads to the acceptance of a sample following a quality inspection. A sampling plan with no valuation parameters will consist only of a sample size.

Q-23:   A. Sampling procedure is specified in the inspection setup for a material master record inspection type

Sampling procedures, sampling schemes and dynamic modification rules are the basic data needed to create the samples used in the inspection process. In particular, a sampling procedure determines how a sample size is calculated, how inspection characteristics are valuated and if a sample size is dynamically modified. The structure of a sampling procedure includes a sampling type, which specifies how a sample size is calculated, and a valuation mode that includes a valuation rule that governs the acceptance or rejection of a characteristic or sample. The structure also includes an inspection points control indicator that determines the number of inspection points that are created for an inspection lot, an inspection point type, as well as a usage control indicator that ensures a particular sampling procedure is not referenced in a task list. The sampling procedure structure also includes a control chart type that governs the characteristics for which a particular control chart can be used, the variables referenced in the chart and the algorithm used to calculate the chart's control limits. Other control indicators in the sampling procedure are the no stage change control indicator that prevents the use of the dynamic modification procedure to determine the inspection scope or sample size and the multiple samples control indicator for independent or dependent multiple samples. The sampling procedure can be assigned to a task list characteristic if an inspection plan is used for the inspection or the inspection setup for a material master record inspection type if an inspection plan is not used for the inspection.

Q-24:   A. Control indicator for independent multiple
samples is set in sampling procedure

Sampling procedures, sampling schemes and dynamic
modification rules are the basic data needed to create the
samples used in the inspection process. In particular, a
sampling procedure determines how a sample size is
calculated, how inspection characteristics are valuated and if
a sample size is dynamically modified. The structure of a
sampling procedure includes a sampling type, which
specifies how a sample size is calculated, and a valuation
mode that includes a valuation rule that governs the
acceptance or rejection of a characteristic or sample. The
structure also includes an inspection points control
indicator that determines the number of inspection points
that are created for an inspection lot, an inspection point
type, as well as a usage control indicator that ensures a
particular sampling procedure is not referenced in a task
list. The sampling procedure structure also includes a
control chart type that governs the characteristics for which
a particular control chart can be used, the variables
referenced in the chart and the algorithm used to calculate
the chart's control limits. Other control indicators in the
sampling procedure are the no stage change control
indicator that prevents the use of the dynamic modification
procedure to determine the inspection scope or sample size
and the multiple samples control indicator for independent
or dependent multiple samples. The multiple samples
control indicator in particular controls a customer's ability
to valuate multiple individual samples prior to valuating a
characteristic. In this case, the customer selects the
independent multiple sampling control indicator and the
valuation rule for independent multiple samples in the

sampling procedure, and specifies the number of independent multiple samples to be valuated. To valuate independent multiple samples requires a valuation mode without valuation parameters, an inspection type other than the 100 percent inspection and a task list in which the inspection points control indicator is not set.

Q-25:   A. Set the dependent multiple samples control indicator in the sampling procedure and D. Define the valuation rule for dependent multiple samples for sampling procedure

Sampling procedures, sampling schemes and dynamic modification rules are the basic data needed to create the samples used in the inspection process. In particular, a sampling procedure determines how a sample size is calculated, how inspection characteristics are valuated and if a sample size is dynamically modified. The structure of a sampling procedure includes a sampling type, which specifies how a sample size is calculated, and a valuation mode that includes a valuation rule that governs the acceptance or rejection of a characteristic or sample. The structure also includes an inspection points control indicator that determines the number of inspection points that are created for an inspection lot, an inspection point type, as well as a usage control indicator that ensures a particular sampling procedure is not referenced in a task list. The sampling procedure structure also includes a control chart type that governs the characteristics for which a particular control chart can be used, the variables referenced in the chart and the algorithm used to calculate the chart's control limits. Other control indicators in the sampling procedure are the no stage change control

indicator that prevents the use of the dynamic modification procedure to determine the inspection scope or sample size and the multiple samples control indicator for independent or dependent multiple samples. The processing of double sampling inspections and multiple sampling inspections is enabled by the dependent multiple samples function control indicator that's set in the sampling procedure. A valuation rule for the function is defined for the valuation mode and i ensures a characteristic is valuated after the dependent multiple samples are valuated. The use of dependent multiple samples requires a sampling type with a sampling scheme, the attributive inspection valuation mode and the definition of a function module for valuating dependent multiple samples in the dependent multiples samples valuation rule.

Q-26:   A. Determine the number of physical samples to be inspected on the basis of an inspection lot size or the number of containers in an inspection lot and C. Specify the valuation parameter for the inspection type for which the sampling scheme is used

When it's not possible to inspect each item produced by a production process, a sample inspection is used to evaluate the quality of the items in an inspection lot. The sample is picked at random from the lot and, on the basis of the information yielded by the sample, a decision is made regarding the disposition of the lot…namely, the lot is accepted or rejected for its intended use. A sampling procedure can be used to select the entities of the sample, which are subsequently evaluated according to an inspection plan. Instructions for drawing the sample, such as the sample's size and the number of samples to be taken,

are documented in a sample drawing procedure that's assigned to the inspection plan. The sampling type, which is defined in the sampling procedure, specifies the method to be used to calculate the sample size. For example, the sampling type may require that a sample size be equal the lot size...namely, 100 percent inspection, a fixed sample size or a size determined by a sampling scheme. If the sampling type requires the use of a sampling scheme, it will consist of individual sampling tables, each of which includes two or more sampling plans that determine a sample size based on the lot size, inspection severity, inspection severity and acceptable quality level, AQL, or the number of containers in an inspection lot. The valuation parameter for which the sampling scheme is created determines the structure of the sampling plan. For instance, the structure of a sampling plan created for an attributive inspection valuation mode will consist of a sample size, acceptance number c, or the maximum number of nonconforming units in a sample that is accepted and a rejection number d, or the least number of nonconforming units in a sample that is rejected. In turn, a sampling plan for a variable inspection will consist of a sample size and k-factor, or acceptability constant that defines the minimum quality score that leads to the acceptance of a sample following a quality inspection. A sampling plan with no valuation parameters will consist only of a sample size.

Q-27:   C. Prevents the assignment of the sampling scheme to a sampling procedure

Sampling procedures, sampling schemes and dynamic modification rules are the basic data needed to create the samples used in the inspection process. In particular, a

sampling procedure determines how a sample size is calculated, how inspection characteristics are valuated and if a sample size is dynamically modified. The structure of a sampling procedure includes a sampling type, which specifies how a sample size is calculated, and a valuation mode that includes a valuation rule that governs the acceptance or rejection of a characteristic or sample. The structure also includes an inspection points control indicator that determines the number of inspection points that are created for an inspection lot, an inspection point type, as well as a usage control indicator that ensures a particular sampling procedure is not referenced in a task list. The sampling procedure structure also includes a control chart type that governs the characteristics for which a particular control chart can be used, the variables referenced in the chart and the algorithm used to calculate the chart's control limits. Other control indicators in the sampling procedure are the no stage change control indicator that prevents the use of the dynamic modification procedure to determine the inspection scope or sample size and the multiple samples control indicator for independent or dependent multiple samples. The sampling procedure can be assigned to a task list characteristic if an inspection plan is used for the inspection or the inspection setup for a material master record inspection type if an inspection plan is not used for the inspection.

Q-28:   B. Valuation mode defined in sampling procedure

When it's not possible to inspect each item produced by a production process, a sample inspection is used to evaluate the quality of the items in an inspection lot. The sample is picked at random from the lot and, on the basis of the

159

information yielded by the sample, a decision is made regarding the disposition of the lot…namely, the lot is accepted or rejected for its intended use. A sampling procedure can be used to select the entities of the sample, which are subsequently evaluated according to an inspection plan. Instructions for drawing the sample, such as the sample's size and the number of samples to be taken, are documented in a sample drawing procedure that's assigned to the inspection plan. The sampling type, which is defined in the sampling procedure, specifies the method to be used to calculate the sample size. For example, the sampling type may require that a sample size be equal the lot size…namely, 100 percent inspection, a fixed sample size or a size determined by a sampling scheme. If the sampling type requires the use of a sampling scheme, it will consist of individual sampling tables, each of which includes two or more sampling plans that determine a sample size based on the lot size, inspection severity, inspection severity and acceptable quality level, AQL, or the number of containers in an inspection lot. The valuation parameter for which the sampling scheme is created determines the structure of the sampling plan. For instance, the structure of a sampling plan created for an attributive inspection valuation mode will consist of a sample size, acceptance number c, or the maximum number of nonconforming units in a sample that is accepted and a rejection number d, or the least number of nonconforming units in a sample that is rejected. In turn, a sampling plan for a variable inspection will consist of a sample size and k-factor, or acceptability constant that defines the minimum quality score that leads to the acceptance of a sample following a quality inspection. A sampling plan with no valuation parameters will consist only of a sample size.

Q-29:   B. Number of nonconforming units in a sample as compared to the acceptance number for each characteristic and D. Number of nonconforming units in a sample as compared to the rejection number for each characteristic

When it's not possible to inspect each item produced by a production process, a sample inspection is used to evaluate the quality of the items in an inspection lot. The sample is picked at random from the lot and, on the basis of the information yielded by the sample, a decision is made regarding the disposition of the lot…namely, the lot is accepted or rejected for its intended use. A sampling procedure can be used to select the entities of the sample, which are subsequently evaluated according to an inspection plan. Instructions for drawing the sample, such as the sample's size and the number of samples to be taken, are documented in a sample drawing procedure that's assigned to the inspection plan. The sampling type, which is defined in the sampling procedure, specifies the method to be used to calculate the sample size. For example, the sampling type may require that a sample size be equal the lot size…namely, 100 percent inspection, a fixed sample size or a size determined by a sampling scheme. If the sampling type requires the use of a sampling scheme that's assigned to the sampling procedure, it will consist of individual sampling tables, each of which includes two or more sampling plans that determine a sample size based on the lot size, inspection severity, inspection severity and acceptable quality level, AQL, or the number of containers in an inspection lot. The valuation parameter for which the sampling scheme is created determines the structure of the sampling plan. For instance, the structure of a sampling plan created for an attributive inspection valuation mode

will consist of a sample size, acceptance number c, or the maximum number of nonconforming units in a sample that is accepted and a rejection number d, or the least number of nonconforming units in a sample that is rejected. In turn, a sampling plan for a variable inspection will consist of a sample size and k-factor, or acceptability constant that defines the minimum quality score that leads to the acceptance of a sample following a quality inspection. A sampling plan with no valuation parameters will consist only of a sample size.

Q-30:   A. 100 percent inspection, C. Sampling scheme and D. Percentage sample

Sampling procedures, sampling schemes and dynamic modification rules are the basic data needed to create the samples used in the inspection process. In particular, a sampling procedure determines how a sample size is calculated, how inspection characteristics are valuated and if a sample size is dynamically modified. The structure of a sampling procedure includes a sampling type, which specifies how a sample size is calculated, and a valuation mode that includes a valuation rule that governs the acceptance or rejection of a characteristic or sample. The structure also includes an inspection points control indicator that determines the number of inspection points that are created for an inspection lot, an inspection point type, as well as a usage control indicator that ensures a particular sampling procedure is not referenced in a task list. The sampling procedure structure also includes a control chart type that governs the characteristics for which a particular control chart can be used, the variables referenced in the chart and the algorithm used to calculate the chart's control limits. Other control indicators in the sampling procedure are the no stage change control indicator that prevents the use of the dynamic modification procedure to determine the inspection scope or sample size and the multiple samples control indicator for independent or dependent multiple samples. The sampling procedure can be assigned to a task list characteristic if an inspection plan is used for the inspection or the inspection setup for a material master record inspection type if an inspection plan is not used for the inspection.

Q-31:   A. Dynamic modification rule stored in inspection plan and sampling procedure and D. Allowed relationship maintained for a sampling procedure and dynamic modification rule

Sampling procedures, sampling schemes and dynamic modification rules are the basic data needed to create the samples used in the inspection process. In particular, a sampling procedure determines how a sample size is calculated, how inspection characteristics are valuated and if a sample size is dynamically modified. The structure of a sampling procedure includes a sampling type, which specifies how a sample size is calculated, and a valuation mode that includes a valuation rule that governs the acceptance or rejection of a characteristic or sample. The structure also includes an inspection points control indicator that determines the number of inspection points that are created for an inspection lot, an inspection point type, as well as a usage control indicator that ensures a particular sampling procedure is not referenced in a task list. The sampling procedure structure also includes a control chart type that governs the characteristics for which

a particular control chart can be used, the variables referenced in the chart and the algorithm used to calculate the chart's control limits. Other control indicators in the sampling procedure are the no stage change control indicator that prevents the use of the dynamic modification procedure to determine the inspection scope or sample size in part on the basis of prior inspection results and the multiple samples control indicator for independent or dependent multiple samples. The sampling procedure can be assigned to a task list characteristic if an inspection plan is used for the inspection or the inspection setup for a material master record inspection type if an inspection plan is not used for the inspection.

Q-32:   A. "100%" inspection control indicator in material master record inspection setup, B. "Fixed percent" control indicator in material master record setup and C. "Sampling procedure" control indicator in material master record setup

Sampling procedures, sampling schemes and dynamic modification rules are the basic data needed to create the samples used in the inspection process. In particular, a sampling procedure determines how a sample size is calculated, how inspection characteristics are valuated and if a sample size is dynamically modified. The structure of a sampling procedure includes a sampling type, which specifies how a sample size is calculated, and a valuation mode that includes a valuation rule that governs the acceptance or rejection of a characteristic or sample. The structure also includes an inspection points control indicator that determines the number of inspection points that are created for an inspection lot, an inspection point

164

type, as well as a usage control indicator that ensures a particular sampling procedure is not referenced in a task list. The sampling procedure structure also includes a control chart type that governs the characteristics for which a particular control chart can be used, the variables referenced in the chart and the algorithm used to calculate the chart's control limits. Other control indicators in the sampling procedure are the no stage change control indicator that prevents the use of the dynamic modification procedure to determine the inspection scope or sample size in part on the basis of prior inspection results and the multiple samples control indicator for independent or dependent multiple samples. The sampling procedure can be assigned to a task list characteristic if an inspection plan is used for the inspection or the inspection setup for a material master record inspection type if an inspection plan is not used for the inspection.

Q-33:   B. Define the number of samples

Sampling procedures, sampling schemes and dynamic modification rules are the basic data needed to create the samples used in the inspection process. In particular, a sampling procedure determines how a sample size is calculated, how inspection characteristics are valuated and if a sample size is dynamically modified. The structure of a sampling procedure includes a sampling type, which specifies how a sample size is calculated, and a valuation mode that includes a valuation rule that governs the acceptance or rejection of a characteristic or sample. The structure also includes an inspection points control indicator that determines the number of inspection points that are created for an inspection lot, an inspection point

type, as well as a usage control indicator that ensures a particular sampling procedure is not referenced in a task list. The sampling procedure structure also includes a control chart type that governs the characteristics for which a particular control chart can be used, the variables referenced in the chart and the algorithm used to calculate the chart's control limits. Other control indicators in the sampling procedure are the no stage change control indicator that prevents the use of the dynamic modification procedure to determine the inspection scope or sample size and the multiple samples control indicator for independent or dependent multiple samples. The multiple samples control indicator in particular controls a customer's ability to valuate multiple individual samples prior to valuating a characteristic. In this case, the customer selects the independent multiple sampling control indicator and the valuation rule for independent multiple samples in the sampling procedure, and specifies the number of independent multiple samples to be valuated.

Q-34: A. Automatic acceptance of samples, C. Automatic rejection of samples and D. Manual rejection of samples

Sampling procedures, sampling schemes and dynamic modification rules are the basic data needed to create the samples used in the inspection process. In particular, a sampling procedure determines how a sample size is calculated, how inspection characteristics are valuated and if a sample size is dynamically modified. The structure of a sampling procedure includes a sampling type, which specifies how a sample size is calculated, and a valuation mode that includes a valuation rule that governs the

acceptance or rejection of a characteristic or sample. The structure also includes an inspection points control indicator that determines the number of inspection points that are created for an inspection lot, an inspection point type, as well as a usage control indicator that ensures a particular sampling procedure is not referenced in a task list. The sampling procedure structure also includes a control chart type that governs the characteristics for which a particular control chart can be used, the variables referenced in the chart and the algorithm used to calculate the chart's control limits. Other control indicators in the sampling procedure are the no stage change control indicator that prevents the use of the dynamic modification procedure to determine the inspection scope or sample size and the multiple samples control indicator for independent or dependent multiple samples. The processing of double sampling inspections and multiple sampling inspections is enabled by the dependent multiple samples function control indicator that's set in the sampling procedure. A valuation rule for the function is defined for the valuation mode and i ensures a characteristic is valuated after the dependent multiple samples are valuated. The use of dependent multiple samples requires a sampling type with a sampling scheme, the attributive inspection valuation mode and the definition of a function module for valuating dependent multiple samples in the dependent multiples samples valuation rule. When valuating inspection results for double inspection samples, the samples can be automatically accepted and automatically or manually rejected.

Q-35:   A. Manual procedure used to valuate the sample

Sampling procedures, sampling schemes and dynamic modification rules are the basic data needed to create the samples used in the inspection process. In particular, a sampling procedure determines how a sample size is calculated, how inspection characteristics are valuated and if a sample size is dynamically modified. The structure of a sampling procedure includes a sampling type, which specifies how a sample size is calculated, and a valuation mode that includes a valuation rule that governs the acceptance or rejection of a characteristic or sample. The structure also includes an inspection points control indicator that determines the number of inspection points that are created for an inspection lot, an inspection point type, as well as a usage control indicator that ensures a particular sampling procedure is not referenced in a task list. The sampling procedure structure also includes a control chart type that governs the characteristics for which a particular control chart can be used, the variables referenced in the chart and the algorithm used to calculate the chart's control limits. Other control indicators in the sampling procedure are the no stage change control indicator that prevents the use of the dynamic modification procedure to determine the inspection scope or sample size and the multiple samples control indicator for independent or dependent multiple samples. The processing of double sampling inspections and multiple sampling inspections is enabled by the dependent multiple samples function control indicator that's set in the sampling procedure. A valuation rule, which is defined for the function is defined for the valuation mode in the sampling procedure, valuates a characteristic after the dependent multiple samples are valuated. The use of dependent multiple samples requires a sampling type with a sampling scheme, the attributive

168

inspection valuation mode and the definition of a function module for valuating dependent multiple samples in the dependent multiples samples valuation rule. When valuating inspection results for double inspection samples, the samples can be automatically accepted and automatically or manually rejected.

Q-36:   A. Sampling procedure for sample calculation for inspection without a task list and D. Sampling scheme in sample-drawing procedure

Sampling procedures, sampling schemes and dynamic modification rules are the basic data needed to create the samples used in the inspection process. The manner in which a sampling procedure is selected for use in a quality inspection is dependent on whether a task list or material specification is used to conduct the inspection. If an inspection plan is used, the sampling procedure can be directly assigned to an inspection characteristic in the plan using the inspection planning functions or the Customizing application. If an inspection plan is not used to conduct the inspection, the sampling procedure can be specified in the inspection setup for a material master record inspection type. In either case, a sampling procedure can be used to select the entities of the sample, which are subsequently evaluated according to an inspection plan. Instructions for drawing the sample, such as the sample's size and the number of samples to be taken, are documented in a sample drawing procedure that's assigned to the inspection plan. If no inspection plan is used to conduct the inspection, the sampling type control indicator is specified in the material master record inspection setup. The sampling type, which is defined in the sampling procedure, specifies the method to be used to calculate the sample size. For example, the sampling type may require that a sample size be equal the lot size…namely, 100 percent inspection, a fixed sample size or a size determined by a sampling scheme. If the sampling type requires the use of a sampling scheme that's assigned to the sampling procedure, it will consist of individual sampling tables, each of which includes two or more sampling plans that determine a sample size based on the lot size, inspection severity, inspection severity and acceptable quality level, AQL, or the number of containers in an inspection lot. The valuation parameter for which the sampling scheme is created determines the structure of the sampling plan. For instance, the structure of a sampling plan created for an attributive inspection valuation mode will consist of a sample size, acceptance number c, or the maximum number of nonconforming units in a sample that is accepted and a rejection number d, or the least number of nonconforming units in a sample that is rejected. In turn, a sampling plan for a variable inspection will consist of a sample size and k-factor, or acceptability constant that defines the minimum quality score that leads to the acceptance of a sample following a quality inspection. A sampling plan with no valuation parameters will consist only of a sample size.

Q-37:   A. Sampling scheme

When it's not possible to inspect each item produced by a production process, a sample inspection is used to evaluate the quality of the items in an inspection lot. The sample is picked at random from the lot and, on the basis of the information yielded by the sample, a decision is made regarding the disposition of the lot…namely, the lot is

accepted or rejected for its intended use. A sampling procedure can be used to select the entities of the sample, which are subsequently evaluated according to an inspection plan. Instructions for drawing the sample, such as the sample's size and the number of samples to be taken, are documented in a sample drawing procedure that's assigned to the inspection plan. The sampling type, which is defined in the sampling procedure, specifies the method to be used to calculate the sample size. For example, the sampling type may require that a sample size be equal the lot size…namely, 100 percent inspection, a fixed sample size or a size determined by a sampling scheme. If the sampling type requires the use of a sampling scheme that's assigned to the sampling procedure, it will consist of individual sampling tables, each of which includes two or more sampling plans that determine a sample size based on the lot size, inspection severity, inspection severity and acceptable quality level, AQL, or the number of containers in an inspection lot. The valuation parameter for which the sampling scheme is created determines the structure of the sampling plan. For instance, the structure of a sampling plan created for an attributive inspection valuation mode will consist of a sample size, acceptance number c, or the maximum number of nonconforming units in a sample that is accepted and a rejection number d, or the least number of nonconforming units in a sample that is rejected. In turn, a sampling plan for a variable inspection will consist of a sample size and k-factor, or acceptability constant that defines the minimum quality score that leads to the acceptance of a sample following a quality inspection. A sampling plan with no valuation parameters will consist only of a sample size.

Q-38:   B. Quality level and D. Dynamic modification rule

Sampling procedures, sampling schemes and dynamic
modification rules are the basic data needed to create the
samples used in the inspection process. In particular, a
sampling procedure determines how a sample size is
calculated, how inspection characteristics are valuated and if
a sample size is dynamically modified. The structure of a
sampling procedure includes a sampling type, which
specifies how a sample size is calculated, and a valuation
mode that includes a valuation rule that governs the
acceptance or rejection of a characteristic or sample. The
structure also includes an inspection points control
indicator that determines the number of inspection points
that are created for an inspection lot, an inspection point
type, as well as a usage control indicator that ensures a
particular sampling procedure is not referenced in a task
list. The sampling procedure structure also includes a
control chart type that governs the characteristics for which
a particular control chart can be used, the variables
referenced in the chart and the algorithm used to calculate
the chart's control limits. Other control indicators in the
sampling procedure are the multiple samples control
indicator for independent or dependent multiple samples
and the no stage change control indicator that prevents the
use of the dynamic modification procedure to determine
the inspection scope or sample size. If the dynamic
modification procedure is used, the inspection severity is
based on a dynamic modification rule and the quality level.

Q-39:   C. Valuation mode defined in a sampling
procedure

Sampling procedures, sampling schemes and dynamic modification rules are the basic data needed to create the samples used in the inspection process. In particular, a sampling procedure determines how a sample size is calculated, how inspection characteristics are valuated and if a sample size is dynamically modified. The structure of a sampling procedure includes a sampling type, which specifies how a sample size is calculated, and a valuation mode that includes a valuation rule that governs the acceptance or rejection of a characteristic or sample. The structure also includes an inspection points control indicator that determines the number of inspection points that are created for an inspection lot, an inspection point type, as well as a usage control indicator that ensures a particular sampling procedure is not referenced in a task list. The sampling procedure structure also includes a control chart type that governs the characteristics for which a particular control chart can be used, the variables referenced in the chart and the algorithm used to calculate the chart's control limits. Other control indicators in the sampling procedure are the multiple samples control indicator for independent or dependent multiple samples and the no stage change control indicator that prevents the use of the dynamic modification procedure to determine the inspection scope or sample size.

Q-40:   D. Percentage sample control indicator in the material master record inspection setting for inspection type

Sampling procedures, sampling schemes and dynamic modification rules are the basic data needed to create the samples used in the inspection process. In particular, a

sampling procedure determines how a sample size is calculated, how inspection characteristics are valuated and if a sample size is dynamically modified. The structure of a sampling procedure includes a sampling type, which specifies how a sample size is calculated, and a valuation mode that includes a valuation rule that governs the acceptance or rejection of a characteristic or sample. The structure also includes an inspection points control indicator that determines the number of inspection points that are created for an inspection lot, an inspection point type, as well as a usage control indicator that ensures a particular sampling procedure is not referenced in a task list. The sampling procedure structure also includes a control chart type that governs the characteristics for which a particular control chart can be used, the variables referenced in the chart and the algorithm used to calculate the chart's control limits. Other control indicators in the sampling procedure are the no stage change control indicator that prevents the use of the dynamic modification procedure to determine the inspection scope or sample size and the multiple samples control indicator for independent or dependent multiple samples. The sampling procedure can be assigned to a task list characteristic if an inspection plan is used for the inspection. If an inspection plan is not used for the inspection, the sampling procedure can be specified in the inspection setup for a material master record inspection type using the material master record inspection setup or the Customizing application.

Q-41:   A. Requirement for fixed sample with valuation on the basis of action limits

Sampling procedures, sampling schemes and dynamic modification rules are the basic data needed to create the samples used in the inspection process. In particular, a sampling procedure determines how a sample size is calculated, how inspection characteristics are valuated and if a sample size is dynamically modified. The structure of a sampling procedure includes a sampling type, which specifies how a sample size is calculated, and a valuation mode that includes a valuation rule, which defines the valuation type and governs the acceptance or rejection of a characteristic or sample. The structure also includes an inspection points control indicator that determines the number of inspection points that are created for an inspection lot, an inspection point type, as well as a usage control indicator that ensures a particular sampling procedure is not referenced in a task list. The sampling procedure structure also includes a control chart type that governs the characteristics for which a particular control chart can be used, the variables referenced in the chart and the algorithm used to calculate the chart's control limits. The entry for the control chart type is required if a fixed sample sampling type and valuation on the basis of action limits are used. Other control indicators in the sampling procedure are the no stage change control indicator that prevents the use of the dynamic modification procedure to determine the inspection scope or sample size and the multiple samples control indicator for independent or dependent multiple samples.

Q-42:   B. Define the valuation type in the valuation mode

Sampling procedures, sampling schemes and dynamic modification rules are the basic data needed to create the

samples used in the inspection process. In particular, a sampling procedure determines how a sample size is calculated, how inspection characteristics are valuated and if a sample size is dynamically modified. The structure of a sampling procedure includes a sampling type, which specifies how a sample size is calculated, and a valuation mode that includes a valuation rule, which defines the valuation type and governs the acceptance or rejection of a characteristic or sample. The structure also includes an inspection points control indicator that determines the number of inspection points that are created for an inspection lot, an inspection point type, as well as a usage control indicator that ensures a particular sampling procedure is not referenced in a task list. The sampling procedure structure also includes a control chart type that governs the characteristics for which a particular control chart can be used, the variables referenced in the chart and the algorithm used to calculate the chart's control limits. Other control indicators in the sampling procedure are the no stage change control indicator that prevents the use of the dynamic modification procedure to determine the inspection scope or sample size and the multiple samples control indicator for independent or dependent multiple samples.

Q-43:   D. Attributive inspection on the basis of nonconforming units valuation mode defined in the sampling procedure

When it's not possible to inspect each item produced by a production process, a sample inspection is used to evaluate the quality of the items in an inspection lot. The sample is picked at random from the lot and, on the basis of the

information yielded by the sample, a decision is made regarding the disposition of the lot...namely, the lot is accepted or rejected for its intended use. A sampling procedure can be used to select the entities of the sample, which are subsequently evaluated according to an inspection plan. Instructions for drawing the sample, such as the sample's size and the number of samples to be taken, are documented in a sample drawing procedure that's assigned to the inspection plan. The sampling type, which is defined in the sampling procedure, specifies the method to be used to calculate the sample size. For example, the sampling type may require that a sample size be equal the lot size...namely, 100 percent inspection, a fixed sample size or a size determined by a sampling scheme. If the sampling type requires the use of a sampling scheme that's assigned to the sampling procedure, it will consist of individual sampling tables, each of which includes two or more sampling plans that determine a sample size based on the lot size, inspection severity, inspection severity and acceptable quality level, AQL, or the number of containers in an inspection lot. The valuation parameter for which the sampling scheme is created determines the structure of the sampling plan. For instance, the structure of a sampling plan created for an attributive inspection valuation mode will consist of a sample size, acceptance number c, or the maximum number of nonconforming units in a sample that is accepted and a rejection number d, or the least number of nonconforming units in a sample that is rejected. In turn, a sampling plan for a variable inspection will consist of a sample size and k-factor, or acceptability constant that defines the minimum quality score that leads to the acceptance of a sample following a quality inspection. A

sampling plan with no valuation parameters will consist only of a sample size.

Q-44:   A. Quality level and B. Dynamic modification rule

Sampling procedures, sampling schemes and dynamic modification rules are the basic data needed to create the samples used in the inspection process. In particular, a sampling procedure determines how a sample size is calculated, how inspection characteristics are valuated and if a sample size is dynamically modified. The structure of a sampling procedure includes a sampling type, which specifies how a sample size is calculated, and a valuation mode that includes a valuation rule that governs the acceptance or rejection of a characteristic or sample. The structure also includes an inspection points control indicator that determines the number of inspection points that are created for an inspection lot, an inspection point type, as well as a usage control indicator that ensures a particular sampling procedure is not referenced in a task list. The sampling procedure structure also includes a control chart type that governs the characteristics for which a particular control chart can be used, the variables referenced in the chart and the algorithm used to calculate the chart's control limits. Other control indicators in the sampling procedure are the multiple samples control indicator for independent or dependent multiple samples and the no stage change control indicator that prevents the use of the dynamic modification procedure to determine the inspection scope or sample size. If the dynamic modification procedure is used, the inspection severity is based on a dynamic modification rule and the quality level.

Q-45:   A. Special control indicator in the sampling procedure

Sampling procedures, sampling schemes and dynamic modification rules are the basic data needed to create the samples used in the inspection process. In particular, a sampling procedure determines how a sample size is calculated, how inspection characteristics are valuated and if a sample size is dynamically modified. The structure of a sampling procedure includes a sampling type, which specifies how a sample size is calculated, and a valuation mode that includes a valuation rule that governs the acceptance or rejection of a characteristic or sample. The structure also includes an inspection points control indicator that determines the number of inspection points that are created for an inspection lot, an inspection point type, as well as a usage control indicator that ensures a particular sampling procedure is not referenced in a task list. The sampling procedure structure also includes a control chart type that governs the characteristics for which a particular control chart can be used, the variables referenced in the chart and the algorithm used to calculate the chart's control limits. Other control indicators in the sampling procedure are the multiple samples control indicator for independent or dependent multiple samples and the no stage change control indicator that prevents the use of the dynamic modification procedure to determine the inspection scope or sample size.

Q-46:   B. Inspection severity and C. Inspection severity and AQL

179

When it's not possible to inspect each item produced by a production process, a sample inspection is used to evaluate the quality of the items in an inspection lot. The sample is picked at random from the lot and, on the basis of the information yielded by the sample, a decision is made regarding the disposition of the lot…namely, the lot is accepted or rejected for its intended use. A sampling procedure can be used to select the entities of the sample, which are subsequently evaluated according to an inspection plan. Instructions for drawing the sample, such as the sample's size and the number of samples to be taken, are documented in a sample drawing procedure that's assigned to the inspection plan. The sampling type, which is defined in the sampling procedure, specifies the method to be used to calculate the sample size. For example, the sampling type may require that a sample size be equal the lot size…namely, 100 percent inspection, a fixed sample size or a size determined by a sampling scheme. If the sampling type requires the use of a sampling scheme that's assigned to the sampling procedure, it will consist of individual sampling tables, each of which includes two or more sampling plans that determine a sample size based on the lot size, inspection severity, inspection severity and acceptable quality level, AQL, or the number of containers in an inspection lot. The valuation parameter for which the sampling scheme is created determines the structure of the sampling plan. For instance, the structure of a sampling plan created for an attributive inspection valuation mode will consist of a sample size, acceptance number c, or the maximum number of nonconforming units in a sample that is accepted and a rejection number d, or the least number of nonconforming units in a sample that is rejected. In turn, a sampling plan for a variable inspection will consist of a

sample size and k-factor, or acceptability constant that defines the minimum quality score that leads to the acceptance of a sample following a quality inspection. A sampling plan with no valuation parameters will consist only of a sample size.

Q-47:   A. Sample Determination

The Sample Determination component can be used to both evaluate samples on the basis of inspection characteristic values and implement statistical process control by means of a control chart. Elements of the Sample Determination component include sampling procedures, sampling schemes and dynamic modification rules, which are the basic data used to create the samples used in the inspection process. In particular, a sampling procedure determines how a sample size is calculated, how inspection characteristics are valuated and if a sample size is dynamically modified. The structure of a sampling procedure includes a sampling type, which specifies how a sample size is calculated, and a valuation mode that includes a valuation rule that governs the acceptance or rejection of a characteristic or sample. The structure also includes an inspection points control indicator that determines the number of inspection points that are created for an inspection lot, an inspection point type, as well as a usage control indicator that ensures a particular sampling procedure is not referenced in a task list. The sampling procedure structure also includes a control chart type that governs the characteristics for which a particular control chart can be used, the variables referenced in the chart and the algorithm used to calculate the chart's control limits. A control chart can be used to evaluate samples on the basis of inspection characteristic values and implement statistical process control. Other control indicators in the sampling procedure are the multiple samples control indicator for independent or dependent multiple samples and the no stage change control indicator that prevents the use of the dynamic modification procedure to determine the inspection scope or sample size.

Q-48:   A. Sampling type and C. Valuation mode

Sampling procedures, sampling schemes and dynamic modification rules are the basic data needed to create the samples used in the inspection process. In particular, a sampling procedure determines how a sample size is calculated, how inspection characteristics are valuated and if a sample size is dynamically modified. The structure of a sampling procedure includes a sampling type, which specifies how a sample size is calculated, and a valuation mode that includes a valuation rule that governs the acceptance or rejection of a characteristic or sample. The structure also includes an inspection points control indicator that determines the number of inspection points that are created for an inspection lot, an inspection point type, as well as a usage control indicator that ensures a particular sampling procedure is not referenced in a task list. The sampling procedure structure also includes a control chart type that governs the characteristics for which a particular control chart can be used, the variables referenced in the chart and the algorithm used to calculate the chart's control limits. Other control indicators in the sampling procedure are the multiple samples control indicator for independent or dependent multiple samples and the no stage change control indicator that prevents the

use of the dynamic modification procedure to determine
the inspection scope or sample size.

Q-49:   B. Select the special control indicator in the
sampling procedure

Sampling procedures, sampling schemes and dynamic
modification rules are the basic data needed to create the
samples used in the inspection process. In particular, a
sampling procedure determines how a sample size is
calculated, how inspection characteristics are valuated and if
a sample size is dynamically modified. The structure of a
sampling procedure includes a sampling type, which
specifies how a sample size is calculated, and a valuation
mode that includes a valuation rule that governs the
acceptance or rejection of a characteristic or sample. The
structure also includes an inspection points control
indicator that determines the number of inspection points
that are created for an inspection lot, an inspection point
type, as well as a usage control indicator that ensures a
particular sampling procedure is not referenced in a task
list. The sampling procedure structure also includes a
control chart type that governs the characteristics for which
a particular control chart can be used, the variables
referenced in the chart and the algorithm used to calculate
the chart's control limits. Other control indicators in the
sampling procedure are the multiple samples control
indicator for independent or dependent multiple samples
and the no stage change control indicator that prevents the
use of the dynamic modification procedure to determine
the inspection scope or sample size.

Q-50:   B. Valuation rule

Sampling procedures, sampling schemes and dynamic modification rules are the basic data needed to create the samples used in the inspection process. In particular, a sampling procedure determines how a sample size is calculated, how inspection characteristics are valuated and if a sample size is dynamically modified. The structure of a sampling procedure includes a sampling type, which specifies how a sample size is calculated, and a valuation mode that includes a valuation rule that governs the acceptance or rejection of a characteristic or sample. The structure also includes an inspection points control indicator that determines the number of inspection points that are created for an inspection lot, an inspection point type, as well as a usage control indicator that ensures a particular sampling procedure is not referenced in a task list. The sampling procedure structure also includes a control chart type that governs the characteristics for which a particular control chart can be used, the variables referenced in the chart and the algorithm used to calculate the chart's control limits. Other control indicators in the sampling procedure are the no stage change control indicator that prevents the use of the dynamic modification procedure to determine the inspection scope or sample size and the multiple samples control indicator for independent or dependent multiple samples. The multiple samples control indicator in particular controls a customer's ability to valuate multiple individual samples prior to valuating a characteristic. In this case, the customer selects the independent multiple sampling control indicator and the valuation rule for independent multiple samples in the sampling procedure, and specifies the number of independent multiple samples to be valuated.

184

Q-51:   A. Relates the allowable number or percentage of nonconforming units to an inspection severity and inspection lot quantity

When it's not possible to inspect each item produced by a production process, a sample inspection is used to evaluate the quality of the items in an inspection lot. The sample is picked at random from the lot and, on the basis of the information yielded by the sample, a decision is made regarding the disposition of the lot... namely, the lot is accepted or rejected for its intended use. A sampling procedure can be used to select the entities of the sample, which are subsequently evaluated according to an inspection plan. Instructions for drawing the sample, such as the sample's size and the number of samples to be taken, are documented in a sample drawing procedure that's assigned to the inspection plan. The sampling type, which is defined in the sampling procedure, specifies the method to be used to calculate the sample size. For example, the sampling type may require that a sample size be equal the lot size...namely, 100 percent inspection, a fixed sample size or a size determined by a sampling scheme. If the sampling type requires the use of a sampling scheme that's assigned to the sampling procedure, it will consist of individual sampling tables, each of which includes two or more sampling plans that determine a sample size based on the lot size, inspection severity, inspection severity and acceptable quality level, AQL, or the number of containers in an inspection lot. The valuation parameter for which the sampling scheme is created determines the structure of the sampling plan. For instance, the structure of a sampling plan created for an attributive inspection valuation mode will consist of a sample size, acceptance number c, or the maximum number of nonconforming units in a sample that is accepted and a rejection number d, or the least number of nonconforming units in a sample that is rejected. In turn, a sampling plan for a variable inspection will consist of a sample size and k-factor, or acceptability constant that defines the minimum quality score that leads to the acceptance of a sample following a quality inspection. A sampling plan with no valuation parameters will consist only of a sample size.

Q-52: A. Text, B. Valuation mode and C. Sampling table variable

When it's not possible to inspect each item produced by a production process, a sample inspection is used to evaluate the quality of the items in an inspection lot. The sample is picked at random from the lot and, on the basis of the information yielded by the sample, a decision is made regarding the disposition of the lot...namely, the lot is accepted or rejected for its intended use. A sampling procedure can be used to select the entities of the sample, which are subsequently evaluated according to an inspection plan. Instructions for drawing the sample, such as the sample's size and the number of samples to be taken, are documented in a sample drawing procedure that's assigned to the inspection plan. The sampling type, which is defined in the sampling procedure, specifies the method to be used to calculate the sample size. For example, the sampling type may require that a sample size be equal the lot size...namely, 100 percent inspection, a fixed sample size or a size determined by a sampling scheme. If the sampling type requires the use of a sampling scheme that's assigned to the sampling procedure, it will consist of

individual sampling tables, each of which includes two or more sampling plans that determine a sample size based on the lot size, inspection severity, inspection severity and acceptable quality level, AQL, or the number of containers in an inspection lot. The valuation parameter for which the sampling scheme is created determines the structure of the sampling plan. For instance, the structure of a sampling plan created for an attributive inspection valuation mode will consist of a sample size, acceptance number c, or the maximum number of nonconforming units in a sample that is accepted and a rejection number d, or the least number of nonconforming units in a sample that is rejected. In turn, a sampling plan for a variable inspection will consist of a sample size and k-factor, or acceptability constant that defines the minimum quality score that leads to the acceptance of a sample following a quality inspection. A sampling plan with no valuation parameters will consist only of a sample size. The header of a sampling scheme requires the entry of text, a valuation mode, a sampling table variable and, if required, a blocking control indicator that prevents the assignment of the sampling scheme to a sampling procedure.

Q-53:   B. Defines the minimum quality score that leads to the acceptance of the sample

When it's not possible to inspect each item produced by a production process, a sample inspection is used to evaluate the quality of the items in an inspection lot. The sample is picked at random from the lot and, on the basis of the information yielded by the sample, a decision is made regarding the disposition of the lot…namely, the lot is accepted or rejected for its intended use. A sampling procedure can be used to select the entities of the sample, which are subsequently evaluated according to an inspection plan. Instructions for drawing the sample, such as the sample's size and the number of samples to be taken, are documented in a sample drawing procedure that's assigned to the inspection plan. The sampling type, which is defined in the sampling procedure, specifies the method to be used to calculate the sample size. For example, the sampling type may require that a sample size be equal the lot size…namely, 100 percent inspection, a fixed sample size or a size determined by a sampling scheme. If the sampling type requires the use of a sampling scheme that's assigned to the sampling procedure, it will consist of individual sampling tables, each of which includes two or more sampling plans that determine a sample size based on the lot size, inspection severity, inspection severity and acceptable quality level, AQL, or the number of containers in an inspection lot. The valuation parameter for which the sampling scheme is created determines the structure of the sampling plan. For instance, the structure of a sampling plan created for an attributive inspection valuation mode will consist of a sample size, acceptance number c, or the maximum number of nonconforming units in a sample that is accepted and a rejection number d, or the least number of nonconforming units in a sample that is rejected. In turn, a sampling plan for a variable inspection will consist of a sample size and k-factor, or acceptability constant that defines the minimum quality score that leads to the acceptance of a sample following a quality inspection. A sampling plan with no valuation parameters will consist only of a sample size. The header of a sampling scheme requires the entry of text, a valuation mode, a sampling table variable and, if required, a blocking control indicator that prevents the assignment of the sampling scheme to a sampling procedure.

Q-54:   A. Sampling type in sampling procedure

Sampling procedures, sampling schemes and dynamic modification rules are the basic data needed to create the samples used in the inspection process. In particular, a sampling procedure determines how a sample size is calculated, how inspection characteristics are valuated and if a sample size is dynamically modified. The structure of a sampling procedure includes a sampling type, which specifies how a sample size is calculated, and a valuation mode that includes a valuation rule that governs the acceptance or rejection of a characteristic or sample. The structure also includes an inspection points control indicator that determines the number of inspection points that are created for an inspection lot, an inspection point type, as well as a usage control indicator that ensures a particular sampling procedure is not referenced in a task list. The sampling procedure structure also includes a control chart type that governs the characteristics for which a particular control chart can be used, the variables referenced in the chart and the algorithm used to calculate the chart's control limits. Other control indicators in the sampling procedure are the no stage change control indicator that prevents the use of the dynamic modification procedure to determine the inspection scope or sample size and the multiple samples control indicator for independent or dependent multiple samples.

Q-55:   A. Control chart type in the sampling procedure

A control chart is used in a quality inspection as a means to monitor controlled production processes. The control chart determines if a process is "in control" or "out of control" on the basis of action limits that are defined for the particular chart and actual measured values acquired during a quality inspection. During a quality inspection, a sample or characteristic is valuated based on the relationship between the control chart action limits and the measured value of the characteristic. Using a valuation rule, a sample or characteristic is rejected if one or more action limits is violated by a characteristic value. To use a control chart to valuate a sample, a control chart type must be defined in the sampling procedure that is, in turn, defined in the inspection characteristic or the inspection settings for the material master record inspection type. In addition, both the fixed sample sampling type and the valuation on the basis of action limits valuation mode must be selected in the sampling procedure. The control chart type governs the characteristics to be referenced in a control chart, the control variables to be included in the chart, as well as the calculation of the chart's control limits.

Q-56:   A. Sampling type

Sampling procedures, sampling schemes and dynamic modification rules are the basic data needed to create the samples used in the inspection process. In particular, a sampling procedure determines how a sample size is calculated, how inspection characteristics are valuated and if a sample size is dynamically modified. The structure of a sampling procedure includes a sampling type, which specifies how a sample size is calculated, and a valuation mode that includes a valuation rule that governs the

acceptance or rejection of a characteristic or sample. The structure also includes an inspection points control indicator that determines the number of inspection points that are created for an inspection lot, an inspection point type, as well as a usage control indicator that ensures a particular sampling procedure is not referenced in a task list. The sampling procedure structure also includes a control chart type that governs the characteristics for which a particular control chart can be used, the variables referenced in the chart and the algorithm used to calculate the chart's control limits. Other control indicators in the sampling procedure are the no stage change control indicator that prevents the use of the dynamic modification procedure to determine the inspection scope or sample size and the multiple samples control indicator for independent or dependent multiple samples.

Q-57:   D. All of the above

Sampling procedures, sampling schemes and dynamic modification rules are the basic data needed to create the samples used in the inspection process. In particular, a sampling procedure determines how a sample size is calculated, how inspection characteristics are valuated and if a sample size is dynamically modified. The structure of a sampling procedure includes a sampling type, which specifies how a sample size is calculated, and a valuation mode that includes a valuation rule that governs the acceptance or rejection of a characteristic or sample. The structure also includes an inspection points control indicator that determines the number of inspection points that are created for an inspection lot, an inspection point type, as well as a usage control indicator that ensures a particular sampling procedure is not referenced in a task list. The sampling procedure structure also includes a control chart type that governs the characteristics for which a particular control chart can be used, the variables referenced in the chart and the algorithm used to calculate the chart's control limits. Other control indicators in the sampling procedure are the no stage change control indicator that prevents the use of the dynamic modification procedure to determine the inspection scope or sample size and the multiple samples control indicator for independent or dependent multiple samples. The processing of double sampling inspections and multiple sampling inspections is enabled by the dependent multiple samples function control indicator that's set in the sampling procedure. A valuation rule for the function is defined for the valuation mode and i ensures a characteristic is valuated after the dependent multiple samples are valuated. The use of dependent multiple samples requires a sampling type with a sampling scheme, the attributive inspection valuation mode and the definition of a function module for valuating dependent multiple samples in the dependent multiples samples valuation rule. Inspection results can be automatically accepted or rejected immediately or not valuated.

Q-58: B. Maximum number of defects per 100 units that does not preclude acceptance of an inspection lot during quality inspection and C. Maximum percentage of defects per 100 units that does not preclude acceptance of an inspection lot during quality inspection

When it's not possible to inspect each item produced by a production process, a sample inspection is used to evaluate the quality of the items in an inspection lot. The sample is picked at random from the lot and, on the basis of the information yielded by the sample, a decision is made regarding the disposition of the lot…namely, the lot is accepted or rejected for its intended use. A sampling procedure can be used to select the entities of the sample, which are subsequently evaluated according to an inspection plan. Instructions for drawing the sample, such as the sample's size and the number of samples to be taken, are documented in a sample drawing procedure that's assigned to the inspection plan. The sampling type, which is defined in the sampling procedure, specifies the method to be used to calculate the sample size. For example, the sampling type may require that a sample size be equal the lot size…namely, 100 percent inspection, a fixed sample size or a size determined by a sampling scheme. If the sampling type requires the use of a sampling scheme that's assigned to the sampling procedure, it will consist of individual sampling tables, each of which includes two or more sampling plans that determine a sample size based on the lot size, inspection severity, inspection severity and acceptable quality level, AQL, or the number of containers in an inspection lot. The valuation parameter for which the sampling scheme is created determines the structure of the sampling plan. For instance, the structure of a sampling plan created for an attributive inspection valuation mode will consist of a sample size, acceptance number c, or the maximum number of nonconforming units in a sample that is accepted and a rejection number d, or the least number of nonconforming units in a sample that is rejected. In turn, a sampling plan for a variable inspection will consist of a sample size and k-factor, or acceptability constant that defines the minimum quality score that leads to the acceptance of a sample following a quality inspection. A sampling plan with no valuation parameters will consist only of a sample size.

Q-59:   A. Sampling type, B. Valuation mode and D. Quality level

Sampling procedures, sampling schemes and dynamic modification rules are the basic data needed to create the samples used in the inspection process. In particular, a sampling procedure determines how a sample size is calculated, how inspection characteristics are valuated and if a sample size is dynamically modified. The structure of a sampling procedure includes a sampling type, which specifies how a sample size is calculated, and a valuation mode that includes a valuation rule that governs the acceptance or rejection of a characteristic or sample. The structure also includes an inspection points control indicator that determines the number of inspection points that are created for an inspection lot, an inspection point type, as well as a usage control indicator that ensures a particular sampling procedure is not referenced in a task list. The sampling procedure structure also includes a control chart type that governs the characteristics for which a particular control chart can be used, the variables referenced in the chart and the algorithm used to calculate the chart's control limits. Other control indicators in the sampling procedure are the multiple samples control indicator for independent or dependent multiple samples and the no stage change control indicator that prevents the use of the dynamic modification procedure to determine the inspection scope or sample size. Prerequisites to the creation of a sampling procedure include the creation of sampling types, valuation modes and quality levels.

Q-60:   A. Acceptance number c

When it's not possible to inspect each item produced by a production process, a sample inspection is used to evaluate the quality of the items in an inspection lot. The sample is picked at random from the lot and, on the basis of the information yielded by the sample, a decision is made regarding the disposition of the lot...namely, the lot is accepted or rejected for its intended use. A sampling procedure can be used to select the entities of the sample, which are subsequently evaluated according to an inspection plan. Instructions for drawing the sample, such as the sample's size and the number of samples to be taken, are documented in a sample drawing procedure that's assigned to the inspection plan. The sampling type, which is defined in the sampling procedure, specifies the method to be used to calculate the sample size. For example, the sampling type may require that a sample size be equal the lot size...namely, 100 percent inspection, a fixed sample size or a size determined by a sampling scheme. If the sampling type requires the use of a sampling scheme that's assigned to the sampling procedure, it will consist of individual sampling tables, each of which includes two or more sampling plans that determine a sample size based on the lot size, inspection severity, inspection severity and acceptable quality level, AQL, or the number of containers in an inspection lot. The valuation parameter for which the sampling scheme is created determines the structure of the sampling plan. For instance, the structure of a sampling plan created for an attributive inspection valuation mode

will consist of a sample size, acceptance number c, or the maximum number of nonconforming units in a sample that is accepted and a rejection number d, or the least number of nonconforming units in a sample that is rejected. In turn, a sampling plan for a variable inspection will consist of a sample size and k-factor, or acceptability constant that defines the minimum quality score that leads to the acceptance of a sample following a quality inspection. A sampling plan with no valuation parameters will consist only of a sample size.

Q-61:   C. Task list characteristic level

Sampling procedures, sampling schemes and dynamic modification rules are the basic data needed to create the samples used in the inspection process. The manner in which a sampling procedure is selected for use in a quality inspection is dependent on whether a task list or material specification is used to conduct the inspection. If an inspection plan is used, the sampling procedure can be directly assigned to an inspection characteristic in the plan using the inspection planning functions or the Customizing application. If an inspection plan is not used to conduct the inspection, the sampling procedure can be specified in the inspection setup for a material master record inspection type.

Q-62:   A. Valuation mode and C. Control chart type

Sampling procedures, sampling schemes and dynamic modification rules are the basic data needed to create the samples used in the inspection process. In particular, a sampling procedure determines how a sample size is calculated, how inspection characteristics are valuated and if a sample size is dynamically modified. The structure of a sampling procedure includes a sampling type, which specifies how a sample size is calculated, and a valuation mode (special condition) that includes a valuation rule, which governs the acceptance or rejection of a characteristic or sample. The structure also includes an inspection points control indicator that determines the number of inspection points that are created for an inspection lot, an inspection point type, as well as a usage control indicator that ensures a particular sampling procedure is not referenced in a task list. The sampling procedure structure also includes a control chart type (special condition) that governs the characteristics for which a particular control chart can be used, the variables referenced in the chart and the algorithm used to calculate the chart's control limits. Other control indicators in the sampling procedure are the multiple samples control indicator for independent or dependent multiple samples and the no stage change control indicator that prevents the use of the dynamic modification procedure to determine the inspection scope or sample size.

Q-63:   A. Sample size and C. Acceptance number

When it's not possible to inspect each item produced by a production process, a sample inspection is used to evaluate the quality of the items in an inspection lot. The sample is picked at random from the lot and, on the basis of the information yielded by the sample, a decision is made regarding the disposition of the lot…namely, the lot is accepted or rejected for its intended use. A sampling procedure can be used to select the entities of the sample, which are subsequently evaluated according to an inspection plan. Instructions for drawing the sample, such as the sample's size and the number of samples to be taken, are documented in a sample drawing procedure that's assigned to the inspection plan. The sampling type, which is defined in the sampling procedure, specifies the method to be used to calculate the sample size. For example, the sampling type may require that a sample size be equal the lot size...namely, 100 percent inspection, a fixed sample size or a size determined by a sampling scheme. If the sampling type requires the use of a sampling scheme that's assigned to the sampling procedure, it will consist of individual sampling tables, each of which includes two or more sampling plans that determine a sample size based on the lot size, inspection severity, inspection severity and acceptable quality level, AQL, or the number of containers in an inspection lot. The valuation parameter for which the sampling scheme is created determines the structure of the sampling plan.

Q-64:   A. Control chart type in the sampling procedure

Sampling procedures, sampling schemes and dynamic modification rules are the basic data needed to create the samples used in the inspection process. In particular, a sampling procedure determines how a sample size is calculated, how inspection characteristics are valuated and if a sample size is dynamically modified. The structure of a sampling procedure includes a sampling type, which specifies how a sample size is calculated, and a valuation mode (special condition) that includes a valuation rule, which governs the acceptance or rejection of a characteristic or sample. The structure also includes an inspection points control indicator that determines the number of inspection points that are created for an inspection lot, an inspection point type, as well as a usage control indicator that ensures a particular sampling procedure is not referenced in a task list. The sampling procedure structure also includes a control chart type (special condition) that governs the characteristics for which a particular control chart can be used and the valuation of a sample on the basis of action limits, the variables referenced in the chart and the algorithm used to calculate the chart's control limits. Other control indicators in the sampling procedure are the multiple samples control indicator for independent or dependent multiple samples and the no stage change control indicator that prevents the use of the dynamic modification procedure to determine the inspection scope or sample size.

Q-65:   C. Enables the valuation of a characteristic following the valuation of a number of dependent multiple samples

Sampling procedures, sampling schemes and dynamic modification rules are the basic data needed to create the samples used in the inspection process. In particular, a sampling procedure determines how a sample size is calculated, how inspection characteristics are valuated and if a sample size is dynamically modified. The structure of a sampling procedure includes a sampling type, which specifies how a sample size is calculated, and a valuation mode that includes a valuation rule that governs the acceptance or rejection of a characteristic or sample. The structure also includes an inspection points control indicator that determines the number of inspection points

that are created for an inspection lot, an inspection point type, as well as a usage control indicator that ensures a particular sampling procedure is not referenced in a task list. The sampling procedure structure also includes a control chart type that governs the characteristics for which a particular control chart can be used, the variables referenced in the chart and the algorithm used to calculate the chart's control limits. Other control indicators in the sampling procedure are the no stage change control indicator that prevents the use of the dynamic modification procedure to determine the inspection scope or sample size and the multiple samples control indicator for independent or dependent multiple samples. The processing of double sampling inspections and multiple sampling inspections is enabled by the dependent multiple samples function control indicator that's set in the sampling procedure. A valuation rule, which is defined for the function is defined for the valuation mode in the sampling procedure, valuates a characteristic after the dependent multiple samples are valuated. The use of dependent multiple samples requires a sampling type with a sampling scheme, the attributive inspection valuation mode and the definition of a function module for valuating dependent multiple samples in the dependent multiples samples valuation rule.

Q-66:   C. AQL value

When it's not possible to inspect each item produced by a production process, a sample inspection is used to evaluate the quality of the items in an inspection lot. The sample is picked at random from the lot and, on the basis of the information yielded by the sample, a decision is made regarding the disposition of the lot…namely, the lot is

accepted or rejected for its intended use. A sampling procedure can be used to select the entities of the sample, which are subsequently evaluated according to an inspection plan. Instructions for drawing the sample, such as the sample's size and the number of samples to be taken, are documented in a sample drawing procedure that's assigned to the inspection plan. The sampling type, which is defined in the sampling procedure, specifies the method to be used to calculate the sample size. For example, the sampling type may require that a sample size be equal the lot size…namely, 100 percent inspection, a fixed sample size or a size determined by a sampling scheme. If the sampling type requires the use of a sampling scheme that's assigned to the sampling procedure, it will consist of individual sampling tables, each of which includes two or more sampling plans that determine a sample size based on the lot size, inspection severity, inspection severity and acceptable quality level, AQL -- the maximum number of defects per 100 units -- or the number of containers in an inspection lot. The valuation parameter for which the sampling scheme is created determines the structure of the sampling plan. For instance, the structure of a sampling plan created for an attributive inspection valuation mode will consist of a sample size, acceptance number c, or the maximum number of nonconforming units in a sample that is accepted and a rejection number d, or the least number of nonconforming units in a sample that is rejected. In turn, a sampling plan for a variable inspection will consist of a sample size and k-factor, or acceptability constant that defines the minimum quality score that leads to the acceptance of a sample following a quality inspection. A sampling plan with no valuation parameters will consist only of a sample size.

Q-67:   A. Independent multiple samples, B. Dependent multiple samples and C. Single samples

When it's not possible to inspect each item produced by a production process, a sample inspection is used to evaluate the quality of the items in an inspection lot. The sample is picked at random from the lot and, on the basis of the information yielded by the sample, a decision is made regarding the disposition of the lot…namely, the lot is accepted or rejected for its intended use. A sampling procedure can be used to select the entities of the sample, which are subsequently evaluated according to an inspection plan. Instructions for drawing the sample, such as the sample's size and the number of samples to be taken, are documented in a sample drawing procedure that's assigned to the inspection plan. The sampling type, which is defined in the sampling procedure, specifies the method to be used to calculate the sample size. For example, the sampling type may require that a sample size be equal the lot size…namely, 100 percent inspection, a fixed sample size or a size determined by a sampling scheme. If the sampling type requires the use of a sampling scheme that's assigned to the sampling procedure, it will consist of individual sampling tables, each of which includes two or more sampling plans that determine a sample size based on the lot size, inspection severity, inspection severity and acceptable quality level, AQL -- the maximum number of defects per 100 units -- or the number of containers in an inspection lot. The valuation parameter for which the sampling scheme is created determines the structure of the sampling plan. For instance, the structure of a sampling plan created for an attributive inspection valuation mode will consist of a sample size, acceptance number c, or the maximum number of nonconforming units in a sample that is accepted and a rejection number d, or the least number of nonconforming units in a sample that is rejected. In turn, a sampling plan for a variable inspection will consist of a sample size and k-factor, or acceptability constant that defines the minimum quality score that leads to the acceptance of a sample following a quality inspection. A sampling plan with no valuation parameters will consist only of a sample size. A sampling scheme can be used for single samples or independent or dependent multiple samples.

Q-68:   B. Sampling type

Sampling procedures, sampling schemes and dynamic modification rules are the basic data needed to create the samples used in the inspection process. In particular, a sampling procedure determines how a sample size is calculated, how inspection characteristics are valuated and if a sample size is dynamically modified. The structure of a sampling procedure includes a sampling type, such as 100 percent inspection, which specifies how a sample size is calculated, and a valuation mode that includes a valuation rule that governs the acceptance or rejection of a characteristic or sample. The structure also includes an inspection points control indicator that determines the number of inspection points that are created for an inspection lot, an inspection point type, as well as a usage control indicator that ensures a particular sampling procedure is not referenced in a task list. The sampling procedure structure also includes a control chart type that governs the characteristics for which a particular control chart can be used, the variables referenced in the chart and the algorithm used to calculate the chart's control limits. Other control indicators in the sampling procedure are the no stage change control indicator that prevents the use of the dynamic modification procedure to determine the inspection scope or sample size and the multiple samples control indicator for independent or dependent multiple samples.

Q-69:   B. Sampling plan

When it's not possible to inspect each item produced by a production process, a sample inspection is used to evaluate the quality of the items in an inspection lot. The sample is picked at random from the lot and, on the basis of the information yielded by the sample, a decision is made regarding the disposition of the lot…namely, the lot is accepted or rejected for its intended use. A sampling procedure can be used to select the entities of the sample, which are subsequently evaluated according to an inspection plan. Instructions for drawing the sample, such as the sample's size and the number of samples to be taken, are documented in a sample drawing procedure that's assigned to the inspection plan. The sampling type, which is defined in the sampling procedure, specifies the method to be used to calculate the sample size. For example, the sampling type may require that a sample size be equal the lot size…namely, 100 percent inspection, a fixed sample size or a size determined by a sampling scheme. If the sampling type requires the use of a sampling scheme that's assigned to the sampling procedure, it will consist of individual sampling tables, each of which includes two or more sampling plans that determine a sample size based on the lot size, inspection severity, inspection severity and acceptable quality level, AQL -- the maximum number of defects per 100 units -- or the number of containers in an inspection lot. The valuation parameter for which the sampling scheme is created determines the structure of the sampling plan. For instance, the structure of a sampling plan created for an attributive inspection valuation mode will consist of a sample size, acceptance number c, or the maximum number of nonconforming units in a sample that is accepted and a rejection number d, or the least number of nonconforming units in a sample that is rejected. In turn, a sampling plan for a variable inspection will consist of a sample size and k-factor, or acceptability constant that defines the minimum quality score that leads to the acceptance of a sample following a quality inspection. A sampling plan with no valuation parameters will consist only of a sample size. A sampling scheme can be used for independent or dependent multiple samples and single samples.

Q-70:   C. Lot size

When it's not possible to inspect each item produced by a production process, a sample inspection is used to evaluate the quality of the items in an inspection lot. The sample is picked at random from the lot and, on the basis of the information yielded by the sample, a decision is made regarding the disposition of the lot...namely, the lot is accepted or rejected for its intended use. A sampling procedure can be used to select the entities of the sample, which are subsequently evaluated according to an inspection plan. Instructions for drawing the sample, such as the sample's size and the number of samples to be taken, are documented in a sample drawing procedure that's assigned to the inspection plan. The sampling type, which is defined in the sampling procedure, specifies the method to be used to calculate the sample size. For example, the sampling type may require that a sample size be equal the lot size...namely, 100 percent inspection, a fixed sample size or a size determined by a sampling scheme. If the sampling type requires the use of a sampling scheme that's assigned to the sampling procedure, it will consist of individual sampling tables, each of which includes two or more sampling plans that determine a sample size based on the lot size that establishes the maximum number of samples, inspection severity, inspection severity and acceptable quality level, AQL -- the maximum number of defects per 100 units -- or the number of containers in an inspection lot. The valuation parameter for which the sampling scheme is created determines the structure of the sampling plan.

Q-71:   C. Sampling procedure

Sampling procedures, sampling schemes and dynamic modification rules are the basic data needed to create the samples used in the inspection process. In particular, a sampling procedure determines how a sample size is calculated, how inspection characteristics are valuated and if a sample size is dynamically modified. The structure of a sampling procedure includes a sampling type, such as 100 percent inspection, which specifies how a sample size is calculated, and a valuation mode that includes a valuation rule that governs the acceptance or rejection of a characteristic or sample. The structure also includes an inspection points control indicator that determines the number of inspection points that are created for an inspection lot, an inspection point type, as well as a usage control indicator that ensures a particular sampling procedure is not referenced in a task list. The sampling procedure structure also includes a control chart type that governs the characteristics for which a particular control chart can be used, the variables referenced in the chart and the algorithm used to calculate the chart's control limits. Other control indicators in the sampling procedure are the no stage change control indicator that prevents the use of the dynamic modification procedure to determine the inspection scope or sample size and the multiple samples control indicator for independent or dependent multiple samples.

Q-72:   C. A parameter used to define the rules for the acceptance or rejection of a characteristic or sample during a quality inspection

Sampling procedures, sampling schemes and dynamic modification rules are the basic data needed to create the samples used in the inspection process. In particular, a sampling procedure determines how a sample size is calculated, how inspection characteristics are valuated and if a sample size is dynamically modified. The structure of a sampling procedure includes a sampling type, such as 100 percent inspection, which specifies how a sample size is calculated, and a valuation mode that includes a valuation rule that governs the acceptance or rejection of a characteristic or sample. The structure also includes an inspection points control indicator that determines the number of inspection points that are created for an inspection lot, an inspection point type, as well as a usage control indicator that ensures a particular sampling procedure is not referenced in a task list. The sampling procedure structure also includes a control chart type that governs the characteristics for which a particular control chart can be used, the variables referenced in the chart and the algorithm used to calculate the chart's control limits. Other control indicators in the sampling procedure are the no stage change control indicator that prevents the use of the dynamic modification procedure to determine the inspection scope or sample size and the multiple samples control indicator for independent or dependent multiple samples.

Q-73: B. A sampling type with a sampling scheme is defined and D. Function module defined to valuate dependent multiple samples in valuation mode

Sampling procedures, sampling schemes and dynamic modification rules are the basic data needed to create the samples used in the inspection process. In particular, a sampling procedure determines how a sample size is calculated, how inspection characteristics are valuated and if a sample size is dynamically modified. The structure of a sampling procedure includes a sampling type, which specifies how a sample size is calculated, and a valuation mode that includes a valuation rule that governs the acceptance or rejection of a characteristic or sample. The structure also includes an inspection points control indicator that determines the number of inspection points that are created for an inspection lot, an inspection point type, as well as a usage control indicator that ensures a particular sampling procedure is not referenced in a task list. The sampling procedure structure also includes a control chart type that governs the characteristics for which

a particular control chart can be used, the variables referenced in the chart and the algorithm used to calculate the chart's control limits. Other control indicators in the sampling procedure are the no stage change control indicator that prevents the use of the dynamic modification procedure to determine the inspection scope or sample size and the multiple samples control indicator for independent or dependent multiple samples. The processing of double sampling inspections and multiple sampling inspections is enabled by the dependent multiple samples function control indicator that's set in the sampling procedure. A valuation rule, which is defined for the function is defined for the valuation mode in the sampling procedure, valuates a characteristic after the dependent multiple samples are valuated. The use of dependent multiple samples requires a sampling type with a sampling scheme, the attributive inspection valuation mode and the definition of a function module for valuating dependent multiple samples in the dependent multiples samples valuation rule.

Q-74:   D. Sampling scheme

When it's not possible to inspect each item produced by a production process, a sample inspection is used to evaluate the quality of the items in an inspection lot. The sample is picked at random from the lot and, on the basis of the information yielded by the sample, a decision is made regarding the disposition of the lot…namely, the lot is accepted or rejected for its intended use. A sampling procedure can be used to select the entities of the sample, which are subsequently evaluated according to an inspection plan. Instructions for drawing the sample, such as the sample's size and the number of samples to be taken,

are documented in a sample drawing procedure that's assigned to the inspection plan. The sampling type, which is defined in the sampling procedure, specifies the method to be used to calculate the sample size. For example, the sampling type may require that a sample size be equal the lot size...namely, 100 percent inspection, a fixed sample size or a size determined by a sampling scheme. If the sampling type requires the use of a sampling scheme that's assigned to the sampling procedure, it will consist of individual sampling tables, each of which includes two or more sampling plans that determine a sample size based on the lot size, inspection severity, inspection severity and acceptable quality level, AQL -- the maximum number of defects per 100 units -- or the number of containers in an inspection lot. The valuation parameter for which the sampling scheme is created determines the structure of the sampling plan. For instance, the structure of a sampling plan created for an attributive inspection valuation mode will consist of a sample size, acceptance number c, or the maximum number of nonconforming units in a sample that is accepted and a rejection number d, or the least number of nonconforming units in a sample that is rejected. In turn, a sampling plan for a variable inspection will consist of a sample size and k-factor, or acceptability constant that defines the minimum quality score that leads to the acceptance of a sample following a quality inspection. A sampling plan with no valuation parameters will consist only of a sample size. A sampling scheme can be used for independent or dependent multiple samples and single samples.

Q-75:   B. Valuation mode and C. Sampling table description

When it's not possible to inspect each item produced by a production process, a sample inspection is used to evaluate the quality of the items in an inspection lot. The sample is picked at random from the lot and, on the basis of the information yielded by the sample, a decision is made regarding the disposition of the lot...namely, the lot is accepted or rejected for its intended use. A sampling procedure can be used to select the entities of the sample, which are subsequently evaluated according to an inspection plan. Instructions for drawing the sample, such as the sample's size and the number of samples to be taken, are documented in a sample drawing procedure that's assigned to the inspection plan. The sampling type, which is defined in the sampling procedure, specifies the method to be used to calculate the sample size. For example, the sampling type may require that a sample size be equal the lot size...namely, 100 percent inspection, a fixed sample size or a size determined by a sampling scheme. If the sampling type requires the use of a sampling scheme that's assigned to the sampling procedure, it will consist of individual sampling tables, each of which includes two or more sampling plans that determine a sample size based on the lot size, inspection severity, inspection severity and acceptable quality level, AQL, or the number of containers in an inspection lot. The valuation parameter for which the sampling scheme is created determines the structure of the sampling plan. For instance, the structure of a sampling plan created for an attributive inspection valuation mode will consist of a sample size, acceptance number c, or the maximum number of nonconforming units in a sample that is accepted and a rejection number d, or the least number of nonconforming units in a sample that is rejected. In turn, a sampling plan for a variable inspection will consist of a

sample size and k-factor, or acceptability constant that
defines the minimum quality score that leads to the
acceptance of a sample following a quality inspection. A
sampling plan with no valuation parameters will consist
only of a sample size. The header of a sampling scheme
requires the entry of text, a valuation mode, a sampling
table variable and, if required, a blocking control indicator
that prevents the assignment of the sampling scheme to a
sampling procedure.

Q-76:   A. Sample size and C. K-factor

When it's not possible to inspect each item produced by a
production process, a sample inspection is used to evaluate
the quality of the items in an inspection lot. The sample is
picked at random from the lot and, on the basis of the
information yielded by the sample, a decision is made
regarding the disposition of the lot…namely, the lot is
accepted or rejected for its intended use. A sampling
procedure can be used to select the entities of the sample,
which are subsequently evaluated according to an
inspection plan. Instructions for drawing the sample, such
as the sample's size and the number of samples to be taken,
are documented in a sample drawing procedure that's
assigned to the inspection plan. The sampling type, which is
defined in the sampling procedure, specifies the method to
be used to calculate the sample size. For example, the
sampling type may require that a sample size be equal the
lot size…namely, 100 percent inspection, a fixed sample
size or a size determined by a sampling scheme. If the
sampling type requires the use of a sampling scheme that's
assigned to the sampling procedure, it will consist of
individual sampling tables, each of which includes two or

more sampling plans that determine a sample size based on the lot size, inspection severity, inspection severity and acceptable quality level, AQL, or the number of containers in an inspection lot. The valuation parameter for which the sampling scheme is created determines the structure of the sampling plan. For instance, the structure of a sampling plan created for an attributive inspection valuation mode will consist of a sample size, acceptance number c, or the maximum number of nonconforming units in a sample that is accepted and a rejection number d, or the least number of nonconforming units in a sample that is rejected. In turn, a sampling plan for a variable inspection will consist of a sample size and k-factor, or acceptability constant that defines the minimum quality score that leads to the acceptance of a sample following a quality inspection. A sampling plan with no valuation parameters will consist only of a sample size.

Q-77:   A. Sampling procedure

Sampling procedures, sampling schemes and dynamic modification rules are the basic data needed to create the samples used in the inspection process. In particular, a sampling procedure determines how a sample size is calculated, how inspection characteristics are valuated and if a sample size is dynamically modified. The structure of a sampling procedure includes a sampling type, which specifies how a sample size is calculated, and a valuation mode that includes a valuation rule that governs the acceptance or rejection of a characteristic or sample. The structure also includes an inspection points control indicator that determines the number of inspection points that are created for an inspection lot, an inspection point

type, as well as a usage control indicator that ensures a particular sampling procedure is not referenced in a task list. The sampling procedure structure also includes a control chart type that governs the characteristics for which a particular control chart can be used, the variables referenced in the chart and the algorithm used to calculate the chart's control limits. Other control indicators in the sampling procedure are the no stage change control indicator that prevents the use of the dynamic modification procedure to determine the inspection scope or sample size and the multiple samples control indicator for independent or dependent multiple samples.

Q-78:   B. Inspection characteristic

Acceptance sampling leads to the acceptance or rejection of materials and lots based on the inspection of samples. A sample of a given size is drawn using a random method and if less than a given number of errors are found, the sample is accepted. If more than the specified number of errors are found, the sample is rejected. A sampling procedure is a process by which the entities of a sample are selected. The sampling procedure also determines how a characteristic or sample is valuated. In the instance that a task list or material specification is used in the conduct of a quality inspection, the sampling procedure is either assigned to the inspection characteristic or it is defined using the Customizing application. The two key elements of a sampling procedure are the sampling type and the valuation mode. The sampling type controls the calculation of the sample size. In turn, the valuation mode governs the acceptance or rejection of a characteristic or sample for its intended use. The structure of a sampling procedure also controls the number of inspection points to be created for an inspection lot, the creation of a control chart for the quality inspection, the dynamic modification of the inspection scope and the creation of a single or multiple independent or dependent samples.

Q-79:   A. Sampling plan, B. Sampling procedure and C. Dynamic modification rule

Sampling procedures, sampling schemes and dynamic modification rules are the basic data needed to create the samples used in the inspection process. In particular, a sampling procedure determines how a sample size is calculated, how inspection characteristics are valuated and if a sample size is dynamically modified. The structure of a sampling procedure includes a sampling type, which specifies how a sample size is calculated, and a valuation mode that includes a valuation rule that governs the acceptance or rejection of a characteristic or sample. The structure also includes an inspection points control indicator that determines the number of inspection points that are created for an inspection lot, an inspection point type, as well as a usage control indicator that ensures a particular sampling procedure is not referenced in a task list. The sampling procedure structure also includes a control chart type that governs the characteristics for which a particular control chart can be used, the variables referenced in the chart and the algorithm used to calculate the chart's control limits. Other control indicators in the sampling procedure are the no stage change control indicator that prevents the use of the dynamic modification procedure to determine the inspection scope or sample size

and the multiple samples control indicator for independent or dependent multiple samples.

Q-80:   A. Sampling procedure

When it's not possible to inspect each item produced by a production process, a sample inspection is used to evaluate the quality of the items in an inspection lot. The sample is picked at random from the lot and, on the basis of the information yielded by the sample, a decision is made regarding the disposition of the lot…namely, the lot is accepted or rejected for its intended use. A sampling procedure can be used to select the entities of the sample, which are subsequently evaluated according to an inspection plan. Instructions for drawing the sample, such as the sample's size and the number of samples to be taken, are documented in a sample drawing procedure that's assigned to the inspection plan. The sampling type, which is defined in the sampling procedure, specifies the method to be used to calculate the sample size. For example, the sampling type may require that a sample size be equal the lot size…namely, 100 percent inspection, a fixed sample size or a size determined by a sampling scheme. If the sampling type requires the use of a sampling scheme that's assigned to the sampling procedure, it will consist of individual sampling tables. Each table will include two or more sampling plans that determine a sample size based on the lot size, inspection severity, inspection severity and acceptable quality level, AQL, or the number of containers in an inspection lot. The valuation parameter for which the sampling scheme is created determines the structure of the sampling plan. For instance, the structure of a sampling plan created for an attributive inspection valuation mode

will consist of a sample size, acceptance number c, or the maximum number of nonconforming units in a sample that is accepted and a rejection number d, or the least number of nonconforming units in a sample that is rejected. In turn, a sampling plan for a variable inspection will consist of a sample size and k-factor, or acceptability constant that defines the minimum quality score that leads to the acceptance of a sample following a quality inspection. A sampling plan with no valuation parameters will consist only of a sample size.

Q-81:   A. Control limits, C. Control chart variables and E. Characteristics

Sampling procedures, sampling schemes and dynamic modification rules are the basic data needed to create the samples used in the inspection process. In particular, a sampling procedure determines how a sample size is calculated, how inspection characteristics are valuated and if a sample size is dynamically modified. The structure of a sampling procedure includes a sampling type, which specifies how a sample size is calculated, and a valuation mode that includes a valuation rule that governs the acceptance or rejection of a characteristic or sample. The structure also includes an inspection points control indicator that determines the number of inspection points that are created for an inspection lot, an inspection point type, as well as a usage control indicator that ensures a particular sampling procedure is not referenced in a task list. The sampling procedure structure also includes a control chart type that governs the characteristics for which a particular control chart can be used, the variables referenced in the chart and the algorithm used to calculate

217

the chart's control limits. Other control indicators in the sampling procedure are the no stage change control indicator that prevents the use of the dynamic modification procedure to determine the inspection scope or sample size and the multiple samples control indicator for independent or dependent multiple samples.

Q-82:   A. Attributive inspection on the basis of nonconforming units

When it's not possible to inspect each item produced by a production process, a sample inspection is used to evaluate the quality of the items in an inspection lot. The sample is picked at random from the lot and, on the basis of the information yielded by the sample, a decision is made regarding the disposition of the lot…namely, the lot is accepted or rejected for its intended use. A sampling procedure can be used to select the entities of the sample, which are subsequently evaluated according to an inspection plan. Instructions for drawing the sample, such as the sample's size and the number of samples to be taken, are documented in a sample drawing procedure that's assigned to the inspection plan. The sampling type, which is defined in the sampling procedure, specifies the method to be used to calculate the sample size. For example, the sampling type may require that a sample size be equal the lot size…namely, 100 percent inspection, a fixed sample size or a size determined by a sampling scheme. If the sampling type requires the use of a sampling scheme that's assigned to the sampling procedure, it will consist of individual sampling tables, each of which includes two or more sampling plans that determine a sample size based on the lot size, inspection severity, inspection severity and acceptable quality level, AQL, or the number of containers in an inspection lot. The valuation parameter for which the sampling scheme is created determines the structure of the sampling plan. For instance, the structure of a sampling plan created for an attributive inspection valuation mode will consist of a sample size, acceptance number c, or the maximum number of nonconforming units in a sample that is accepted and a rejection number d, or the least number of nonconforming units in a sample that is rejected. In turn, a sampling plan for a variable inspection will consist of a sample size and k-factor, or acceptability constant that defines the minimum quality score that leads to the acceptance of a sample following a quality inspection. A sampling plan with no valuation parameters will consist only of a sample size.

Q-83:   B. Sampling type with sampling scheme, C. Attributive inspection valuation mode and E. Dependent multiple samples control indicator

Sampling procedures, sampling schemes and dynamic modification rules are the basic data needed to create the samples used in the inspection process. In particular, a sampling procedure determines how a sample size is calculated, how inspection characteristics are valuated and if a sample size is dynamically modified. The structure of a sampling procedure includes a sampling type, which specifies how a sample size is calculated, and a valuation mode that includes a valuation rule that governs the acceptance or rejection of a characteristic or sample. The structure also includes an inspection points control indicator that determines the number of inspection points that are created for an inspection lot, an inspection point

type, as well as a usage control indicator that ensures a particular sampling procedure is not referenced in a task list. The sampling procedure structure also includes a control chart type that governs the characteristics for which a particular control chart can be used, the variables referenced in the chart and the algorithm used to calculate the chart's control limits. Other control indicators in the sampling procedure are the no stage change control indicator that prevents the use of the dynamic modification procedure to determine the inspection scope or sample size and the multiple samples control indicator for independent or dependent multiple samples. The processing of double sampling inspections and multiple sampling inspections is enabled by the dependent multiple samples function control indicator that's set in the sampling procedure. A valuation rule, which is defined for the function is defined for the valuation mode in the sampling procedure, valuates a characteristic after the dependent multiple samples are valuated. The use of dependent multiple samples requires a sampling type with a sampling scheme, the attributive inspection valuation mode and the definition of a function module for valuating dependent multiple samples in the dependent multiples samples valuation rule.

Q-84:   B. Sampling plan

Sampling procedures, sampling schemes and dynamic modification rules are the basic data needed to create the samples used in the inspection process. In particular, a sampling procedure determines how a sample size is calculated, how inspection characteristics are valuated and if a sample size is dynamically modified. The structure of a sampling procedure includes a sampling type, which specifies how a sample size is calculated, and a valuation mode that includes a valuation rule that governs the acceptance or rejection of a characteristic or sample. The structure also includes an inspection points control indicator that determines the number of inspection points that are created for an inspection lot, an inspection point type, as well as a usage control indicator that ensures a particular sampling procedure is not referenced in a task list. The sampling procedure structure also includes a control chart type that governs the characteristics for which a particular control chart can be used, the variables referenced in the chart and the algorithm used to calculate the chart's control limits. Other control indicators in the sampling procedure are the no stage change control indicator that prevents the use of the dynamic modification procedure to determine the inspection scope or sample size and the multiple samples control indicator for independent or dependent multiple samples.

Q-85:   A. Quality level and B. Dynamic modification rule

Sampling procedures, sampling schemes and dynamic modification rules are the basic data needed to create the samples used in the inspection process. In particular, a sampling procedure determines how a sample size is calculated, how inspection characteristics are valuated and if a sample size is dynamically modified. The structure of a sampling procedure includes a sampling type, which specifies how a sample size is calculated, and a valuation mode that includes a valuation rule that governs the acceptance or rejection of a characteristic or sample. The structure also includes an inspection points control indicator that determines the number of inspection points

that are created for an inspection lot, an inspection point type, as well as a usage control indicator that ensures a particular sampling procedure is not referenced in a task list. The sampling procedure structure also includes a control chart type that governs the characteristics for which a particular control chart can be used, the variables referenced in the chart and the algorithm used to calculate the chart's control limits. Other control indicators in the sampling procedure are the no stage change control indicator that prevents the use of the dynamic modification procedure to determine the inspection scope or sample size, which means the sampling procedure determines the inspection severity that influences the sample size. In turn, the inspection severity that's used in the sampling scheme is influenced by the quality level and dynamic modification rule. The sampling procedure also contains the multiple samples control indicator for independent or dependent multiple samples.

Q-86:   C. Structure includes an acceptance number c for an attributive inspection

When it's not possible to inspect each item produced by a production process, a sample inspection is used to evaluate the quality of the items in an inspection lot. The sample is picked at random from the lot and, on the basis of the information yielded by the sample, a decision is made regarding the disposition of the lot…namely, the lot is accepted or rejected for its intended use. A sampling procedure can be used to select the entities of the sample, which are subsequently evaluated according to an inspection plan. Instructions for drawing the sample, such as the sample's size and the number of samples to be taken,

are documented in a sample drawing procedure that's assigned to the inspection plan. The sampling type, which is defined in the sampling procedure, specifies the method to be used to calculate the sample size. For example, the sampling type may require that a sample size be equal the lot size…namely, 100 percent inspection, a fixed sample size or a size determined by a sampling scheme. If the sampling type requires the use of a sampling scheme that's assigned to the sampling procedure, it will consist of individual sampling tables, each of which includes two or more sampling plans that determine a sample size based on the lot size, inspection severity, inspection severity and acceptable quality level, AQL, or the number of containers in an inspection lot. The valuation parameter for which the sampling scheme is created determines the structure of the sampling plan. For instance, the structure of a sampling plan created for an attributive inspection valuation mode will consist of a sample size, acceptance number c, or the maximum number of nonconforming units in a sample that is accepted and a rejection number d, or the least number of nonconforming units in a sample that is rejected. In turn, a sampling plan for a variable inspection will consist of a sample size and k-factor, or acceptability constant that defines the minimum quality score that leads to the acceptance of a sample following a quality inspection. A sampling plan with no valuation parameters will consist only of a sample size.

Q-87:   C. Rejection number d

When it's not possible to inspect each item produced by a production process, a sample inspection is used to evaluate the quality of the items in an inspection lot. The sample is picked at random from the lot and, on the basis of the information yielded by the sample, a decision is made regarding the disposition of the lot…namely, the lot is accepted or rejected for its intended use. A sampling procedure can be used to select the entities of the sample, which are subsequently evaluated according to an inspection plan. Instructions for drawing the sample, such as the sample's size and the number of samples to be taken, are documented in a sample drawing procedure that's assigned to the inspection plan. The sampling type, which is defined in the sampling procedure, specifies the method to be used to calculate the sample size. For example, the sampling type may require that a sample size be equal the lot size…namely, 100 percent inspection, a fixed sample size or a size determined by a sampling scheme. If the sampling type requires the use of a sampling scheme that's assigned to the sampling procedure, it will consist of individual sampling tables, each of which includes two or more sampling plans that determine a sample size based on the lot size, inspection severity, inspection severity and acceptable quality level, AQL, or the number of containers in an inspection lot. The valuation parameter for which the sampling scheme is created determines the structure of the sampling plan. For instance, the structure of a sampling plan created for an attributive inspection valuation mode will consist of a sample size, acceptance number c, or the maximum number of nonconforming units in a sample that is accepted and a rejection number d, or the least number of nonconforming units in a sample that is rejected. In turn, a sampling plan for a variable inspection will consist of a sample size and k-factor, or acceptability constant that defines the minimum quality score that leads to the acceptance of a sample following a quality inspection. A

sampling plan with no valuation parameters will consist only of a sample size.

Q-88:   A. Sampling procedure

Sampling procedures, sampling schemes and dynamic modification rules are the basic data needed to create the samples used in the inspection process. In particular, a sampling procedure determines how a sample size is calculated, how inspection characteristics are valuated and if a sample size is dynamically modified. The structure of a sampling procedure includes a sampling type, which specifies how a sample size is calculated, and a valuation mode that includes a valuation rule that governs the acceptance or rejection of a characteristic or sample. The structure also includes an inspection points control indicator that determines the number of inspection points that are created for an inspection lot, an inspection point type, as well as a usage control indicator that ensures a particular sampling procedure is not referenced in a task list. The sampling procedure structure also includes a control chart type that governs the characteristics for which a particular control chart can be used, the variables referenced in the chart and the algorithm used to calculate the chart's control limits. Other control indicators in the sampling procedure are the no stage change control indicator that prevents the use of the dynamic modification procedure to determine the inspection scope or sample size, which means the sampling procedure determines the inspection severity that influences the sample size. In turn, the inspection severity is influenced by the quality level and dynamic modification rule. The sampling procedure also contains the multiple samples control indicator for independent or dependent multiple samples.

Q-89:   A. Characteristics, B. Control variables and C. Calculation of control limits

Sampling procedures, sampling schemes and dynamic modification rules are the basic data needed to create the samples used in the inspection process. In particular, a sampling procedure determines how a sample size is calculated, how inspection characteristics are valuated and if a sample size is dynamically modified. The structure of a sampling procedure includes a sampling type, which specifies how a sample size is calculated, and a valuation mode that includes a valuation rule that governs the acceptance or rejection of a characteristic or sample. The structure also includes an inspection points control indicator that determines the number of inspection points that are created for an inspection lot, an inspection point type, as well as a usage control indicator that ensures a particular sampling procedure is not referenced in a task list. The sampling procedure structure also includes a control chart type that governs the characteristics for which a particular control chart can be used, the variables referenced in the chart and the algorithm used to calculate the chart's control limits. Other control indicators in the sampling procedure are the no stage change control indicator that prevents the use of the dynamic modification procedure to determine the inspection scope or sample size, which means the sampling procedure determines the inspection severity that influences the sample size. In turn, the inspection severity is influenced by the quality level and dynamic modification rule. The sampling procedure also contains the multiple samples control indicator for independent or dependent multiple samples.

Q-90:   B. Dependent multiple samples control indicator in sampling procedure

Sampling procedures, sampling schemes and dynamic modification rules are the basic data needed to create the samples used in the inspection process. In particular, a sampling procedure determines how a sample size is calculated, how inspection characteristics are valuated and if a sample size is dynamically modified. The structure of a sampling procedure includes a sampling type, which specifies how a sample size is calculated, and a valuation mode that includes a valuation rule that governs the acceptance or rejection of a characteristic or sample. The structure also includes an inspection points control indicator that determines the number of inspection points that are created for an inspection lot, an inspection point type, as well as a usage control indicator that ensures a particular sampling procedure is not referenced in a task list. The sampling procedure structure also includes a control chart type that governs the characteristics for which a particular control chart can be used, the variables referenced in the chart and the algorithm used to calculate the chart's control limits. Other control indicators in the sampling procedure are the no stage change control indicator that prevents the use of the dynamic modification procedure to determine the inspection scope or sample size and the multiple samples control indicator for independent or dependent multiple samples. The processing of double sampling inspections and multiple sampling inspections is enabled by the dependent multiple samples function control indicator that's set in the sampling procedure. A valuation rule, which is defined for the function is defined for the valuation mode in the sampling procedure, valuates a characteristic after the dependent multiple samples are valuated. The use of dependent multiple samples requires a sampling type with a sampling scheme, the attributive inspection valuation mode and the definition of a function module for valuating dependent multiple samples in the dependent multiples samples valuation rule.

Q-91:   A. Selection of normal, reduced or tightened inspection, B. Means of adjusting the inspection effort to reflect the current quality of material as measured by inspection results and C. Means of adjusting the probability of acceptance of a material during quality inspection

Sampling procedures, sampling schemes and dynamic modification rules are the basic data needed to create the samples used in the inspection process. In particular, a sampling procedure determines how a sample size is calculated, how inspection characteristics are valuated and if a sample size is dynamically modified. The structure of a sampling procedure includes a sampling type, which specifies how a sample size is calculated, and a valuation mode that includes a valuation rule that governs the acceptance or rejection of a characteristic or sample. The structure also includes an inspection points control indicator that determines the number of inspection points that are created for an inspection lot, an inspection point type, as well as a usage control indicator that ensures a particular sampling procedure is not referenced in a task list. The sampling procedure structure also includes a control chart type that governs the characteristics for which

a particular control chart can be used, the variables referenced in the chart and the algorithm used to calculate the chart's control limits. Other control indicators in the sampling procedure are the no stage change control indicator that prevents the use of the dynamic modification procedure to determine the inspection scope or sample size, which means the sampling procedure determines the inspection severity that controls the sample size. The inspection severity determines if a normal, reduced or tightened inspection is performed, which is a way to adjust the inspection effort to reflect the current quality of the material as reflected in inspection results. The inspection severity is also a way to adjust the probability of acceptance of a material during a quality inspection. The sampling procedure also contains the multiple samples control indicator for independent or dependent multiple samples.

Q-92:   B. Create a sampling scheme for a variable inspection

When it's not possible to inspect each item produced by a production process, a sample inspection is used to evaluate the quality of the items in an inspection lot. The sample is picked at random from the lot and, on the basis of the information yielded by the sample, a decision is made regarding the disposition of the lot…namely, the lot is accepted or rejected for its intended use. A sampling procedure can be used to select the entities of the sample, which are subsequently evaluated according to an inspection plan. Instructions for drawing the sample, such as the sample's size and the number of samples to be taken, are documented in a sample drawing procedure that's assigned to the inspection plan. The sampling type, which is defined in the sampling procedure, specifies the method to be used to calculate the sample size. For example, the sampling type may require that a sample size be equal the lot size…namely, 100 percent inspection, a fixed sample size or a size determined by a sampling scheme. If the sampling type requires the use of a sampling scheme that's assigned to the sampling procedure, it will consist of individual sampling tables, each of which includes two or more sampling plans that determine a sample size based on the lot size, inspection severity, inspection severity and acceptable quality level, AQL, or the number of containers in an inspection lot. The valuation parameter for which the sampling scheme is created determines the structure of the sampling plan. For instance, the structure of a sampling plan created for an attributive inspection valuation mode will consist of a sample size, acceptance number c, or the maximum number of nonconforming units in a sample that is accepted and a rejection number d, or the least number of nonconforming units in a sample that is rejected. In turn, a sampling plan for a variable inspection will consist of a sample size and k-factor, or acceptability constant that defines the minimum quality score that leads to the acceptance of a sample following a quality inspection. A sampling plan with no valuation parameters will consist only of a sample size.

Q-93:   A. An acceptability constant determines the minimum quality score that leads to the acceptance of a sample and an acceptance number c determines the maximum number of defects that leads to the acceptance of a sample

When it's not possible to inspect each item produced by a production process, a sample inspection is used to evaluate the quality of the items in an inspection lot. The sample is picked at random from the lot and, on the basis of the information yielded by the sample, a decision is made regarding the disposition of the lot...namely, the lot is accepted or rejected for its intended use. A sampling procedure can be used to select the entities of the sample, which are subsequently evaluated according to an inspection plan. Instructions for drawing the sample, such as the sample's size and the number of samples to be taken, are documented in a sample drawing procedure that's assigned to the inspection plan. The sampling type, which is defined in the sampling procedure, specifies the method to be used to calculate the sample size. For example, the sampling type may require that a sample size be equal the lot size...namely, 100 percent inspection, a fixed sample size or a size determined by a sampling scheme. If the sampling type requires the use of a sampling scheme that's assigned to the sampling procedure, it will consist of individual sampling tables, each of which includes two or more sampling plans that determine a sample size based on the lot size, inspection severity, inspection severity and acceptable quality level, AQL, or the number of containers in an inspection lot. The valuation parameter for which the sampling scheme is created determines the structure of the sampling plan. For instance, the structure of a sampling plan created for an attributive inspection valuation mode will consist of a sample size, acceptance number c, or the maximum number of nonconforming units in a sample that is accepted and a rejection number d, or the least number of nonconforming units in a sample that is rejected. In turn, a sampling plan for a variable inspection will consist of a

sample size and k-factor, or acceptability constant that defines the minimum quality score that leads to the acceptance of a sample following a quality inspection. A sampling plan with no valuation parameters will consist only of a sample size.

Q-94:   B. Entry of the control chart type in the sampling procedure, D. Selection of the fixed sample sampling type and E. Selection of the valuation on basis of action limits valuation mode

A control chart is used in a quality inspection as a means to monitor controlled production processes. The control chart determines if a process is "in control" or "out of control" on the basis of action limits that are defined for the particular chart and actual measured values acquired during a quality inspection. During a quality inspection, a sample or characteristic is valuated based on the relationship between the control chart action limits and the measured value of the characteristic. Using a valuation rule, a sample or characteristic is rejected if one or more action limits is violated by a characteristic value. To use a control chart to valuate a sample, a control chart type must be defined in the sampling procedure that is, in turn, defined in the inspection characteristic or the inspection settings for the material master record inspection type. In addition, both the fixed sample sampling type and the valuation on the basis of action limits valuation mode must be selected in the sampling procedure. The control chart type governs the characteristics to be referenced in a control chart, the control variables to be included in the chart, as well as the calculation of the chart's control limits.

Q-95:   B. Variable inspection according to s-method

When it's not possible to inspect each item produced by a production process, a sample inspection is used to evaluate the quality of the items in an inspection lot. The sample is picked at random from the lot and, on the basis of the information yielded by the sample, a decision is made regarding the disposition of the lot…namely, the lot is accepted or rejected for its intended use. A sampling procedure can be used to select the entities of the sample, which are subsequently evaluated according to an inspection plan. Instructions for drawing the sample, such as the sample's size and the number of samples to be taken, are documented in a sample drawing procedure that's assigned to the inspection plan. The sampling type, which is defined in the sampling procedure, specifies the method to be used to calculate the sample size. For example, the sampling type may require that a sample size be equal the lot size…namely, 100 percent inspection, a fixed sample size or a size determined by a sampling scheme. If the sampling type requires the use of a sampling scheme that's assigned to the sampling procedure, it will consist of individual sampling tables, each of which includes two or more sampling plans that determine a sample size based on the lot size, inspection severity, inspection severity and acceptable quality level, AQL, or the number of containers in an inspection lot. The valuation parameter for which the sampling scheme is created determines the structure of the sampling plan. For instance, the structure of a sampling plan created for an attributive inspection valuation mode will consist of a sample size, acceptance number c, or the maximum number of nonconforming units in a sample that is accepted and a rejection number d, or the least number of nonconforming units in a sample that is rejected. In turn, a sampling plan for a variable inspection will consist of a sample size and k-factor, or acceptability constant that defines the minimum quality score that leads to the acceptance of a sample following a quality inspection. A sampling plan with no valuation parameters will consist only of a sample size. The variable inspection according to the s-method is used for quantitative inspections.

Q-96:   A. Dependent multiple samples control indicator in sampling procedure

Sampling procedures, sampling schemes and dynamic modification rules are the basic data needed to create the samples used in the inspection process. In particular, a sampling procedure determines how a sample size is calculated, how inspection characteristics are valuated and if a sample size is dynamically modified. The structure of a sampling procedure includes a sampling type, which specifies how a sample size is calculated, and a valuation mode that includes a valuation rule that governs the acceptance or rejection of a characteristic or sample. The structure also includes an inspection points control indicator that determines the number of inspection points that are created for an inspection lot, an inspection point type, as well as a usage control indicator that ensures a particular sampling procedure is not referenced in a task list. The sampling procedure structure also includes a control chart type that governs the characteristics for which a particular control chart can be used, the variables referenced in the chart and the algorithm used to calculate the chart's control limits. Other control indicators in the sampling procedure are the no stage change control

indicator that prevents the use of the dynamic modification procedure to determine the inspection scope or sample size and the multiple samples control indicator for independent or dependent multiple samples. The processing of double sampling inspections and multiple sampling inspections is enabled by the dependent multiple samples function control indicator that's set in the sampling procedure. A valuation rule, which is defined for the function is defined for the valuation mode in the sampling procedure, valuates a characteristic after the dependent multiple samples are valuated. The use of dependent multiple samples requires a sampling type with a sampling scheme, the attributive inspection valuation mode and the definition of a function module for valuating dependent multiple samples in the dependent multiples samples valuation rule.

Q-97:   B. Inspection severity

Sampling procedures, sampling schemes and dynamic modification rules are the basic data needed to create the samples used in the inspection process. In particular, a sampling procedure determines how a sample size is calculated, how inspection characteristics are valuated and if a sample size is dynamically modified. The structure of a sampling procedure includes a sampling type, which specifies how a sample size is calculated, and a valuation mode that includes a valuation rule that governs the acceptance or rejection of a characteristic or sample. The structure also includes an inspection points control indicator that determines the number of inspection points that are created for an inspection lot, an inspection point type, as well as a usage control indicator that ensures a particular sampling procedure is not referenced in a task

235

list. The sampling procedure structure also includes a control chart type that governs the characteristics for which a particular control chart can be used, the variables referenced in the chart and the algorithm used to calculate the chart's control limits. Other control indicators in the sampling procedure are the no stage change control indicator that prevents the use of the dynamic modification procedure to determine the inspection scope or sample size, which means the sampling procedure determines the inspection severity that controls the sample size. The inspection severity determines if a normal, reduced or tightened inspection is performed, which is a way to adjust the inspection effort to reflect the current quality of the material as reflected in inspection results. The inspection severity is also a way to adjust the probability of acceptance of a material during a quality inspection. The sampling procedure also contains the multiple samples control indicator for independent or dependent multiple samples.

Q-98:   A. Sample size, C. Acceptance number and D. Rejection number

When it's not possible to inspect each item produced by a production process, a sample inspection is used to evaluate the quality of the items in an inspection lot. The sample is picked at random from the lot and, on the basis of the information yielded by the sample, a decision is made regarding the disposition of the lot…namely, the lot is accepted or rejected for its intended use. A sampling procedure can be used to select the entities of the sample, which are subsequently evaluated according to an inspection plan. Instructions for drawing the sample, such as the sample's size and the number of samples to be taken,

are documented in a sample drawing procedure that's assigned to the inspection plan. The sampling type, which is defined in the sampling procedure, specifies the method to be used to calculate the sample size. For example, the sampling type may require that a sample size be equal the lot size...namely, 100 percent inspection, a fixed sample size or a size determined by a sampling scheme. If the sampling type requires the use of a sampling scheme that's assigned to the sampling procedure, it will consist of individual sampling tables, each of which includes two or more sampling plans that determine a sample size based on the lot size, inspection severity, inspection severity and acceptable quality level, AQL, or the number of containers in an inspection lot. The valuation parameter for which the sampling scheme is created determines the structure of the sampling plan. For instance, the structure of a sampling plan created for an attributive inspection valuation mode will consist of a sample size, acceptance number c, or the maximum number of nonconforming units in a sample that is accepted and a rejection number d, or the least number of nonconforming units in a sample that is rejected. In turn, a sampling plan for a variable inspection will consist of a sample size and k-factor, or acceptability constant that defines the minimum quality score that leads to the acceptance of a sample following a quality inspection. A sampling plan with no valuation parameters will consist only of a sample size.

Q-99:   A. Create sampling scheme function and B. Copy sampling scheme function

When it's not possible to inspect each item produced by a production process, a sample inspection is used to evaluate the quality of the items in an inspection lot. The sample is picked at random from the lot and, on the basis of the information yielded by the sample, a decision is made regarding the disposition of the lot…namely, the lot is accepted or rejected for its intended use. A sampling procedure can be used to select the entities of the sample, which are subsequently evaluated according to an inspection plan. Instructions for drawing the sample, such as the sample's size and the number of samples to be taken, are documented in a sample drawing procedure that's assigned to the inspection plan. The sampling type, which is defined in the sampling procedure, specifies the method to be used to calculate the sample size. For example, the sampling type may require that a sample size be equal the lot size…namely, 100 percent inspection, a fixed sample size or a size determined by a sampling scheme. If the sampling type requires the use of a sampling scheme, it will consist of individual sampling tables, each of which includes two or more sampling plans that determine a sample size based on the lot size, inspection severity, inspection severity and acceptable quality level, AQL, or the number of containers in an inspection lot. The valuation parameter for which the sampling scheme is created determines the structure of the sampling plan. Functions used to create a sampling scheme include the Create Sampling Scheme, Copy Sampling Scheme and Reference Sampling Scheme functions.

Q-100:   B. The acceptability constant is the minimum quality score that leads to an acceptance of a sample and D. The rejection number d is the minimum number of nonconforming units in a sample that leads to the rejection of a sample

When it's not possible to inspect each item produced by a production process, a sample inspection is used to evaluate the quality of the items in an inspection lot. The sample is picked at random from the lot and, on the basis of the information yielded by the sample, a decision is made regarding the disposition of the lot...namely, the lot is accepted or rejected for its intended use. A sampling procedure can be used to select the entities of the sample, which are subsequently evaluated according to an inspection plan. Instructions for drawing the sample, such as the sample's size and the number of samples to be taken, are documented in a sample drawing procedure that's assigned to the inspection plan. The sampling type, which is defined in the sampling procedure, specifies the method to be used to calculate the sample size. For example, the sampling type may require that a sample size be equal the lot size...namely, 100 percent inspection, a fixed sample size or a size determined by a sampling scheme. If the sampling type requires the use of a sampling scheme that's assigned to the sampling procedure, it will consist of individual sampling tables, each of which includes two or more sampling plans that determine a sample size based on the lot size, inspection severity, inspection severity and acceptable quality level, AQL, or the number of containers in an inspection lot. The valuation parameter for which the sampling scheme is created determines the structure of the sampling plan. For instance, the structure of a sampling plan created for an attributive inspection valuation mode will consist of a sample size, acceptance number c, or the maximum number of nonconforming units in a sample that is accepted and a rejection number d, or the least number of nonconforming units in a sample that is rejected. In turn, a sampling plan for a variable inspection will consist of a

sample size and k-factor, or acceptability constant that defines the minimum quality score that leads to the acceptance of a sample following a quality inspection. A sampling plan with no valuation parameters will consist only of a sample size.

Q-101:   B. Valuation mode in sampling procedure

When it's not possible to inspect each item produced by a production process, a sample inspection is used to evaluate the quality of the items in an inspection lot. The sample is picked at random from the lot and, on the basis of the information yielded by the sample, a decision is made regarding the disposition of the lot…namely, the lot is accepted or rejected for its intended use. A sampling procedure can be used to select the entities of the sample, which are subsequently evaluated according to an inspection plan. Instructions for drawing the sample, such as the sample's size and the number of samples to be taken, are documented in a sample drawing procedure that's assigned to the inspection plan. The sampling type, which is defined in the sampling procedure, specifies the method to be used to calculate the sample size. For example, the sampling type may require that a sample size be equal the lot size…namely, 100 percent inspection, a fixed sample size or a size determined by a sampling scheme. If the sampling type requires the use of a sampling scheme that's assigned to the sampling procedure, it will consist of individual sampling tables, each of which includes two or more sampling plans that determine a sample size based on the lot size, inspection severity, inspection severity and acceptable quality level, AQL, or the number of containers in an inspection lot. The valuation parameter for which the sampling scheme is created determines the structure of the sampling plan. For instance, the structure of a sampling plan created for an attributive inspection valuation mode will consist of a sample size, acceptance number c, or the maximum number of nonconforming units in a sample that is accepted and a rejection number d, or the least number of nonconforming units in a sample that is rejected. In turn, a sampling plan for a variable inspection will consist of a sample size and k-factor, or acceptability constant that defines the minimum quality score that leads to the acceptance of a sample following a quality inspection. A sampling plan with no valuation parameters will consist only of a sample size.

Q-102:   A. No stage change control indicator in the sampling procedure

Sampling procedures, sampling schemes and dynamic modification rules are the basic data needed to create the samples used in the inspection process. In particular, a sampling procedure determines how a sample size is calculated, how inspection characteristics are valuated and if a sample size is dynamically modified. The structure of a sampling procedure includes a sampling type, which specifies how a sample size is calculated, and a valuation mode that includes a valuation rule that governs the acceptance or rejection of a characteristic or sample. The structure also includes an inspection points control indicator that determines the number of inspection points that are created for an inspection lot, an inspection point type, as well as a usage control indicator that ensures a particular sampling procedure is not referenced in a task list. The sampling procedure structure also includes a

241

control chart type that governs the characteristics for which a particular control chart can be used, the variables referenced in the chart and the algorithm used to calculate the chart's control limits. Other control indicators in the sampling procedure are the no stage change control indicator that prevents the use of the dynamic modification procedure to determine the inspection scope or sample size and the multiple samples control indicator for independent or dependent multiple samples.

Q-103:   A. Valuation mode that determines the rules for the acceptance or rejection of a characteristic or sample

When it's not possible to inspect each item produced by a production process, a sample inspection is used to evaluate the quality of the items in an inspection lot. The sample is picked at random from the lot and, on the basis of the information yielded by the sample, a decision is made regarding the disposition of the lot...namely, the lot is accepted or rejected for its intended use. A sampling procedure can be used to select the entities of the sample, which are subsequently evaluated according to an inspection plan. Instructions for drawing the sample, such as the sample's size and the number of samples to be taken, are documented in a sample drawing procedure that's assigned to the inspection plan. The sampling type, which is defined in the sampling procedure, specifies the method to be used to calculate the sample size. For example, the sampling type may require that a sample size be equal the lot size...namely, 100 percent inspection, a fixed sample size or a size determined by a sampling scheme. If the sampling type requires the use of a sampling scheme that's assigned to the sampling procedure, it will consist of

individual sampling tables, each of which includes two or more sampling plans that determine a sample size based on the lot size, inspection severity, inspection severity and acceptable quality level, AQL, or the number of containers in an inspection lot. The valuation parameter for which the sampling scheme is created determines the structure of the sampling plan. For instance, the structure of a sampling plan created for an attributive inspection valuation mode will consist of a sample size, acceptance number c, or the maximum number of nonconforming units in a sample that is accepted and a rejection number d, or the least number of nonconforming units in a sample that is rejected. In turn, a sampling plan for a variable inspection will consist of a sample size and k-factor, or acceptability constant that defines the minimum quality score that leads to the acceptance of a sample following a quality inspection. A sampling plan with no valuation parameters will consist only of a sample size.

Q-104: B. Sampling type with a sampling scheme and D. Function module for the valuation of dependent multiple samples is defined in the valuation rule for dependent multiple samples

Sampling procedures, sampling schemes and dynamic modification rules are the basic data needed to create the samples used in the inspection process. In particular, a sampling procedure determines how a sample size is calculated, how inspection characteristics are valuated and if a sample size is dynamically modified. The structure of a sampling procedure includes a sampling type, which specifies how a sample size is calculated, and a valuation mode that includes a valuation rule that governs the

acceptance or rejection of a characteristic or sample. The structure also includes an inspection points control indicator that determines the number of inspection points that are created for an inspection lot, an inspection point type, as well as a usage control indicator that ensures a particular sampling procedure is not referenced in a task list. The sampling procedure structure also includes a control chart type that governs the characteristics for which a particular control chart can be used, the variables referenced in the chart and the algorithm used to calculate the chart's control limits. Other control indicators in the sampling procedure are the no stage change control indicator that prevents the use of the dynamic modification procedure to determine the inspection scope or sample size and the multiple samples control indicator for independent or dependent multiple samples. The processing of double sampling inspections and multiple sampling inspections is enabled by the dependent multiple samples function control indicator that's set in the sampling procedure. A valuation rule, which is defined for the function is defined for the valuation mode in the sampling procedure, valuates a characteristic after the dependent multiple samples are valuated. The use of dependent multiple samples requires a sampling type with a sampling scheme, the attributive inspection valuation mode and the definition of a function module for valuating dependent multiple samples in the dependent multiples samples valuation rule.

Q-105: C. Display master inspection characteristic and D. Display inspection type

A sampling procedure is directly referenced in a task list or material specification. To determine the objects in which a particular sampling procedure is referenced, a where-used list for a sampling procedure is created. Data elements that appear in the where-used list include sampling procedure name, key date, total number of times used and number of times used in task lists. Also included are the number of times used in material specifications, the number of times used in material master record inspection setups, task lists, operations and characteristics. Other elements included are the characteristic description, Also included are the number of times used in material specifications, the number of times used in material master record inspection setups, task lists, operations and characteristics. Other elements included are the characteristic description, master inspection characteristic and dynamic modification rule. Additional functions that can be accessed from the where-used list include "Replace sampling procedure in task list," "Display master inspection characteristic" and " Display inspection type."

Q-106: A. The probability of acceptance of the inspection lot and the anticipated inspection effort based on an existing quality level

When it's not possible to inspect each item produced by a production process, a sample inspection is used to evaluate the quality of the items in an inspection lot. The sample is picked at random from the lot and, on the basis of the information yielded by the sample, a decision is made regarding the disposition of the lot…namely, the lot is accepted or rejected for its intended use. A sampling procedure can be used to select the entities of the sample, which are subsequently evaluated according to an inspection plan. Instructions for drawing the sample, such as the sample's size and the number of samples to be taken, are documented in a sample drawing procedure that's assigned to the inspection plan. The sampling type, which is defined in the sampling procedure, specifies the method to be used to calculate the sample size. For example, the sampling type may require that a sample size be equal the lot size...namely, 100 percent inspection, a fixed sample size or a size determined by a sampling scheme. If the sampling type requires the use of a sampling scheme that's assigned to the sampling procedure, it will consist of individual sampling tables, each of which includes two or more sampling plans that determine a sample size based on the lot size, inspection severity, inspection severity and acceptable quality level, AQL, or the number of containers in an inspection lot. The inspection severity, in particular, reflects the probability of acceptance of the inspection lot and the anticipated inspection effort based on an existing quality level.

Q-107:   A. A means to select the appropriate sampling plan in a sampling scheme

When it's not possible to inspect each item produced by a production process, a sample inspection is used to evaluate the quality of the items in an inspection lot. The sample is picked at random from the lot and, on the basis of the information yielded by the sample, a decision is made regarding the disposition of the lot...namely, the lot is accepted or rejected for its intended use. A sampling procedure can be used to select the entities of the sample, which are subsequently evaluated according to an inspection plan. Instructions for drawing the sample, such as the sample's size and the number of samples to be taken, are documented in a sample drawing procedure that's assigned to the inspection plan. The sampling type, which is defined in the sampling procedure, specifies the method to be used to calculate the sample size. For example, the sampling type may require that a sample size be equal the lot size…namely, 100 percent inspection, a fixed sample size or a size determined by a sampling scheme. If the sampling type requires the use of a sampling scheme that's assigned to the sampling procedure, it will consist of individual sampling tables, each of which includes two or more sampling plans that determine a sample size based on the lot size, inspection severity, inspection severity and acceptable quality level, AQL, or the number of containers in an inspection lot. The inspection severity, in particular, reflects the probability of acceptance of the inspection lot and the anticipated inspection effort based on an existing quality level.

Q-108:   A. Document lot size, sample size, and acceptability constant or acceptance number used to determine if a sample is accepted or rejected

When it's not possible to inspect each item produced by a production process, a sample inspection is used to evaluate the quality of the items in an inspection lot. The sample is picked at random from the lot and, on the basis of the information yielded by the sample, a decision is made regarding the disposition of the lot…namely, the lot is accepted or rejected for its intended use. A sampling procedure can be used to select the entities of the sample, which are subsequently evaluated according to an inspection plan. Instructions for drawing the sample, such as the sample's size and the number of samples to be taken,

are documented in a sample drawing procedure that's assigned to the inspection plan. The sampling type, which is defined in the sampling procedure, specifies the method to be used to calculate the sample size. For example, the sampling type may require that a sample size be equal the lot size…namely, 100 percent inspection, a fixed sample size or a size determined by a sampling scheme. If the sampling type requires the use of a sampling scheme that's assigned to the sampling procedure, it will consist of individual sampling tables, each of which includes two or more sampling plans that determine a sample size based on the lot size, inspection severity, inspection severity and acceptable quality level, AQL, or the number of containers in an inspection lot. The valuation parameter for which the sampling scheme is created determines the structure of the sampling plan. For instance, the structure of a sampling plan created for an attributive inspection valuation mode will consist of a sample size, acceptance number c, or the maximum number of nonconforming units in a sample that is accepted and a rejection number d, or the least number of nonconforming units in a sample that is rejected. In turn, a sampling plan for a variable inspection will consist of a sample size and k-factor, or acceptability constant that defines the minimum quality score that leads to the acceptance of a sample following a quality inspection. A sampling plan with no valuation parameters will consist only of a sample size.

Q-109:   C. Sampling procedure parameters

When it's not possible to inspect each item produced by a production process, a sample inspection is used to evaluate the quality of the items in an inspection lot. The sample is picked at random from the lot and, on the basis of the information yielded by the sample, a decision is made regarding the disposition of the lot…namely, the lot is accepted or rejected for its intended use. A sampling procedure can be used to select the entities of the sample, which are subsequently evaluated according to an inspection plan. Instructions for drawing the sample, such as the sample's size and the number of samples to be taken, are documented in a sample drawing procedure that's assigned to the inspection plan. The sampling type, which is defined in the sampling procedure, specifies the method to be used to calculate the sample size. For example, the sampling type may require that a sample size be equal the lot size…namely, 100 percent inspection, a fixed sample size or a size determined by a sampling scheme. If the sampling type requires the use of a sampling scheme that's assigned to the sampling procedure, it will consist of individual sampling tables, each of which includes two or more sampling plans that determine a sample size based on the lot size, inspection severity, inspection severity and acceptable quality level, AQL, or the number of containers in an inspection lot. The valuation parameter for which the sampling scheme is created determines the structure of the sampling plan. For instance, the structure of a sampling plan created for an attributive inspection valuation mode will consist of a sample size, acceptance number c, or the maximum number of nonconforming units in a sample that is accepted and a rejection number d, or the least number of nonconforming units in a sample that is rejected. In turn, a sampling plan for a variable inspection will consist of a sample size and k-factor, or acceptability constant that defines the minimum quality score that leads to the acceptance of a sample following a quality inspection. A

sampling plan with no valuation parameters will consist only of a sample size.

Q-110:   A. Special control indicator in the sampling procedure

Sampling procedures, sampling schemes and dynamic modification rules are the basic data needed to create the samples used in the inspection process. In particular, a sampling procedure determines how a sample size is calculated, how inspection characteristics are valuated and if a sample size is dynamically modified. The structure of a sampling procedure includes a sampling type, which specifies how a sample size is calculated, and a valuation mode that includes a valuation rule that governs the acceptance or rejection of a characteristic or sample. The structure also includes an inspection points control indicator that determines the number of inspection points that are created for an inspection lot, an inspection point type, as well as a usage control indicator that ensures a particular sampling procedure is not referenced in a task list. The sampling procedure structure also includes a control chart type that governs the characteristics for which a particular control chart can be used, the variables referenced in the chart and the algorithm used to calculate the chart's control limits. Other control indicators in the sampling procedure are the no stage change control indicator that prevents the use of the dynamic modification procedure to determine the inspection scope or sample size and the multiple samples control indicator for independent or dependent multiple samples.

Q-111:   Variable inspection according to s-method

When it's not possible to inspect each item produced by a production process, a sample inspection is used to evaluate the quality of the items in an inspection lot. The sample is picked at random from the lot and, on the basis of the information yielded by the sample, a decision is made regarding the disposition of the lot...namely, the lot is accepted or rejected for its intended use. A sampling procedure can be used to select the entities of the sample, which are subsequently evaluated according to an inspection plan. Instructions for drawing the sample, such as the sample's size and the number of samples to be taken, are documented in a sample drawing procedure that's assigned to the inspection plan. The sampling type, which is defined in the sampling procedure, specifies the method to be used to calculate the sample size. For example, the sampling type may require that a sample size be equal the lot size...namely, 100 percent inspection, a fixed sample size or a size determined by a sampling scheme. If the sampling type requires the use of a sampling scheme that's assigned to the sampling procedure, it will consist of individual sampling tables, each of which includes two or more sampling plans that determine a sample size based on the lot size, inspection severity, inspection severity and acceptable quality level, AQL, or the number of containers in an inspection lot. The valuation parameter for which the sampling scheme is created determines the structure of the sampling plan. For instance, the structure of a sampling plan created for an attributive inspection valuation mode will consist of a sample size, acceptance number c, or the maximum number of nonconforming units in a sample that is accepted and a rejection number d, or the least number of nonconforming units in a sample that is rejected. In turn, a sampling plan for a variable inspection according to s method consists of a sample size and k-factor, or acceptability constant that defines the minimum quality score that leads to the acceptance of a sample following a quality inspection. A sampling plan with no valuation parameters will consist only of a sample size.

Q-112:   B. Number of times used and D. Operation number

A sampling procedure is directly referenced in a task list or material specification. To determine the objects in which a particular sampling procedure is referenced, a where-used list for a sampling procedure is created. Data elements that appear in the where-used list include sampling procedure name, key date, total number of times used and number of times used in task lists. Also included are the number of times used in material specifications, the number of times used in material master record inspection setups, task lists, operations and characteristics. Other elements included are the characteristic description, master inspection characteristic and dynamic modification rule. Additional functions that can be accessed from the where-used list include "Replace sampling procedure in task list," "Display master inspection characteristic" and " Display inspection type."

Q-113:   B. Inspection severity defined in a sampling table in a sampling scheme

When it's not possible to inspect each item produced by a production process, a sample inspection is used to evaluate the quality of the items in an inspection lot. The sample is picked at random from the lot and, on the basis of the

information yielded by the sample, a decision is made regarding the disposition of the lot...namely, the lot is accepted or rejected for its intended use. A sampling procedure can be used to select the entities of the sample, which are subsequently evaluated according to an inspection plan. Instructions for drawing the sample, such as the sample's size and the number of samples to be taken, are documented in a sample drawing procedure that's assigned to the inspection plan. The sampling type, which is defined in the sampling procedure, specifies the method to be used to calculate the sample size. For example, the sampling type may require that a sample size be equal the lot size...namely, 100 percent inspection, a fixed sample size or a size determined by a sampling scheme. If the sampling type requires the use of a sampling scheme that's assigned to the sampling procedure, it will consist of individual sampling tables, each of which includes two or more sampling plans that determine a sample size based on the lot size, inspection severity, inspection severity and acceptable quality level, AQL, or the number of containers in an inspection lot. The inspection severity is used to adjust the probability of acceptance of an inspection lot, as well as the effort employed to inspect a material. The valuation parameter for which the sampling scheme is created determines the structure of the sampling plan. For instance, the structure of a sampling plan created for an attributive inspection valuation mode will consist of a sample size, acceptance number c, or the maximum number of nonconforming units in a sample that is accepted and a rejection number d, or the least number of nonconforming units in a sample that is rejected. In turn, a sampling plan for a variable inspection will consist of a sample size and k-factor, or acceptability constant that defines the minimum quality score that leads to the acceptance of a sample following a quality inspection. A sampling plan with no valuation parameters will consist only of a sample size.

Q-114:   A. The quality level and dynamic modification rule determine an inspection severity and the inspection severity leads to the sampling plan

When it's not possible to inspect each item produced by a production process, a sample inspection is used to evaluate the quality of the items in an inspection lot. The sample is picked at random from the lot and, on the basis of the information yielded by the sample, a decision is made regarding the disposition of the lot…namely, the lot is accepted or rejected for its intended use. A sampling procedure can be used to select the entities of the sample, which are subsequently evaluated according to an inspection plan. Instructions for drawing the sample, such as the sample's size and the number of samples to be taken, are documented in a sample drawing procedure that's assigned to the inspection plan. The sampling type, which is defined in the sampling procedure, specifies the method to be used to calculate the sample size. For example, the sampling type may require that a sample size be equal the lot size…namely, 100 percent inspection, a fixed sample size or a size determined by a sampling scheme. If the sampling type requires the use of a sampling scheme that's assigned to the sampling procedure, it will consist of individual sampling tables, each of which includes two or more sampling plans that determine a sample size based on the lot size, inspection severity, inspection severity and acceptable quality level, AQL, or the number of containers in an inspection lot. The quality level and the dynamic modification rule control the inspection severity, which determines the sampling plan in the sampling scheme. The inspection severity is used to adjust the probability of acceptance of an inspection lot, as well as the effort employed to inspect a material. The valuation parameter for which the sampling scheme is created determines the structure of the sampling plan. For instance, the structure of a sampling plan created for an attributive inspection valuation mode will consist of a sample size, acceptance number c, or the maximum number of nonconforming units in a sample that is accepted and a rejection number d, or the least number of nonconforming units in a sample that is rejected. In turn, a sampling plan for a variable inspection will consist of a sample size and k-factor, or acceptability constant that defines the minimum quality score that leads to the acceptance of a sample following a quality inspection. A sampling plan with no valuation parameters will consist only of a sample size.

Q-115: A. Attributive inspection, B. Variable inspection and C. Inspection without valuation parameters

When it's not possible to inspect each item produced by a production process, a sample inspection is used to evaluate the quality of the items in an inspection lot. The sample is picked at random from the lot and, on the basis of the information yielded by the sample, a decision is made regarding the disposition of the lot…namely, the lot is accepted or rejected for its intended use. A sampling procedure can be used to select the entities of the sample, which are subsequently evaluated according to an inspection plan. Instructions for drawing the sample, such as the sample's size and the number of samples to be taken, are documented in a sample drawing procedure that's assigned to the inspection plan. The sampling type, which is defined in the sampling procedure, specifies the method to be used to calculate the sample size. For example, the sampling type may require that a sample size be equal the lot size...namely, 100 percent inspection, a fixed sample size or a size determined by a sampling scheme. If the sampling type requires the use of a sampling scheme that's assigned to the sampling procedure, it will consist of individual sampling tables, each of which includes two or more sampling plans that determine a sample size based on the lot size, inspection severity, inspection severity and acceptable quality level, AQL, or the number of containers in an inspection lot. The quality level and the dynamic modification rule control the inspection severity, which determines the sampling plan in the sampling scheme. The inspection severity is used to adjust the probability of acceptance of an inspection lot, as well as the effort employed to inspect a material. The valuation parameter for which the sampling scheme is created determines the structure of the sampling plan. For instance, the structure of a sampling plan created for an attributive inspection valuation mode will consist of a sample size, acceptance number c, or the maximum number of nonconforming units in a sample that is accepted and a rejection number d, or the least number of nonconforming units in a sample that is rejected. In turn, a sampling plan for a variable inspection will consist of a sample size and k-factor, or acceptability constant that defines the minimum quality score that leads to the acceptance of a sample following a quality inspection. A sampling plan with no valuation parameters will consist only of a sample size.

Q-116:   A. Acceptability constant

When it's not possible to inspect each item produced by a production process, a sample inspection is used to evaluate the quality of the items in an inspection lot. The sample is picked at random from the lot and, on the basis of the information yielded by the sample, a decision is made regarding the disposition of the lot…namely, the lot is accepted or rejected for its intended use. A sampling procedure can be used to select the entities of the sample, which are subsequently evaluated according to an inspection plan. Instructions for drawing the sample, such as the sample's size and the number of samples to be taken, are documented in a sample drawing procedure that's assigned to the inspection plan. The sampling type, which is defined in the sampling procedure, specifies the method to be used to calculate the sample size. For example, the sampling type may require that a sample size be equal the lot size…namely, 100 percent inspection, a fixed sample size or a size determined by a sampling scheme. If the sampling type requires the use of a sampling scheme that's assigned to the sampling procedure, it will consist of individual sampling tables, each of which includes two or more sampling plans that determine a sample size based on the lot size, inspection severity, inspection severity and acceptable quality level, AQL, or the number of containers in an inspection lot. The quality level and the dynamic modification rule control the inspection severity, which determines the sampling plan in the sampling scheme. The inspection severity is used to adjust the probability of acceptance of an inspection lot, as well as the effort employed to inspect a material. The valuation parameter for which the sampling scheme is created determines the structure of the sampling plan. For instance, the structure of a sampling plan created for an attributive inspection valuation mode will consist of a sample size, acceptance number c, or the maximum number of nonconforming units in a sample that is accepted and a rejection number d, or the least number of nonconforming units in a sample that is rejected. In turn, a sampling plan for a variable inspection will consist of a sample size and k-factor, or acceptability constant that defines the minimum quality score that leads to the acceptance of a sample following a quality inspection. A sampling plan with no valuation parameters will consist only of a sample size.

Q-117: B. Sampling procedure

Sampling procedures, sampling schemes and dynamic modification rules are the basic data needed to create the samples used in the inspection process. In particular, a sampling procedure determines how a sample size is calculated, how inspection characteristics are valuated and if a sample size is dynamically modified. The structure of a sampling procedure includes a sampling type, which specifies how a sample size is calculated, and a valuation mode that includes a valuation rule that governs the acceptance or rejection of a characteristic or sample. The structure also includes an inspection points control indicator that determines the number of inspection points that are created for an inspection lot, an inspection point type, as well as a usage control indicator that ensures a particular sampling procedure is not referenced in a task list. The sampling procedure structure also includes a control chart type that governs the characteristics for which a particular control chart can be used, the variables

referenced in the chart and the algorithm used to calculate the chart's control limits. Other control indicators in the sampling procedure are the no stage change control indicator that prevents the use of the dynamic modification procedure to determine the inspection scope or sample size and the multiple samples control indicator for independent or dependent multiple samples.

Q-118: B. Control chart type in sampling procedure

Sampling procedures, sampling schemes and dynamic modification rules are the basic data needed to create the samples used in the inspection process. In particular, a sampling procedure determines how a sample size is calculated, how inspection characteristics are valuated and if a sample size is dynamically modified. The structure of a sampling procedure includes a sampling type, which specifies how a sample size is calculated, and a valuation mode that includes a valuation rule that governs the acceptance or rejection of a characteristic or sample. The structure also includes an inspection points control indicator that determines the number of inspection points that are created for an inspection lot, an inspection point type, as well as a usage control indicator that ensures a particular sampling procedure is not referenced in a task list. The sampling procedure structure also includes a control chart type that governs the characteristics for which a particular control chart can be used, the variables referenced in the chart and the algorithm used to calculate the chart's control limits. Other control indicators in the sampling procedure are the no stage change control indicator that prevents the use of the dynamic modification procedure to determine the inspection scope or sample size

and the multiple samples control indicator for independent or dependent multiple samples.

Q-119:   A. Dynamic modification rule

A sampling procedure is directly referenced in a task list or material specification. To determine the objects in which a particular sampling procedure is referenced, a where-used list for a sampling procedure is created. Data elements that appear in the where-used list include sampling procedure name, key date, total number of times used and number of times used in task lists. Also included are the number of times used in material specifications, the number of times used in material master record inspection setups, task lists, operations and characteristics. Other elements included are the characteristic description, master inspection characteristic and dynamic modification rule. Additional functions that can be accessed from the where-used list include "Replace sampling procedure in task list," "Display master inspection characteristic" and " Display inspection type."

Q-120:   B. Inspection scope

When it's not possible to inspect each item produced by a production process, a sample inspection is used to evaluate the quality of the items in an inspection lot. The sample is picked at random from the lot and, on the basis of the information yielded by the sample, a decision is made regarding the disposition of the lot…namely, the lot is accepted or rejected for its intended use. A sampling procedure can be used to select the entities of the sample, which are subsequently evaluated according to an inspection plan. Instructions for drawing the sample, such as the sample's size and the number of samples to be taken, are documented in a sample drawing procedure that's assigned to the inspection plan. The sampling type, which is defined in the sampling procedure, specifies the method to be used to calculate the sample size. For example, the sampling type may require that a sample size be equal the lot size…namely, 100 percent inspection, a fixed sample size or a size determined by a sampling scheme. If the sampling type requires the use of a sampling scheme that's assigned to the sampling procedure, it will consist of individual sampling tables, each of which includes two or more sampling plans that determine a sample size based on the lot size, inspection severity, inspection severity and acceptable quality level, AQL, or the number of containers in an inspection lot. The quality level and the dynamic modification rule control the inspection severity, which determines the sampling plan in the sampling scheme. The inspection severity is used to adjust the probability of acceptance of an inspection lot, as well as the effort employed to inspect a material. The valuation parameter for which the sampling scheme is created determines the structure of the sampling plan. For instance, the structure of a sampling plan created for an attributive inspection valuation mode will consist of a sample size, acceptance number c, or the maximum number of nonconforming units in a sample that is accepted and a rejection number d, or the least number of nonconforming units in a sample that is rejected. In turn, a sampling plan for a variable inspection will consist of a sample size and k-factor, or acceptability constant that defines the minimum quality score that leads to the acceptance of a sample following a quality inspection. A sampling plan with no valuation parameters will consist only of a sample size.

Q-121: B. Define maximum number of defects permitted per 100 units for the lot to be accepted and D. Define the maximum fraction of nonconforming units permitted for lot to be accepted

When it's not possible to inspect each item produced by a production process, a sample inspection is used to evaluate the quality of the items in an inspection lot. The sample is picked at random from the lot and, on the basis of the information yielded by the sample, a decision is made regarding the disposition of the lot...namely, the lot is accepted or rejected for its intended use. A sampling procedure can be used to select the entities of the sample, which are subsequently evaluated according to an inspection plan. Instructions for drawing the sample, such as the sample's size and the number of samples to be taken, are documented in a sample drawing procedure that's assigned to the inspection plan. The sampling type, which is defined in the sampling procedure, specifies the method to be used to calculate the sample size. For example, the sampling type may require that a sample size be equal the lot size...namely, 100 percent inspection, a fixed sample size or a size determined by a sampling scheme. If the sampling type requires the use of a sampling scheme that's assigned to the sampling procedure, it will consist of individual sampling tables, each of which includes two or more sampling plans that determine a sample size based on the lot size, inspection severity, inspection severity and acceptable quality level, AQL, or the number of containers in an inspection lot. The quality level and the dynamic modification rule control the inspection severity, which determines the sampling plan in the sampling scheme. The inspection severity is used to adjust the probability of acceptance of an inspection lot, as well as the effort employed to inspect a material. The valuation parameter for which the sampling scheme is created determines the structure of the sampling plan. For instance, the structure of a sampling plan created for an attributive inspection valuation mode will consist of a sample size, acceptance number c, or the maximum number of nonconforming units in a sample that is accepted and a rejection number d, or the least number of nonconforming units in a sample that is rejected. In turn, a sampling plan for a variable inspection will consist of a sample size and k-factor, or acceptability constant that defines the minimum quality score that leads to the acceptance of a sample following a quality inspection. A sampling plan with no valuation parameters will consist only of a sample size.

Q-122:   B. Sampling scheme

When it's not possible to inspect each item produced by a production process, a sample inspection is used to evaluate the quality of the items in an inspection lot. The sample is picked at random from the lot and, on the basis of the information yielded by the sample, a decision is made regarding the disposition of the lot…namely, the lot is accepted or rejected for its intended use. A sampling procedure can be used to select the entities of the sample, which are subsequently evaluated according to an inspection plan. Instructions for drawing the sample, such as the sample's size and the number of samples to be taken, are documented in a sample drawing procedure that's assigned to the inspection plan. The sampling type, which is defined in the sampling procedure, specifies the method to be used to calculate the sample size. For example, the sampling type may require that a sample size be equal the lot size…namely, 100 percent inspection, a fixed sample size or a size determined by a sampling scheme. If the sampling type requires the use of a sampling scheme that's assigned to the sampling procedure, it will consist of individual sampling tables, each of which includes two or more sampling plans that determine a sample size based on the lot size, inspection severity, inspection severity and acceptable quality level, AQL, or the number of containers in an inspection lot. The quality level and the dynamic modification rule control the inspection severity, which determines the sampling plan in the sampling scheme. The inspection severity is used to adjust the probability of acceptance of an inspection lot, as well as the effort employed to inspect a material. The valuation parameter for which the sampling scheme is created determines the structure of the sampling plan. For instance, the structure of a sampling plan created for an attributive inspection valuation mode will consist of a sample size, acceptance number c, or the maximum number of nonconforming units in a sample that is accepted and a rejection number d, or the least number of nonconforming units in a sample that is rejected. In turn, a sampling plan for a variable inspection will consist of a sample size and k-factor, or acceptability constant that defines the minimum quality score that leads to the acceptance of a sample following a quality inspection. A sampling plan with no valuation parameters will consist only of a sample size.

Q-123:   A. Defines rules that determine the acceptance or rejection of a characteristic or sample during a quality inspection

Sampling procedures, sampling schemes and dynamic modification rules are the basic data needed to create the samples used in the inspection process. In particular, a sampling procedure determines how a sample size is calculated, how inspection characteristics are valuated and if a sample size is dynamically modified. The structure of a sampling procedure includes a sampling type, which specifies how a sample size is calculated, and a valuation mode that includes a valuation rule that governs the acceptance or rejection of a characteristic or sample. The structure also includes an inspection points control indicator that determines the number of inspection points that are created for an inspection lot, an inspection point type, as well as a usage control indicator that ensures a particular sampling procedure is not referenced in a task list. The sampling procedure structure also includes a control chart type that governs the characteristics for which a particular control chart can be used, the variables referenced in the chart and the algorithm used to calculate the chart's control limits. Other control indicators in the sampling procedure are the no stage change control indicator that prevents the use of the dynamic modification procedure to determine the inspection scope or sample size and the multiple samples control indicator for independent or dependent multiple samples.

Q-124:   B. Special indicator in the sampling procedure

Sampling procedures, sampling schemes and dynamic modification rules are the basic data needed to create the samples used in the inspection process. In particular, a sampling procedure determines how a sample size is calculated, how inspection characteristics are valuated and if a sample size is dynamically modified. The structure of a sampling procedure includes a sampling type, which specifies how a sample size is calculated, and a valuation mode that includes a valuation rule that governs the acceptance or rejection of a characteristic or sample. The structure also includes an inspection points control indicator that determines the number of inspection points that are created for an inspection lot, an inspection point type, as well as a usage control indicator that ensures a particular sampling procedure is not referenced in a task list. The sampling procedure structure also includes a control chart type that governs the characteristics for which a particular control chart can be used, the variables referenced in the chart and the algorithm used to calculate the chart's control limits. Other control indicators in the sampling procedure are the no stage change control indicator that prevents the use of the dynamic modification procedure to determine the inspection scope or sample size and the multiple samples control indicator for independent or dependent multiple samples.

Q-125:   A. Valuation mode

Sampling procedures, sampling schemes and dynamic modification rules are the basic data needed to create the samples used in the inspection process. In particular, a sampling procedure determines how a sample size is calculated, how inspection characteristics are valuated and if a sample size is dynamically modified. The structure of a sampling procedure includes a sampling type, which specifies how a sample size is calculated, and a valuation mode that includes a valuation rule that governs the acceptance or rejection of a characteristic or sample. The structure also includes an inspection points control indicator that determines the number of inspection points that are created for an inspection lot, an inspection point type, as well as a usage control indicator that ensures a particular sampling procedure is not referenced in a task list. The sampling procedure structure also includes a control chart type that governs the characteristics for which a particular control chart can be used, the variables referenced in the chart and the algorithm used to calculate the chart's control limits. Other control indicators in the sampling procedure are the no stage change control indicator that prevents the use of the dynamic modification procedure to determine the inspection scope or sample size and the multiple samples control indicator for independent or dependent multiple samples.

Q-126:   A. Key date, B. Number of times the sampling procedure is referenced in the material master record inspection set-up and D. Master inspection characteristic

A sampling procedure is directly referenced in a task list or material specification. To determine the objects in which a particular sampling procedure is referenced, a where-used list for a sampling procedure is created. Data elements that appear in the where-used list include sampling procedure name, key date, total number of times used and number of times used in task lists. Also included are the number of times used in material specifications, the number of times used in material master record inspection setups, task lists, operations and characteristics. Other elements included are the characteristic description, master inspection characteristic and dynamic modification rule. Additional functions that can be accessed from the where-used list include "Replace sampling procedure in task list," "Display master inspection characteristic" and " Display inspection type."

Q-127:   A. Sampling plan

When it's not possible to inspect each item produced by a production process, a sample inspection is used to evaluate the quality of the items in an inspection lot. The sample is picked at random from the lot and, on the basis of the information yielded by the sample, a decision is made regarding the disposition of the lot...namely, the lot is accepted or rejected for its intended use. A sampling procedure can be used to select the entities of the sample, which are subsequently evaluated according to an inspection plan. Instructions for drawing the sample, such as the sample's size and the number of samples to be taken, are documented in a sample drawing procedure that's assigned to the inspection plan. The sampling type, which is defined in the sampling procedure, specifies the method to be used to calculate the sample size. For example, the sampling type may require that a sample size be equal the lot size...namely, 100 percent inspection, a fixed sample size or a size determined by a sampling scheme. If the sampling type requires the use of a sampling scheme that's assigned to the sampling procedure, it will consist of individual sampling tables, each of which includes two or more sampling plans that determine a sample size based on the lot size, inspection severity, inspection severity and acceptable quality level, AQL, or the number of containers in an inspection lot. The quality level and the dynamic modification rule control the inspection severity, which determines the sampling plan in the sampling scheme. The inspection severity is used to adjust the probability of acceptance of an inspection lot, as well as the effort employed to inspect a material. The valuation parameter for which the sampling scheme is created determines the structure of the sampling plan. For instance, the structure of a sampling plan created for an attributive inspection valuation mode will consist of a sample size, acceptance number c, or the maximum number of nonconforming units in a sample that is accepted and a rejection number d, or the least number of nonconforming units in a sample that is rejected. In turn, a sampling plan for a variable inspection will consist of a sample size and k-factor, or acceptability constant that defines the minimum quality score that leads to the acceptance of a sample following a quality inspection. A sampling plan with no valuation parameters will consist only of a sample size.

Q-128:   A. Sample size and D. Rejection number d

When it's not possible to inspect each item produced by a production process, a sample inspection is used to evaluate the quality of the items in an inspection lot. The sample is picked at random from the lot and, on the basis of the information yielded by the sample, a decision is made regarding the disposition of the lot...namely, the lot is accepted or rejected for its intended use. A sampling procedure can be used to select the entities of the sample, which are subsequently evaluated according to an inspection plan. Instructions for drawing the sample, such as the sample's size and the number of samples to be taken, are documented in a sample drawing procedure that's assigned to the inspection plan. The sampling type, which is defined in the sampling procedure, specifies the method to be used to calculate the sample size. For example, the sampling type may require that a sample size be equal the lot size...namely, 100 percent inspection, a fixed sample size or a size determined by a sampling scheme. If the sampling type requires the use of a sampling scheme that's assigned to the sampling procedure, it will consist of individual sampling tables, each of which includes two or more sampling plans that determine a sample size based on the lot size, inspection severity, inspection severity and acceptable quality level, AQL, or the number of containers in an inspection lot. The quality level and the dynamic modification rule control the inspection severity, which determines the sampling plan in the sampling scheme. The inspection severity is used to adjust the probability of acceptance of an inspection lot, as well as the effort employed to inspect a material. The valuation parameter for which the sampling scheme is created determines the structure of the sampling plan. For instance, the structure of a sampling plan created for an attributive inspection valuation mode will consist of a sample size, acceptance number c, or the maximum number of nonconforming units in a sample that is accepted and a rejection number d, or the least number of nonconforming units in a sample that is rejected. In turn, a sampling plan for a variable inspection will consist of a sample size and k-factor, or acceptability constant that defines the minimum quality score that leads to the acceptance of a sample following a quality inspection. A sampling plan with no valuation parameters will consist only of a sample size.

Q-129:   A. Sampling plan table

When it's not possible to inspect each item produced by a production process, a sample inspection is used to evaluate the quality of the items in an inspection lot. The sample is picked at random from the lot and, on the basis of the information yielded by the sample, a decision is made regarding the disposition of the lot…namely, the lot is accepted or rejected for its intended use. A sampling procedure can be used to select the entities of the sample, which are subsequently evaluated according to an inspection plan. Instructions for drawing the sample, such as the sample's size and the number of samples to be taken, are documented in a sample drawing procedure that's assigned to the inspection plan. The sampling type, which is defined in the sampling procedure, specifies the method to be used to calculate the sample size. For example, the sampling type may require that a sample size be equal the lot size…namely, 100 percent inspection, a fixed sample size or a size determined by a sampling scheme. If the sampling type requires the use of a sampling scheme that's assigned to the sampling procedure, it will consist of individual sampling tables, each of which includes two or more sampling plans that determine a sample size based on the lot size, inspection severity, inspection severity and acceptable quality level, AQL, or the number of containers in an inspection lot. The quality level and the dynamic modification rule control the inspection severity, which determines the sampling plan in the sampling scheme. The inspection severity is used to adjust the probability of

acceptance of an inspection lot, as well as the effort employed to inspect a material. The valuation parameter for which the sampling scheme is created determines the structure of the sampling plan. For instance, the structure of a sampling plan created for an attributive inspection valuation mode will consist of a sample size, acceptance number c, or the maximum number of nonconforming units in a sample that is accepted and a rejection number d, or the least number of nonconforming units in a sample that is rejected. In turn, a sampling plan for a variable inspection will consist of a sample size and k-factor, or acceptability constant that defines the minimum quality score that leads to the acceptance of a sample following a quality inspection. A sampling plan with no valuation parameters will consist only of a sample size.

Q-130:   A. Specify the rules used to calculate a sample size

Sampling procedures, sampling schemes and dynamic modification rules are the basic data needed to create the samples used in the inspection process. In particular, a sampling procedure determines how a sample size is calculated, how inspection characteristics are valuated and if a sample size is dynamically modified. The structure of a sampling procedure includes a sampling type, which specifies how a sample size is calculated, and a valuation mode that includes a valuation rule that governs the acceptance or rejection of a characteristic or sample. The structure also includes an inspection points control indicator that determines the number of inspection points that are created for an inspection lot, an inspection point type, as well as a usage control indicator that ensures a particular sampling procedure is not referenced in a task

272

list. The sampling procedure structure also includes a control chart type that governs the characteristics for which a particular control chart can be used, the variables referenced in the chart and the algorithm used to calculate the chart's control limits. Other control indicators in the sampling procedure are the no stage change control indicator that prevents the use of the dynamic modification procedure to determine the inspection scope or sample size and the multiple samples control indicator for independent or dependent multiple samples.

Q-131:   B. Inspection characteristics referenced in the control chart, C. Control variables referenced in the control chart and D. Algorithm used to calculate control limits

Sampling procedures, sampling schemes and dynamic modification rules are the basic data needed to create the samples used in the inspection process. In particular, a sampling procedure determines how a sample size is calculated, how inspection characteristics are valuated and if a sample size is dynamically modified. The structure of a sampling procedure includes a sampling type, which specifies how a sample size is calculated, and a valuation mode that includes a valuation rule that governs the acceptance or rejection of a characteristic or sample. The structure also includes an inspection points control indicator that determines the number of inspection points that are created for an inspection lot, an inspection point type, as well as a usage control indicator that ensures a particular sampling procedure is not referenced in a task list. The sampling procedure structure also includes a control chart type that governs the characteristics for which a particular control chart can be used, the variables

273

referenced in the chart and the algorithm used to calculate the chart's control limits. Other control indicators in the sampling procedure are the no stage change control indicator that prevents the use of the dynamic modification procedure to determine the inspection scope or sample size and the multiple samples control indicator for independent or dependent multiple samples.

Q-132: A. Attributive inspection

When it's not possible to inspect each item produced by a production process, a sample inspection is used to evaluate the quality of the items in an inspection lot. The sample is picked at random from the lot and, on the basis of the information yielded by the sample, a decision is made regarding the disposition of the lot...namely, the lot is accepted or rejected for its intended use. A sampling procedure can be used to select the entities of the sample, which are subsequently evaluated according to an inspection plan. Instructions for drawing the sample, such as the sample's size and the number of samples to be taken, are documented in a sample drawing procedure that's assigned to the inspection plan. The sampling type, which is defined in the sampling procedure, specifies the method to be used to calculate the sample size. For example, the sampling type may require that a sample size be equal the lot size...namely, 100 percent inspection, a fixed sample size or a size determined by a sampling scheme. If the sampling type requires the use of a sampling scheme that's assigned to the sampling procedure, it will consist of individual sampling tables, each of which includes two or more sampling plans that determine a sample size based on the lot size, inspection severity, inspection severity and acceptable quality level, AQL, or the number of containers in an inspection lot. The quality level and the dynamic modification rule control the inspection severity, which determines the sampling plan in the sampling scheme. The inspection severity is used to adjust the probability of acceptance of an inspection lot, as well as the effort employed to inspect a material. The valuation parameter for which the sampling scheme is created determines the structure of the sampling plan. For instance, the structure of a sampling plan created for an attributive inspection valuation mode will consist of a sample size, acceptance number c, or the maximum number of nonconforming units in a sample that is accepted and a rejection number d, or the least number of nonconforming units in a sample that is rejected. In turn, a sampling plan for a variable inspection will consist of a sample size and k-factor, or acceptability constant that defines the minimum quality score that leads to the acceptance of a sample following a quality inspection. A sampling plan with no valuation parameters will consist only of a sample size.

Q-133:   B. Display replacement log

Acceptance sampling leads to the acceptance or rejection of materials and lots based on the inspection of samples. A sample of a given size is drawn using a random method and if less than a given number of errors are found, the sample is accepted. If more than the specified number of errors are found, the sample is rejected. A sampling procedure is a process by which the entities of a sample are selected. The sampling procedure also determines how a characteristic or sample is valuated. In the instance that a task list or material specification is used in the conduct of a quality inspection, the sampling procedure is either assigned to the inspection characteristic or it is defined using the Customizing application. In the event that one sampling procedure replaces another in the sampling procedure, the replacement log can be reviewed to confirm the replacement was successful.

Q-134:   D. Acceptance number c and E. Sample size

When it's not possible to inspect each item produced by a production process, a sample inspection is used to evaluate the quality of the items in an inspection lot. The sample is picked at random from the lot and, on the basis of the information yielded by the sample, a decision is made regarding the disposition of the lot…namely, the lot is accepted or rejected for its intended use. A sampling procedure can be used to select the entities of the sample, which are subsequently evaluated according to an inspection plan. Instructions for drawing the sample, such as the sample's size and the number of samples to be taken, are documented in a sample drawing procedure that's assigned to the inspection plan. The sampling type, which is defined in the sampling procedure, specifies the method to be used to calculate the sample size. For example, the sampling type may require that a sample size be equal the lot size…namely, 100 percent inspection, a fixed sample size or a size determined by a sampling scheme. If the sampling type requires the use of a sampling scheme that's assigned to the sampling procedure, it will consist of individual sampling tables, each of which includes two or more sampling plans that determine a sample size based on the lot size, inspection severity, inspection severity and acceptable quality level, AQL, or the number of containers in an inspection lot. The quality level and the dynamic modification rule control the inspection severity, which determines the sampling plan in the sampling scheme. The inspection severity is used to adjust the probability of acceptance of an inspection lot, as well as the effort employed to inspect a material. The valuation parameter for which the sampling scheme is created determines the structure of the sampling plan. For instance, the structure of a sampling plan created for an attributive inspection valuation mode will consist of a sample size, acceptance number c, or the maximum number of nonconforming units in a sample that is accepted and a rejection number d, or the least number of nonconforming units in a sample that is rejected. In turn, a sampling plan for a variable inspection will consist of a sample size and k-factor, or acceptability constant that defines the minimum quality score that leads to the acceptance of a sample following a quality inspection. A sampling plan with no valuation parameters will consist only of a sample size.

Q-135:   C. Sampling plan

When it's not possible to inspect each item produced by a production process, a sample inspection is used to evaluate the quality of the items in an inspection lot. The sample is picked at random from the lot and, on the basis of the information yielded by the sample, a decision is made regarding the disposition of the lot…namely, the lot is accepted or rejected for its intended use. A sampling procedure can be used to select the entities of the sample, which are subsequently evaluated according to an inspection plan. Instructions for drawing the sample, such as the sample's size and the number of samples to be taken,

are documented in a sample drawing procedure that's assigned to the inspection plan. The sampling type, which is defined in the sampling procedure, specifies the method to be used to calculate the sample size. For example, the sampling type may require that a sample size be equal the lot size...namely, 100 percent inspection, a fixed sample size or a size determined by a sampling scheme. If the sampling type requires the use of a sampling scheme that's assigned to the sampling procedure, it will consist of individual sampling tables, each of which includes two or more sampling plans that determine a sample size based on the lot size, inspection severity, inspection severity and acceptable quality level, AQL, or the number of containers in an inspection lot. The quality level and the dynamic modification rule control the inspection severity, which determines the sampling plan in the sampling scheme. The inspection severity is used to adjust the probability of acceptance of an inspection lot, as well as the effort employed to inspect a material. The valuation parameter for which the sampling scheme is created determines the structure of the sampling plan. For instance, the structure of a sampling plan created for an attributive inspection valuation mode will consist of a sample size, acceptance number c, or the maximum number of nonconforming units in a sample that is accepted and a rejection number d, or the least number of nonconforming units in a sample that is rejected. In turn, a sampling plan for a variable inspection will consist of a sample size and k-factor, or acceptability constant that defines the minimum quality score that leads to the acceptance of a sample following a quality inspection. A sampling plan with no valuation parameters will consist only of a sample size.

Q-136:   A. Acceptance constant in sampling plan

When it's not possible to inspect each item produced by a
production process, a sample inspection is used to evaluate
the quality of the items in an inspection lot. The sample is
picked at random from the lot and, on the basis of the
information yielded by the sample, a decision is made
regarding the disposition of the lot...namely, the lot is
accepted or rejected for its intended use. A sampling
procedure can be used to select the entities of the sample,
which are subsequently evaluated according to an
inspection plan. Instructions for drawing the sample, such
as the sample's size and the number of samples to be taken,
are documented in a sample drawing procedure that's
assigned to the inspection plan. The sampling type, which is
defined in the sampling procedure, specifies the method to
be used to calculate the sample size. For example, the
sampling type may require that a sample size be equal the
lot size...namely, 100 percent inspection, a fixed sample
size or a size determined by a sampling scheme. If the
sampling type requires the use of a sampling scheme that's
assigned to the sampling procedure, it will consist of
individual sampling tables, each of which includes two or
more sampling plans that determine a sample size based on
the lot size, inspection severity, inspection severity and
acceptable quality level, AQL, or the number of containers
in an inspection lot. The quality level and the dynamic
modification rule control the inspection severity, which
determines the sampling plan in the sampling scheme. The
inspection severity is used to adjust the probability of
acceptance of an inspection lot, as well as the effort
employed to inspect a material. The valuation parameter for
which the sampling scheme is created determines the

structure of the sampling plan. For instance, the structure of a sampling plan created for an attributive inspection valuation mode will consist of a sample size, acceptance number c, or the maximum number of nonconforming units in a sample that is accepted and a rejection number d, or the least number of nonconforming units in a sample that is rejected. In turn, a sampling plan for a variable inspection will consist of a sample size and k-factor, or acceptability constant that defines the minimum quality score that leads to the acceptance of a sample following a quality inspection. A sampling plan with no valuation parameters will consist only of a sample size.

Q-137: B. Sampling type

Sampling procedures, sampling schemes and dynamic modification rules are the basic data needed to create the samples used in the inspection process. In particular, a sampling procedure determines how a sample size is calculated, how inspection characteristics are valuated and if a sample size is dynamically modified. The structure of a sampling procedure includes a sampling type, which specifies how a sample size is calculated, and a valuation mode that includes a valuation rule that governs the acceptance or rejection of a characteristic or sample. The structure also includes an inspection points control indicator that determines the number of inspection points that are created for an inspection lot, an inspection point type, as well as a usage control indicator that ensures a particular sampling procedure is not referenced in a task list. The sampling procedure structure also includes a control chart type that governs the characteristics for which a particular control chart can be used, the variables

referenced in the chart and the algorithm used to calculate the chart's control limits. Other control indicators in the sampling procedure are the no stage change control indicator that prevents the use of the dynamic modification procedure to determine the inspection scope or sample size and the multiple samples control indicator for independent or dependent multiple samples.

Q-138:   B. Sampling type

When it's not possible to inspect each item produced by a production process, a sample inspection is used to evaluate the quality of the items in an inspection lot. The sample is picked at random from the lot and, on the basis of the information yielded by the sample, a decision is made regarding the disposition of the lot...namely, the lot is accepted or rejected for its intended use. A sampling procedure can be used to select the entities of the sample, which are subsequently evaluated according to an inspection plan. Instructions for drawing the sample, such as the sample's size and the number of samples to be taken, are documented in a sample drawing procedure that's assigned to the inspection plan. The sampling type, which is defined in the sampling procedure, specifies the method to be used to calculate the sample size. For example, the sampling type may require that a sample size be equal the lot size...namely, 100 percent inspection, a fixed sample size or a size determined by a sampling scheme. If the sampling type requires the use of a sampling scheme that's assigned to the sampling procedure, it will consist of individual sampling tables, each of which includes two or more sampling plans that determine a sample size based on the lot size, inspection severity, inspection severity and acceptable quality level, AQL, or the number of containers in an inspection lot. The quality level and the dynamic modification rule control the inspection severity, which determines the sampling plan in the sampling scheme. The inspection severity is used to adjust the probability of acceptance of an inspection lot, as well as the effort employed to inspect a material. The valuation parameter for which the sampling scheme is created determines the structure of the sampling plan. For instance, the structure of a sampling plan created for an attributive inspection valuation mode will consist of a sample size, acceptance number c, or the maximum number of nonconforming units in a sample that is accepted and a rejection number d, or the least number of nonconforming units in a sample that is rejected. In turn, a sampling plan for a variable inspection will consist of a sample size and k-factor, or acceptability constant that defines the minimum quality score that leads to the acceptance of a sample following a quality inspection. A sampling plan with no valuation parameters will consist only of a sample size.

Q-139:   B. Multiple samples control indicator

Sampling procedures, sampling schemes and dynamic modification rules are the basic data needed to create the samples used in the inspection process. In particular, a sampling procedure determines how a sample size is calculated, how inspection characteristics are valuated and if a sample size is dynamically modified. The structure of a sampling procedure includes a sampling type, which specifies how a sample size is calculated, and a valuation mode that includes a valuation rule that governs the acceptance or rejection of a characteristic or sample. The

282

structure also includes an inspection points control indicator that determines the number of inspection points that are created for an inspection lot, an inspection point type, as well as a usage control indicator that ensures a particular sampling procedure is not referenced in a task list. The sampling procedure structure also includes a control chart type that governs the characteristics for which a particular control chart can be used, the variables referenced in the chart and the algorithm used to calculate the chart's control limits. Other control indicators in the sampling procedure are the no stage change control indicator that prevents the use of the dynamic modification procedure to determine the inspection scope or sample size and the multiple samples control indicator for independent or dependent multiple samples.

Q-140:   A. Attributive inspection, B. Variable inspection and C. No valuation parameter

When it's not possible to inspect each item produced by a production process, a sample inspection is used to evaluate the quality of the items in an inspection lot. The sample is picked at random from the lot and, on the basis of the information yielded by the sample, a decision is made regarding the disposition of the lot…namely, the lot is accepted or rejected for its intended use. A sampling procedure can be used to select the entities of the sample, which are subsequently evaluated according to an inspection plan. Instructions for drawing the sample, such as the sample's size and the number of samples to be taken, are documented in a sample drawing procedure that's assigned to the inspection plan. The sampling type, which is defined in the sampling procedure, specifies the method to be used to calculate the sample size. For example, the sampling type may require that a sample size be equal the lot size...namely, 100 percent inspection, a fixed sample size or a size determined by a sampling scheme. If the sampling type requires the use of a sampling scheme that's assigned to the sampling procedure, it will consist of individual sampling tables, each of which includes two or more sampling plans that determine a sample size based on the lot size, inspection severity, inspection severity and acceptable quality level, AQL, or the number of containers in an inspection lot. The quality level and the dynamic modification rule control the inspection severity, which determines the sampling plan in the sampling scheme. The inspection severity is used to adjust the probability of acceptance of an inspection lot, as well as the effort employed to inspect a material. The valuation parameter for which the sampling scheme is created determines the structure of the sampling plan. For instance, the structure of a sampling plan created for an attributive inspection valuation mode will consist of a sample size, acceptance number c, or the maximum number of nonconforming units in a sample that is accepted and a rejection number d, or the least number of nonconforming units in a sample that is rejected. In turn, a sampling plan for a variable inspection will consist of a sample size and k-factor, or acceptability constant that defines the minimum quality score that leads to the acceptance of a sample following a quality inspection. A sampling plan with no valuation parameters will consist only of a sample size.

Q-141:   A. Sample size and C. Acceptance number

When it's not possible to inspect each item produced by a production process, a sample inspection is used to evaluate the quality of the items in an inspection lot. The sample is picked at random from the lot and, on the basis of the information yielded by the sample, a decision is made regarding the disposition of the lot…namely, the lot is accepted or rejected for its intended use. A sampling procedure can be used to select the entities of the sample, which are subsequently evaluated according to an inspection plan. Instructions for drawing the sample, such as the sample's size and the number of samples to be taken, are documented in a sample drawing procedure that's assigned to the inspection plan. The sampling type, which is defined in the sampling procedure, specifies the method to be used to calculate the sample size. For example, the sampling type may require that a sample size be equal the lot size…namely, 100 percent inspection, a fixed sample size or a size determined by a sampling scheme. If the sampling type requires the use of a sampling scheme that's assigned to the sampling procedure, it will consist of individual sampling tables, each of which includes two or more sampling plans that determine a sample size based on the lot size, inspection severity, inspection severity and acceptable quality level, AQL, or the number of containers in an inspection lot. The quality level and the dynamic modification rule control the inspection severity, which determines the sampling plan in the sampling scheme. The inspection severity is used to adjust the probability of acceptance of an inspection lot, as well as the effort employed to inspect a material. The valuation parameter for which the sampling scheme is created determines the structure of the sampling plan. For instance, the structure of a sampling plan created for an attributive inspection

valuation mode will consist of a sample size, acceptance number c, or the maximum number of nonconforming units in a sample that is accepted and a rejection number d, or the least number of nonconforming units in a sample that is rejected. In turn, a sampling plan for a variable inspection will consist of a sample size and k-factor, or acceptability constant that defines the minimum quality score that leads to the acceptance of a sample following a quality inspection. A sampling plan with no valuation parameters will consist only of a sample size.

Q-142:   C. Valuation mode defined for sampling procedure

When it's not possible to inspect each item produced by a production process, a sample inspection is used to evaluate the quality of the items in an inspection lot. The sample is picked at random from the lot and, on the basis of the information yielded by the sample, a decision is made regarding the disposition of the lot...namely, the lot is accepted or rejected for its intended use. A sampling procedure can be used to select the entities of the sample, which are subsequently evaluated according to an inspection plan. Instructions for drawing the sample, such as the sample's size and the number of samples to be taken, are documented in a sample drawing procedure that's assigned to the inspection plan. The sampling type, which is defined in the sampling procedure, specifies the method to be used to calculate the sample size. For example, the sampling type may require that a sample size be equal the lot size....namely, 100 percent inspection, a fixed sample size or a size determined by a sampling scheme. If the sampling type requires the use of a sampling scheme that's assigned to the sampling procedure, it will consist of individual sampling tables, each of which includes two or more sampling plans that determine a sample size based on the lot size, inspection severity, inspection severity and acceptable quality level, AQL, or the number of containers in an inspection lot. The quality level and the dynamic modification rule control the inspection severity, which determines the sampling plan in the sampling scheme. The inspection severity is used to adjust the probability of acceptance of an inspection lot, as well as the effort employed to inspect a material. The valuation parameter for which the sampling scheme is created determines the structure of the sampling plan. For instance, the structure of a sampling plan created for an attributive inspection valuation mode will consist of a sample size, acceptance number c, or the maximum number of nonconforming units in a sample that is accepted and a rejection number d, or the least number of nonconforming units in a sample that is rejected. In turn, a sampling plan for a variable inspection will consist of a sample size and k-factor, or acceptability constant that defines the minimum quality score that leads to the acceptance of a sample following a quality inspection. A sampling plan with no valuation parameters will consist only of a sample size.

Q-143:   A. Sampling type and C. Inspection points

Sampling procedures, sampling schemes and dynamic modification rules are the basic data needed to create the samples used in the inspection process. In particular, a sampling procedure determines how a sample size is calculated, how inspection characteristics are valuated and if a sample size is dynamically modified. The structure of a sampling procedure includes a sampling type, which specifies how a sample size is calculated and is defined at the characteristic level, and a valuation mode that includes a valuation rule that governs the acceptance or rejection of a characteristic or sample. The structure also includes an inspection points control indicator that determines the number of inspection points that are created for an inspection lot, an inspection point type, as well as a usage control indicator that ensures a particular sampling procedure is not referenced in a task list. The sampling procedure structure also includes a control chart type that governs the characteristics for which a particular control chart can be used, the variables referenced in the chart and the algorithm used to calculate the chart's control limits. Other control indicators in the sampling procedure are the no stage change control indicator that prevents the use of the dynamic modification procedure to determine the inspection scope or sample size and the multiple samples control indicator for independent or dependent multiple samples.

Q-144:   C. Inspection characteristic level

Sampling procedures, sampling schemes and dynamic modification rules are the basic data needed to create the samples used in the inspection process. In particular, a sampling procedure determines how a sample size is calculated, how inspection characteristics are valuated and if a sample size is dynamically modified. The structure of a sampling procedure includes a sampling type, which specifies how a sample size is calculated and is defined at the characteristic level, and a valuation mode that includes a valuation rule that governs the acceptance or rejection of a characteristic or sample. The structure also includes an inspection points control indicator that determines the number of inspection points that are created for an inspection lot, an inspection point type, as well as a usage control indicator that ensures a particular sampling procedure is not referenced in a task list. The sampling procedure structure also includes a control chart type that governs the characteristics for which a particular control chart can be used, the variables referenced in the chart and the algorithm used to calculate the chart's control limits. Other control indicators in the sampling procedure are the no stage change control indicator that prevents the use of the dynamic modification procedure to determine the inspection scope or sample size and the multiple samples control indicator for independent or dependent multiple samples.

Q-145:   B. Sampling type was not entered in the material master record inspection setup

Sampling procedures, sampling schemes and dynamic modification rules are the basic data needed to create the samples used in the inspection process. In particular, a sampling procedure determines how a sample size is calculated, how inspection characteristics are valuated and if a sample size is dynamically modified. The structure of a sampling procedure includes a sampling type, which specifies how a sample size is calculated, and a valuation mode that includes a valuation rule that governs the acceptance or rejection of a characteristic or sample. The structure also includes an inspection points control indicator that determines the number of inspection points that are created for an inspection lot, an inspection point

type, as well as a usage control indicator that ensures a particular sampling procedure is not referenced in a task list. The sampling procedure structure also includes a control chart type that governs the characteristics for which a particular control chart can be used, the variables referenced in the chart and the algorithm used to calculate the chart's control limits. Other control indicators in the sampling procedure are the no stage change control indicator that prevents the use of the dynamic modification procedure to determine the inspection scope or sample size and the multiple samples control indicator for independent or dependent multiple samples. The sampling procedure can be assigned to a task list characteristic if an inspection plan is used for the inspection or the inspection setup for a material master record inspection type if an inspection plan is not used for the inspection.

Q-146:   B. Variable inspection valuation mode in sampling procedure

When it's not possible to inspect each item produced by a production process, a sample inspection is used to evaluate the quality of the items in an inspection lot. The sample is picked at random from the lot and, on the basis of the information yielded by the sample, a decision is made regarding the disposition of the lot...namely, the lot is accepted or rejected for its intended use. A sampling procedure can be used to select the entities of the sample, which are subsequently evaluated according to an inspection plan. Instructions for drawing the sample, such as the sample's size and the number of samples to be taken, are documented in a sample drawing procedure that's assigned to the inspection plan. The sampling type, which is defined in the sampling procedure, specifies the method to be used to calculate the sample size. For example, the sampling type may require that a sample size be equal the lot size…namely, 100 percent inspection, a fixed sample size or a size determined by a sampling scheme. If the sampling type requires the use of a sampling scheme that's assigned to the sampling procedure, it will consist of individual sampling tables, each of which includes two or more sampling plans that determine a sample size based on the lot size, inspection severity, inspection severity and acceptable quality level, AQL, or the number of containers in an inspection lot. The quality level and the dynamic modification rule control the inspection severity, which determines the sampling plan in the sampling scheme. The inspection severity is used to adjust the probability of acceptance of an inspection lot, as well as the effort employed to inspect a material. The valuation parameter for which the sampling scheme is created determines the structure of the sampling plan. For instance, the structure of a sampling plan created for an attributive inspection valuation mode will consist of a sample size, acceptance number c, or the maximum number of nonconforming units in a sample that is accepted and a rejection number d, or the least number of nonconforming units in a sample that is rejected. In turn, a sampling plan for a variable inspection will consist of a sample size and k-factor, or acceptability constant that defines the minimum quality score that leads to the acceptance of a sample following a quality inspection. A sampling plan with no valuation parameters will consist only of a sample size.

Q-147:   C. Sampling scheme

291

When it's not possible to inspect each item produced by a production process, a sample inspection is used to evaluate the quality of the items in an inspection lot. The sample is picked at random from the lot and, on the basis of the information yielded by the sample, a decision is made regarding the disposition of the lot...namely, the lot is accepted or rejected for its intended use. A sampling procedure can be used to select the entities of the sample, which are subsequently evaluated according to an inspection plan. Instructions for drawing the sample, such as the sample's size and the number of samples to be taken, are documented in a sample drawing procedure that's assigned to the inspection plan. The sampling type, which is defined in the sampling procedure, specifies the method to be used to calculate the sample size. For example, the sampling type may require that a sample size be equal the lot size...namely, 100 percent inspection, a fixed sample size or a size determined by a sampling scheme. If the sampling type requires the use of a sampling scheme that's assigned to the sampling procedure, it will consist of individual sampling tables, each of which includes two or more sampling plans that determine a sample size based on the lot size, inspection severity, inspection severity and acceptable quality level, AQL, or the number of containers in an inspection lot. The quality level and the dynamic modification rule control the inspection severity, which determines the sampling plan in the sampling scheme. The inspection severity is used to adjust the probability of acceptance of an inspection lot, as well as the effort employed to inspect a material. The valuation parameter for which the sampling scheme is created determines the structure of the sampling plan. For instance, the structure of a sampling plan created for an attributive inspection

valuation mode will consist of a sample size, acceptance number c, or the maximum number of nonconforming units in a sample that is accepted and a rejection number d, or the least number of nonconforming units in a sample that is rejected. In turn, a sampling plan for a variable inspection will consist of a sample size and k-factor, or acceptability constant that defines the minimum quality score that leads to the acceptance of a sample following a quality inspection. A sampling plan with no valuation parameters will consist only of a sample size.

Q-148:   A. Inspection lot size and D. AQL

When it's not possible to inspect each item produced by a production process, a sample inspection is used to evaluate the quality of the items in an inspection lot. The sample is picked at random from the lot and, on the basis of the information yielded by the sample, a decision is made regarding the disposition of the lot...namely, the lot is accepted or rejected for its intended use. A sampling procedure can be used to select the entities of the sample, which are subsequently evaluated according to an inspection plan. Instructions for drawing the sample, such as the sample's size and the number of samples to be taken, are documented in a sample drawing procedure that's assigned to the inspection plan. The sampling type, which is defined in the sampling procedure, specifies the method to be used to calculate the sample size. For example, the sampling type may require that a sample size be equal the lot size...namely, 100 percent inspection, a fixed sample size or a size determined by a sampling scheme. If the sampling type requires the use of a sampling scheme that's assigned to the sampling procedure, it will consist of

individual sampling tables, each of which includes two or more sampling plans that determine a sample size based on the lot size, inspection severity, inspection severity and acceptable quality level, AQL, or the number of containers in an inspection lot. The quality level and the dynamic modification rule control the inspection severity, which determines the sampling plan in the sampling scheme. The inspection severity is used to adjust the probability of acceptance of an inspection lot, as well as the effort employed to inspect a material. The valuation parameter for which the sampling scheme is created determines the structure of the sampling plan. For instance, the structure of a sampling plan created for an attributive inspection valuation mode will consist of a sample size, acceptance number c, or the maximum number of nonconforming units in a sample that is accepted and a rejection number d, or the least number of nonconforming units in a sample that is rejected. In turn, a sampling plan for a variable inspection will consist of a sample size and k-factor, or acceptability constant that defines the minimum quality score that leads to the acceptance of a sample following a quality inspection. A sampling plan with no valuation parameters will consist only of a sample size.

Q-149:   D. Sampling procedure

Sampling procedures, sampling schemes and dynamic modification rules are the basic data needed to create the samples used in the inspection process. In particular, a sampling procedure determines how a sample size is calculated, how inspection characteristics are valuated and if a sample size is dynamically modified. The structure of a sampling procedure includes a sampling type, which specifies how a sample size is calculated, and a valuation mode that includes a valuation rule that governs the acceptance or rejection of a characteristic or sample. The structure also includes an inspection points control indicator that determines the number of inspection points that are created for an inspection lot, an inspection point type, as well as a usage control indicator that ensures a particular sampling procedure is not referenced in a task list. The sampling procedure structure also includes a control chart type that governs the characteristics for which a particular control chart can be used, the variables referenced in the chart and the algorithm used to calculate the chart's control limits. Other control indicators in the sampling procedure are the no stage change control indicator that prevents the use of the dynamic modification procedure to determine the inspection scope or sample size and the multiple samples control indicator for independent or dependent multiple samples.

Q-150:   B. Sample size and k-factor

When it's not possible to inspect each item produced by a production process, a sample inspection is used to evaluate the quality of the items in an inspection lot. The sample is picked at random from the lot and, on the basis of the information yielded by the sample, a decision is made regarding the disposition of the lot…namely, the lot is accepted or rejected for its intended use. A sampling procedure can be used to select the entities of the sample, which are subsequently evaluated according to an inspection plan. Instructions for drawing the sample, such as the sample's size and the number of samples to be taken, are documented in a sample drawing procedure that's assigned to the inspection plan. The sampling type, which is defined in the sampling procedure, specifies the method to be used to calculate the sample size. For example, the sampling type may require that a sample size be equal the lot size...namely, 100 percent inspection, a fixed sample size or a size determined by a sampling scheme. If the sampling type requires the use of a sampling scheme that's assigned to the sampling procedure, it will consist of individual sampling tables, each of which includes two or more sampling plans that determine a sample size based on the lot size, inspection severity, inspection severity and acceptable quality level, AQL, or the number of containers in an inspection lot. The quality level and the dynamic modification rule control the inspection severity, which determines the sampling plan in the sampling scheme. The inspection severity is used to adjust the probability of acceptance of an inspection lot, as well as the effort employed to inspect a material. The valuation parameter for which the sampling scheme is created determines the structure of the sampling plan. For instance, the structure of a sampling plan created for an attributive inspection valuation mode will consist of a sample size, acceptance number c, or the maximum number of nonconforming units in a sample that is accepted and a rejection number d, or the least number of nonconforming units in a sample that is rejected. In turn, a sampling plan for a variable inspection will consist of a sample size and k-factor, or acceptability constant that defines the minimum quality score that leads to the acceptance of a sample following a quality inspection. A sampling plan with no valuation parameters will consist only of a sample size.

Q-151:   B. Customizing application

The entities of a sample are selected by means of a sampling procedure. The two key elements of a sampling procedure structure are the sampling type and the valuation mode. The sampling type controls the calculation of the sample size. In turn, the valuation mode defines the rules that govern the acceptance or rejection of a characteristic or sample for its intended use. The valuation mode is defined with the Customizing application.

Q-152:   A. Change in inspection scope and B. Change in probability of acceptance

Sampling procedures, sampling schemes and dynamic modification rules are the basic data needed to create the samples used in the inspection process. In particular, a sampling procedure determines how a sample size is calculated, how inspection characteristics are valuated and if a sample size is dynamically modified. The structure of a sampling procedure includes a sampling type, which specifies how a sample size is calculated, and a valuation mode that includes a valuation rule that governs the acceptance or rejection of a characteristic or sample. The structure also includes an inspection points control indicator that determines the number of inspection points that are created for an inspection lot, an inspection point type, as well as a usage control indicator that ensures a particular sampling procedure is not referenced in a task list. The sampling procedure structure also includes a control chart type that governs the characteristics for which a particular control chart can be used, the variables referenced in the chart and the algorithm used to calculate the chart's control limits. Other control indicators in the

sampling procedure are the no stage change control indicator that prevents the use of the dynamic modification procedure to determine the inspection scope or sample size, which means the sampling procedure determines the inspection severity that controls the sample size. The inspection severity determines if a normal, reduced or tightened inspection is performed, which is a way to adjust the inspection effort to reflect the current quality of the material as reflected in inspection results. The inspection severity is also a way to adjust the probability of acceptance of a material during a quality inspection. The sampling procedure also contains the multiple samples control indicator for independent or dependent multiple samples.

Q-153: B. Define the minimum quality score that leads to an acceptance of the sample for a variable inspection

When it's not possible to inspect each item produced by a production process, a sample inspection is used to evaluate the quality of the items in an inspection lot. The sample is picked at random from the lot and, on the basis of the information yielded by the sample, a decision is made regarding the disposition of the lot…namely, the lot is accepted or rejected for its intended use. A sampling procedure can be used to select the entities of the sample, which are subsequently evaluated according to an inspection plan. Instructions for drawing the sample, such as the sample's size and the number of samples to be taken, are documented in a sample drawing procedure that's assigned to the inspection plan. The sampling type, which is defined in the sampling procedure, specifies the method to be used to calculate the sample size. For example, the sampling type may require that a sample size be equal the lot size…namely, 100 percent inspection, a fixed sample size or a size determined by a sampling scheme. If the sampling type requires the use of a sampling scheme that's assigned to the sampling procedure, it will consist of individual sampling tables, each of which includes two or more sampling plans that determine a sample size based on the lot size, inspection severity, inspection severity and acceptable quality level, AQL, or the number of containers in an inspection lot. The quality level and the dynamic modification rule control the inspection severity, which determines the sampling plan in the sampling scheme. The inspection severity is used to adjust the probability of acceptance of an inspection lot, as well as the effort employed to inspect a material. The valuation parameter for which the sampling scheme is created determines the structure of the sampling plan. For instance, the structure of a sampling plan created for an attributive inspection valuation mode will consist of a sample size, acceptance number c, or the maximum number of nonconforming units in a sample that is accepted and a rejection number d, or the least number of nonconforming units in a sample that is rejected. In turn, a sampling plan for a variable inspection will consist of a sample size and k-factor, or acceptability constant that defines the minimum quality score that leads to the acceptance of a sample following a quality inspection. A sampling plan with no valuation parameters will consist only of a sample size.

Q-154:   A. Prevents the reference of a sampling procedure by a task list

Sampling procedures, sampling schemes and dynamic modification rules are the basic data needed to create the

samples used in the inspection process. In particular, a sampling procedure determines how a sample size is calculated, how inspection characteristics are valuated and if a sample size is dynamically modified. The structure of a sampling procedure includes a sampling type, which specifies how a sample size is calculated, and a valuation mode that includes a valuation rule that governs the acceptance or rejection of a characteristic or sample. The structure also includes an inspection points control indicator that determines the number of inspection points that are created for an inspection lot, an inspection point type, as well as a usage control indicator that ensures a particular sampling procedure is not referenced in a task list. The sampling procedure structure also includes a control chart type that governs the characteristics for which a particular control chart can be used, the variables referenced in the chart and the algorithm used to calculate the chart's control limits. Other control indicators in the sampling procedure are the no stage change control indicator that prevents the use of the dynamic modification procedure to determine the inspection scope or sample size and the multiple samples control indicator for independent or dependent multiple samples.

Q-155:   A. Assign sampling procedure to the inspection characteristic and B. Maintain allowed relationship for sampling procedure and dynamic modification rule

When it's not possible to inspect each item produced by a production process, a sample inspection is used to evaluate the quality of the items in an inspection lot. The sample is picked at random from the lot and, on the basis of the information yielded by the sample, a decision is made regarding the disposition of the lot…namely, the lot is accepted or rejected for its intended use. A sampling procedure can be used to select the entities of the sample, which are subsequently evaluated according to an inspection plan. Instructions for drawing the sample, such as the sample's size and the number of samples to be taken, are documented in a sample drawing procedure that's assigned to the inspection characteristics in the inspection plan. If the dynamic modification of the inspection scope is implemented, an allowed relationship between the sampling procedure and the dynamic modification rule must also be maintained. The sampling type, which is defined in the sampling procedure, specifies the method to be used to calculate the sample size. For example, the sampling type may require that a sample size be equal the lot size…namely, 100 percent inspection, a fixed sample size or a size determined by a sampling scheme. If the sampling type requires the use of a sampling scheme that's assigned to the sampling procedure, it will consist of individual sampling tables, each of which includes two or more sampling plans that determine a sample size based on the lot size, inspection severity, inspection severity and acceptable quality level, AQL, or the number of containers in an inspection lot. The quality level and the dynamic modification rule control the inspection severity, which determines the sampling plan in the sampling scheme. The inspection severity is used to adjust the probability of acceptance of an inspection lot, as well as the effort employed to inspect a material. The valuation parameter for which the sampling scheme is created determines the structure of the sampling plan. For instance, the structure of a sampling plan created for an attributive inspection valuation mode will consist of a sample size, acceptance

301

number c, or the maximum number of nonconforming units in a sample that is accepted and a rejection number d, or the least number of nonconforming units in a sample that is rejected. In turn, a sampling plan for a variable inspection will consist of a sample size and k-factor, or acceptability constant that defines the minimum quality score that leads to the acceptance of a sample following a quality inspection. A sampling plan with no valuation parameters will consist only of a sample size.

Q-156:　　A. Qualitative inspection characteristic and D. Attributive inspection

When it's not possible to inspect each item produced by a production process, a sample inspection is used to evaluate the quality of the items in an inspection lot. The sample is picked at random from the lot and, on the basis of the information yielded by the sample, a decision is made regarding the disposition of the lot…namely, the lot is accepted or rejected for its intended use. A sampling procedure can be used to select the entities of the sample, which are subsequently evaluated according to an inspection plan. Instructions for drawing the sample, such as the sample's size and the number of samples to be taken, are documented in a sample drawing procedure that's assigned to the inspection plan. The sampling type, which is defined in the sampling procedure, specifies the method to be used to calculate the sample size. For example, the sampling type may require that a sample size be equal the lot size…namely, 100 percent inspection, a fixed sample size or a size determined by a sampling scheme. If the sampling type requires the use of a sampling scheme that's assigned to the sampling procedure, it will consist of individual sampling tables, each of which includes two or more sampling plans that determine a sample size based on the lot size, inspection severity, inspection severity and acceptable quality level, AQL, or the number of containers in an inspection lot. The quality level and the dynamic modification rule control the inspection severity, which determines the sampling plan in the sampling scheme. The inspection severity is used to adjust the probability of acceptance of an inspection lot, as well as the effort employed to inspect a material. The valuation parameter for which the sampling scheme is created determines the structure of the sampling plan. For instance, the structure of a sampling plan created for an attributive, or qualitative, inspection valuation mode will consist of a sample size, acceptance number c, or the maximum number of nonconforming units in a sample that is accepted and a rejection number d, or the least number of nonconforming units in a sample that is rejected. In turn, a sampling plan for a variable inspection will consist of a sample size and k-factor, or acceptability constant that defines the minimum quality score that leads to the acceptance of a sample following a quality inspection. A sampling plan with no valuation parameters will consist only of a sample size.

Q-157:   B. Sample size and D. Acceptance number

When it's not possible to inspect each item produced by a production process, a sample inspection is used to evaluate the quality of the items in an inspection lot. The sample is picked at random from the lot and, on the basis of the information yielded by the sample, a decision is made regarding the disposition of the lot…namely, the lot is accepted or rejected for its intended use. A sampling procedure can be used to select the entities of the sample, which are subsequently evaluated according to an inspection plan. Instructions for drawing the sample, such as the sample's size and the number of samples to be taken, are documented in a sample drawing procedure that's assigned to the inspection plan. The sampling type, which is defined in the sampling procedure, specifies the method to be used to calculate the sample size. For example, the sampling type may require that a sample size be equal the lot size...namely, 100 percent inspection, a fixed sample size or a size determined by a sampling scheme. If the sampling type requires the use of a sampling scheme that's assigned to the sampling procedure, it will consist of individual sampling tables, each of which includes two or more sampling plans that determine a sample size based on the lot size, inspection severity, inspection severity and acceptable quality level, AQL, or the number of containers in an inspection lot. The quality level and the dynamic modification rule control the inspection severity, which determines the sampling plan in the sampling scheme. The inspection severity is used to adjust the probability of acceptance of an inspection lot, as well as the effort employed to inspect a material. The valuation parameter for which the sampling scheme is created determines the structure of the sampling plan. For instance, the structure of a sampling plan created for an attributive inspection valuation mode will consist of a sample size, acceptance number c, or the maximum number of nonconforming units in a sample that is accepted and a rejection number d, or the least number of nonconforming units in a sample that is rejected. In turn, a sampling plan for a variable inspection will consist of a sample size and k-factor, or acceptability constant that defines the minimum quality score that leads to the acceptance of a sample following a quality inspection. A sampling plan with no valuation parameters will consist only of a sample size.

Q-158:   B. Inspection points, C. Valuation mode and E. Sampling type

Sampling procedures, sampling schemes and dynamic modification rules are the basic data needed to create the samples used in the inspection process. In particular, a sampling procedure determines how a sample size is calculated, how inspection characteristics are valuated and if a sample size is dynamically modified. The structure of a sampling procedure includes a sampling type, which specifies how a sample size is calculated, and a valuation mode that includes a valuation rule that governs the acceptance or rejection of a characteristic or sample. The structure also includes an inspection points control indicator that determines the number of inspection points that are created for an inspection lot, an inspection point type, as well as a usage control indicator that ensures a particular sampling procedure is not referenced in a task list. The sampling procedure structure also includes a control chart type that governs the characteristics for which a particular control chart can be used, the variables referenced in the chart and the algorithm used to calculate the chart's control limits. Other control indicators in the sampling procedure are the no stage change control indicator that prevents the use of the dynamic modification procedure to determine the inspection scope or sample size and the multiple samples control indicator for independent or dependent multiple samples.

Q-159:   C. Maintain the inspection type in the material
master record inspection setup

Sampling procedures, sampling schemes and dynamic
modification rules are the basic data needed to create the
samples used in the inspection process. In particular, a
sampling procedure determines how a sample size is
calculated, how inspection characteristics are valuated and if
a sample size is dynamically modified. The structure of a
sampling procedure includes a sampling type, which
specifies how a sample size is calculated, and a valuation
mode that includes a valuation rule that governs the
acceptance or rejection of a characteristic or sample. The
structure also includes an inspection points control
indicator that determines the number of inspection points
that are created for an inspection lot, an inspection point
type, as well as a usage control indicator that ensures a
particular sampling procedure is not referenced in a task
list. The sampling procedure structure also includes a
control chart type that governs the characteristics for which
a particular control chart can be used, the variables
referenced in the chart and the algorithm used to calculate
the chart's control limits. Other control indicators in the
sampling procedure are the no stage change control
indicator that prevents the use of the dynamic modification
procedure to determine the inspection scope or sample size
and the multiple samples control indicator for independent
or dependent multiple samples. The sampling procedure
can be assigned to a task list characteristic if an inspection
plan is used for the inspection or the inspection setup for a
material master record inspection type if an inspection plan
is not used for the inspection.

Q-160:   C. Maintain the 100 percent inspection type in the material master record inspection setup

Sampling procedures, sampling schemes and dynamic modification rules are the basic data needed to create the samples used in the inspection process. In particular, a sampling procedure determines how a sample size is calculated, how inspection characteristics are valuated and if a sample size is dynamically modified. The structure of a sampling procedure includes a sampling type, which specifies how a sample size is calculated, and a valuation mode that includes a valuation rule that governs the acceptance or rejection of a characteristic or sample. The structure also includes an inspection points control indicator that determines the number of inspection points that are created for an inspection lot, an inspection point type, as well as a usage control indicator that ensures a particular sampling procedure is not referenced in a task list. The sampling procedure structure also includes a control chart type that governs the characteristics for which a particular control chart can be used, the variables referenced in the chart and the algorithm used to calculate the chart's control limits. Other control indicators in the sampling procedure are the no stage change control indicator that prevents the use of the dynamic modification procedure to determine the inspection scope or sample size and the multiple samples control indicator for independent or dependent multiple samples. The sampling procedure can be assigned to a task list characteristic if an inspection plan is used for the inspection or the inspection setup for a material master record inspection type if an inspection plan is not used for the inspection.

Q-161:   B. Attributive inspection on the basis of nonconforming units

When it's not possible to inspect each item produced by a production process, a sample inspection is used to evaluate the quality of the items in an inspection lot. The sample is picked at random from the lot and, on the basis of the information yielded by the sample, a decision is made regarding the disposition of the lot...namely, the lot is accepted or rejected for its intended use. A sampling procedure can be used to select the entities of the sample, which are subsequently evaluated according to an inspection plan. Instructions for drawing the sample, such as the sample's size and the number of samples to be taken, are documented in a sample drawing procedure that's assigned to the inspection plan. The sampling type, which is defined in the sampling procedure, specifies the method to be used to calculate the sample size. For example, the sampling type may require that a sample size be equal the lot size...namely, 100 percent inspection, a fixed sample size or a size determined by a sampling scheme. If the sampling type requires the use of a sampling scheme that's assigned to the sampling procedure, it will consist of individual sampling tables, each of which includes two or more sampling plans that determine a sample size based on the lot size, inspection severity, inspection severity and acceptable quality level, AQL, or the number of containers in an inspection lot. The quality level and the dynamic modification rule control the inspection severity, which determines the sampling plan in the sampling scheme. The inspection severity is used to adjust the probability of acceptance of an inspection lot, as well as the effort employed to inspect a material. The valuation parameter for which the sampling scheme is created determines the structure of the sampling plan. For instance, the structure of a sampling plan created for an attributive inspection valuation mode will consist of a sample size, acceptance number c, or the maximum number of nonconforming units in a sample that is accepted and a rejection number d, or the least number of nonconforming units in a sample that is rejected. In turn, a sampling plan for a variable inspection will consist of a sample size and k-factor, or acceptability constant that defines the minimum quality score that leads to the acceptance of a sample following a quality inspection. A sampling plan with no valuation parameters will consist only of a sample size.

Q-162:   B. Prevent reference of sampling procedure in task list

Sampling procedures, sampling schemes and dynamic modification rules are the basic data needed to create the samples used in the inspection process. In particular, a sampling procedure determines how a sample size is calculated, how inspection characteristics are valuated and if a sample size is dynamically modified. The structure of a sampling procedure includes a sampling type, which specifies how a sample size is calculated, and a valuation mode that includes a valuation rule that governs the acceptance or rejection of a characteristic or sample. The structure also includes an inspection points control indicator that determines the number of inspection points that are created for an inspection lot, an inspection point type, as well as a usage control indicator that ensures a particular sampling procedure is not referenced in a task list. The sampling procedure structure also includes a

control chart type that governs the characteristics for which a particular control chart can be used, the variables referenced in the chart and the algorithm used to calculate the chart's control limits. Other control indicators in the sampling procedure are the no stage change control indicator that prevents the use of the dynamic modification procedure to determine the inspection scope or sample size and the multiple samples control indicator for independent or dependent multiple samples.

Q-163:   B. Sampling type in the material master record

Sampling procedures, sampling schemes and dynamic modification rules are the basic data needed to create the samples used in the inspection process. In particular, a sampling procedure determines how a sample size is calculated, how inspection characteristics are valuated and if a sample size is dynamically modified. The structure of a sampling procedure includes a sampling type, which specifies how a sample size is calculated, and a valuation mode that includes a valuation rule that governs the acceptance or rejection of a characteristic or sample. The structure also includes an inspection points control indicator that determines the number of inspection points that are created for an inspection lot, an inspection point type, as well as a usage control indicator that ensures a particular sampling procedure is not referenced in a task list. The sampling procedure structure also includes a control chart type that governs the characteristics for which a particular control chart can be used, the variables referenced in the chart and the algorithm used to calculate the chart's control limits. Other control indicators in the sampling procedure are the no stage change control

indicator that prevents the use of the dynamic modification procedure to determine the inspection scope or sample size and the multiple samples control indicator for independent or dependent multiple samples. The sampling procedure can be assigned to a task list characteristic if an inspection plan is used for the inspection or the inspection setup for a material master record inspection type if an inspection plan is not used for the inspection.

Q-164:   A. Define sampling type that controls the calculation of a sample size and B. Define a valuation mode that governs the acceptance or rejection of a characteristic

Sampling procedures, sampling schemes and dynamic modification rules are the basic data needed to create the samples used in the inspection process. In particular, a sampling procedure determines how a sample size is calculated, how inspection characteristics are valuated and if a sample size is dynamically modified. The structure of a sampling procedure includes a sampling type, which specifies how a sample size is calculated, and a valuation mode that includes a valuation rule that governs the acceptance or rejection of a characteristic or sample. The structure also includes an inspection points control indicator that determines the number of inspection points that are created for an inspection lot, an inspection point type, as well as a usage control indicator that ensures a particular sampling procedure is not referenced in a task list. The sampling procedure structure also includes a control chart type that governs the characteristics for which a particular control chart can be used, the variables referenced in the chart and the algorithm used to calculate the chart's control limits. Other control indicators in the

sampling procedure are the no stage change control indicator that prevents the use of the dynamic modification procedure to determine the inspection scope or sample size and the multiple samples control indicator for independent or dependent multiple samples.

Q-165:   A. Control chart type in a sampling procedure

Sampling procedures, sampling schemes and dynamic modification rules are the basic data needed to create the samples used in the inspection process. In particular, a sampling procedure determines how a sample size is calculated, how inspection characteristics are valuated and if a sample size is dynamically modified. The structure of a sampling procedure includes a sampling type, which specifies how a sample size is calculated, and a valuation mode that includes a valuation rule that governs the acceptance or rejection of a characteristic or sample. The structure also includes an inspection points control indicator that determines the number of inspection points that are created for an inspection lot, an inspection point type, as well as a usage control indicator that ensures a particular sampling procedure is not referenced in a task list. The sampling procedure structure also includes a control chart type that governs the characteristics for which a particular control chart can be used, the variables referenced in the chart and the algorithm used to calculate the chart's control limits. Other control indicators in the sampling procedure are the no stage change control indicator that prevents the use of the dynamic modification procedure to determine the inspection scope or sample size and the multiple samples control indicator for independent or dependent multiple samples.

Q-166:   A. Determine the number of defects or nonconforming units in a sample and B. Accept characteristic if the number of defects is less than a predefined number of defects

When it's not possible to inspect each item produced by a production process, a sample inspection is used to evaluate the quality of the items in an inspection lot. The sample is picked at random from the lot and, on the basis of the information yielded by the sample, a decision is made regarding the disposition of the lot...namely, the lot is accepted or rejected for its intended use. A sampling procedure can be used to select the entities of the sample, which are subsequently evaluated according to an inspection plan. Instructions for drawing the sample, such as the sample's size and the number of samples to be taken, are documented in a sample drawing procedure that's assigned to the inspection plan. The sampling type, which is defined in the sampling procedure, specifies the method to be used to calculate the sample size. For example, the sampling type may require that a sample size be equal the lot size...namely, 100 percent inspection, a fixed sample size or a size determined by a sampling scheme. If the sampling type requires the use of a sampling scheme that's assigned to the sampling procedure, it will consist of individual sampling tables, each of which includes two or more sampling plans that determine a sample size based on the lot size, inspection severity, inspection severity and acceptable quality level, AQL, or the number of containers in an inspection lot. The quality level and the dynamic modification rule control the inspection severity, which determines the sampling plan in the sampling scheme. The inspection severity is used to adjust the probability of

acceptance of an inspection lot, as well as the effort employed to inspect a material. The valuation parameter for which the sampling scheme is created determines the structure of the sampling plan. For instance, the structure of a sampling plan created for an attributive inspection valuation mode will consist of a sample size, acceptance number c, or the maximum number of nonconforming units in a sample that is accepted and a rejection number d, or the least number of nonconforming units in a sample that is rejected. In turn, a sampling plan for a variable inspection will consist of a sample size and k-factor, or acceptability constant that defines the minimum quality score that leads to the acceptance of a sample following a quality inspection. A sampling plan with no valuation parameters will consist only of a sample size.

Q-167:   B. The maximum number of permitted defects per 100 units that allows an acceptance valuation of an inspection lot

When it's not possible to inspect each item produced by a production process, a sample inspection is used to evaluate the quality of the items in an inspection lot. The sample is picked at random from the lot and, on the basis of the information yielded by the sample, a decision is made regarding the disposition of the lot…namely, the lot is accepted or rejected for its intended use. A sampling procedure can be used to select the entities of the sample, which are subsequently evaluated according to an inspection plan. Instructions for drawing the sample, such as the sample's size and the number of samples to be taken, are documented in a sample drawing procedure that's assigned to the inspection plan. The sampling type, which is defined in the sampling procedure, specifies the method to be used to calculate the sample size. For example, the sampling type may require that a sample size be equal the lot size...namely, 100 percent inspection, a fixed sample size or a size determined by a sampling scheme. If the sampling type requires the use of a sampling scheme that's assigned to the sampling procedure, it will consist of individual sampling tables, each of which includes two or more sampling plans that determine a sample size based on the lot size, inspection severity, inspection severity and acceptable quality level, AQL, or the number of containers in an inspection lot. The quality level and the dynamic modification rule control the inspection severity, which determines the sampling plan in the sampling scheme. The inspection severity is used to adjust the probability of acceptance of an inspection lot, as well as the effort employed to inspect a material. The valuation parameter for which the sampling scheme is created determines the structure of the sampling plan. For instance, the structure of a sampling plan created for an attributive inspection valuation mode will consist of a sample size, acceptance number c, or the maximum number of nonconforming units in a sample that is accepted and a rejection number d, or the least number of nonconforming units in a sample that is rejected. In turn, a sampling plan for a variable inspection will consist of a sample size and k-factor, or acceptability constant that defines the minimum quality score that leads to the acceptance of a sample following a quality inspection. A sampling plan with no valuation parameters will consist only of a sample size.

Q-168: A. The minimum quality score that results in the acceptance of the sample for a variable inspection

When it's not possible to inspect each item produced by a production process, a sample inspection is used to evaluate the quality of the items in an inspection lot. The sample is picked at random from the lot and, on the basis of the information yielded by the sample, a decision is made regarding the disposition of the lot…namely, the lot is accepted or rejected for its intended use. A sampling procedure can be used to select the entities of the sample, which are subsequently evaluated according to an inspection plan. Instructions for drawing the sample, such as the sample's size and the number of samples to be taken, are documented in a sample drawing procedure that's assigned to the inspection plan. The sampling type, which is defined in the sampling procedure, specifies the method to be used to calculate the sample size. For example, the sampling type may require that a sample size be equal the lot size…namely, 100 percent inspection, a fixed sample size or a size determined by a sampling scheme. If the sampling type requires the use of a sampling scheme that's assigned to the sampling procedure, it will consist of individual sampling tables, each of which includes two or more sampling plans that determine a sample size based on the lot size, inspection severity, inspection severity and acceptable quality level, AQL, or the number of containers in an inspection lot. The quality level and the dynamic modification rule control the inspection severity, which determines the sampling plan in the sampling scheme. The inspection severity is used to adjust the probability of acceptance of an inspection lot, as well as the effort employed to inspect a material. The valuation parameter for which the sampling scheme is created determines the structure of the sampling plan. For instance, the structure of a sampling plan created for an attributive inspection

valuation mode will consist of a sample size, acceptance number c, or the maximum number of nonconforming units in a sample that is accepted and a rejection number d, or the least number of nonconforming units in a sample that is rejected. In turn, a sampling plan for a variable inspection will consist of a sample size and k-factor, or acceptability constant that defines the minimum quality score that leads to the acceptance of a sample following a quality inspection. A sampling plan with no valuation parameters will consist only of a sample size.

Q-169:   C. Inspection characteristic

Sampling procedures, sampling schemes and dynamic modification rules are the basic data needed to create the samples used in the inspection process. The manner in which a sampling procedure is selected for use in a quality inspection is dependent on whether a task list or material specification is used to conduct the inspection. If an inspection plan is used, the sampling procedure can be directly assigned to an inspection characteristic in the plan using the inspection planning functions or the Customizing application. If an inspection plan is not used to conduct the inspection, the sampling procedure can be specified in the inspection setup for a material master record inspection type.

Q-170:   C. Select the "Inspection points for sample management" control indicator in the sampling procedure

Sampling procedures, sampling schemes and dynamic modification rules are the basic data needed to create the samples used in the inspection process. In particular, a

sampling procedure determines how a sample size is calculated, how inspection characteristics are valuated and if a sample size is dynamically modified. The structure of a sampling procedure includes a sampling type, which specifies how a sample size is calculated, and a valuation mode that includes a valuation rule that governs the acceptance or rejection of a characteristic or sample. The structure also includes an inspection points control indicator that determines the number of inspection points that are created for an inspection lot, an inspection point type, as well as a usage control indicator that ensures a particular sampling procedure is not referenced in a task list. The sampling procedure structure also includes a control chart type that governs the characteristics for which a particular control chart can be used, the variables referenced in the chart and the algorithm used to calculate the chart's control limits. Other control indicators in the sampling procedure are the no stage change control indicator that prevents the use of the dynamic modification procedure to determine the inspection scope or sample size and the multiple samples control indicator for independent or dependent multiple samples.

Q-171:   B. Control chart type

Sampling procedures, sampling schemes and dynamic modification rules are the basic data needed to create the samples used in the inspection process. In particular, a sampling procedure determines how a sample size is calculated, how inspection characteristics are valuated and if a sample size is dynamically modified. The structure of a sampling procedure includes a sampling type, which specifies how a sample size is calculated, and a valuation mode that includes a valuation rule that governs the acceptance or rejection of a characteristic or sample. The structure also includes an inspection points control indicator that determines the number of inspection points that are created for an inspection lot, an inspection point type, as well as a usage control indicator that ensures a particular sampling procedure is not referenced in a task list. The sampling procedure structure also includes a control chart type that governs the characteristics for which a particular control chart can be used, the variables referenced in the chart and the algorithm used to calculate the chart's control limits. Other control indicators in the sampling procedure are the no stage change control indicator that prevents the use of the dynamic modification procedure to determine the inspection scope or sample size and the multiple samples control indicator for independent or dependent multiple samples.

Q-172:   B. Free inspection points and C. Inspection points for sample management

Sampling procedures, sampling schemes and dynamic modification rules are the basic data needed to create the samples used in the inspection process. In particular, a sampling procedure determines how a sample size is calculated, how inspection characteristics are valuated and if a sample size is dynamically modified. The structure of a sampling procedure includes a sampling type, which specifies how a sample size is calculated, and a valuation mode that includes a valuation rule that governs the acceptance or rejection of a characteristic or sample. The structure also includes an inspection points control indicator that determines the number of inspection points

that are created for an inspection lot, an inspection point type, as well as a usage control indicator that ensures a particular sampling procedure is not referenced in a task list. Inspection point types include without inspection points, free inspection points, plant maintenance and sample management. The sampling procedure structure also includes a control chart type that governs the characteristics for which a particular control chart can be used, the variables referenced in the chart and the algorithm used to calculate the chart's control limits. Other control indicators in the sampling procedure are the no stage change control indicator that prevents the use of the dynamic modification procedure to determine the inspection scope or sample size and the multiple samples control indicator for independent or dependent multiple samples.

Q-173: B. Sampling plan table

When it's not possible to inspect each item produced by a production process, a sample inspection is used to evaluate the quality of the items in an inspection lot. The sample is picked at random from the lot and, on the basis of the information yielded by the sample, a decision is made regarding the disposition of the lot...namely, the lot is accepted or rejected for its intended use. A sampling procedure can be used to select the entities of the sample, which are subsequently evaluated according to an inspection plan. Instructions for drawing the sample, such as the sample's size and the number of samples to be taken, are documented in a sample drawing procedure that's assigned to the inspection plan. The sampling type, which is defined in the sampling procedure, specifies the method to be used to calculate the sample size. For example, the sampling type may require that a sample size be equal the lot size...namely, 100 percent inspection, a fixed sample size or a size determined by a sampling scheme. If the sampling type requires the use of a sampling scheme that's assigned to the sampling procedure, it will consist of individual sampling tables, each of which includes two or more sampling plans that determine a sample size based on the lot size, inspection severity, inspection severity and acceptable quality level, AQL, or the number of containers in an inspection lot. The quality level and the dynamic modification rule control the inspection severity, which determines the sampling plan in the sampling scheme. The inspection severity is used to adjust the probability of acceptance of an inspection lot, as well as the effort employed to inspect a material. The valuation parameter for which the sampling scheme is created determines the structure of the sampling plan. For instance, the structure of a sampling plan created for an attributive inspection valuation mode will consist of a sample size, acceptance number c, or the maximum number of nonconforming units in a sample that is accepted and a rejection number d, or the least number of nonconforming units in a sample that is rejected. In turn, a sampling plan for a variable inspection will consist of a sample size and k-factor, or acceptability constant that defines the minimum quality score that leads to the acceptance of a sample following a quality inspection. A sampling plan with no valuation parameters will consist only of a sample size.

Q-174:   B. Acceptance number c and C. Rejection number d

When it's not possible to inspect each item produced by a production process, a sample inspection is used to evaluate the quality of the items in an inspection lot. The sample is picked at random from the lot and, on the basis of the information yielded by the sample, a decision is made regarding the disposition of the lot...namely, the lot is accepted or rejected for its intended use. A sampling procedure can be used to select the entities of the sample, which are subsequently evaluated according to an inspection plan. Instructions for drawing the sample, such as the sample's size and the number of samples to be taken, are documented in a sample drawing procedure that's assigned to the inspection plan. The sampling type, which is defined in the sampling procedure, specifies the method to be used to calculate the sample size. For example, the sampling type may require that a sample size be equal the lot size...namely, 100 percent inspection, a fixed sample size or a size determined by a sampling scheme. If the sampling type requires the use of a sampling scheme that's assigned to the sampling procedure, it will consist of individual sampling tables, each of which includes two or more sampling plans that determine a sample size based on the lot size, inspection severity, inspection severity and acceptable quality level, AQL, or the number of containers in an inspection lot. The quality level and the dynamic modification rule control the inspection severity, which determines the sampling plan in the sampling scheme. The inspection severity is used to adjust the probability of acceptance of an inspection lot, as well as the effort employed to inspect a material. The valuation parameter for which the sampling scheme is created determines the structure of the sampling plan. For instance, the structure of a sampling plan created for an attributive inspection

valuation mode will consist of a sample size, acceptance number c, or the maximum number of nonconforming units in a sample that is accepted and a rejection number d, or the least number of nonconforming units in a sample that is rejected. In turn, a sampling plan for a variable inspection will consist of a sample size and k-factor, or acceptability constant that defines the minimum quality score that leads to the acceptance of a sample following a quality inspection. A sampling plan with no valuation parameters will consist only of a sample size.

Q-175: A. Define sampling procedure at characteristic level of task list

Sampling procedures, sampling schemes and dynamic modification rules are the basic data needed to create the samples used in the inspection process. In particular, a sampling procedure determines how a sample size is calculated, how inspection characteristics are valuated and if a sample size is dynamically modified. The structure of a sampling procedure includes a sampling type, which specifies how a sample size is calculated, and a valuation mode that includes a valuation rule that governs the acceptance or rejection of a characteristic or sample. The structure also includes an inspection points control indicator that determines the number of inspection points that are created for an inspection lot, an inspection point type, as well as a usage control indicator that ensures a particular sampling procedure is not referenced in a task list. The sampling procedure structure also includes a control chart type that governs the characteristics for which a particular control chart can be used, the variables referenced in the chart and the algorithm used to calculate

323

the chart's control limits. Other control indicators in the sampling procedure are the no stage change control indicator that prevents the use of the dynamic modification procedure to determine the inspection scope or sample size and the multiple samples control indicator for independent or dependent multiple samples.

Q-176:   A. Allowed relationship between a sampling procedure and the dynamic modification rule

Sampling procedures, sampling schemes and dynamic modification rules are the basic data needed to create the samples used in the inspection process. In particular, a sampling procedure determines how a sample size is calculated, how inspection characteristics are valuated and if a sample size is dynamically modified. The structure of a sampling procedure includes a sampling type, which specifies how a sample size is calculated, and a valuation mode that includes a valuation rule that governs the acceptance or rejection of a characteristic or sample. The structure also includes an inspection points control indicator that determines the number of inspection points that are created for an inspection lot, an inspection point type, as well as a usage control indicator that ensures a particular sampling procedure is not referenced in a task list. The sampling procedure structure also includes a control chart type that governs the characteristics for which a particular control chart can be used, the variables referenced in the chart and the algorithm used to calculate the chart's control limits. Other control indicators in the sampling procedure are the no stage change control indicator that prevents the use of the dynamic modification procedure to determine the inspection scope or sample size

and the multiple samples control indicator for independent or dependent multiple samples. The dynamic modification of an inspection scope requires an allowed relationship between a sampling procedure and the dynamic modification rules.

Q-177:   B. "Free inspection points" control indicator in the sampling procedure and C. "Inspection points for sample management" control indicator in sampling procedure

Sampling procedures, sampling schemes and dynamic modification rules are the basic data needed to create the samples used in the inspection process. In particular, a sampling procedure determines how a sample size is calculated, how inspection characteristics are valuated and if a sample size is dynamically modified. The structure of a sampling procedure includes a sampling type, which specifies how a sample size is calculated, and a valuation mode that includes a valuation rule that governs the acceptance or rejection of a characteristic or sample. The sampling procedure structure also includes a control chart type that governs the characteristics for which a particular control chart can be used, the variables referenced in the chart and the algorithm used to calculate the chart's control limits. Other control indicators in the sampling procedure are the no stage change control indicator that prevents the use of the dynamic modification procedure to determine the inspection scope or sample size and the multiple samples control indicator for independent or dependent multiple samples. The structure also includes an inspection points control indicator that determines the number of inspection points that are created for an inspection lot, an inspection point type, as well as a usage control indicator that ensures a particular sampling procedure is not referenced in a task list. Inspection point types include without inspection points, free inspection points, plant maintenance and sample management. The inspection point types "without inspection points", "free inspection points" and "inspection points for sample management" are used with an inspection plan. In turn, "free inspection points" and "inspection points for sample management" are used with a routing. For a master recipe, the "free inspection points" and "inspection points for sample management" inspection point types are used. In addition, for a maintenance task list, the "inspection points for plant maintenance" inspection point type is used.

Q-178:   A. Sample size

When it's not possible to inspect each item produced by a production process, a sample inspection is used to evaluate the quality of the items in an inspection lot. The sample is picked at random from the lot and, on the basis of the information yielded by the sample, a decision is made regarding the disposition of the lot…namely, the lot is accepted or rejected for its intended use. A sampling procedure can be used to select the entities of the sample, which are subsequently evaluated according to an inspection plan. Instructions for drawing the sample, such as the sample's size and the number of samples to be taken, are documented in a sample drawing procedure that's assigned to the inspection plan. The sampling type, which is defined in the sampling procedure, specifies the method to be used to calculate the sample size. For example, the sampling type may require that a sample size be equal the lot size…namely, 100 percent inspection, a fixed sample size or a size determined by a sampling scheme. If the sampling type requires the use of a sampling scheme that's assigned to the sampling procedure, it will consist of individual sampling tables, each of which includes two or more sampling plans that determine a sample size based on the lot size, inspection severity, inspection severity and acceptable quality level, AQL, or the number of containers in an inspection lot. The quality level and the dynamic modification rule control the inspection severity, which determines the sampling plan in the sampling scheme. The inspection severity is used to adjust the probability of acceptance of an inspection lot, as well as the effort employed to inspect a material. The valuation parameter for which the sampling scheme is created determines the structure of the sampling plan. For instance, the structure of a sampling plan created for an attributive inspection valuation mode will consist of a sample size, acceptance number c, or the maximum number of nonconforming units in a sample that is accepted and a rejection number d, or the least number of nonconforming units in a sample that is rejected. In turn, a sampling plan for a variable inspection will consist of a sample size and k-factor, or acceptability constant that defines the minimum quality score that leads to the acceptance of a sample following a quality inspection. A sampling plan with no valuation parameters will consist only of a sample size.

Q-179:   B. Prevents the reference of the sampling procedure in a task list

Sampling procedures, sampling schemes and dynamic modification rules are the basic data needed to create the

samples used in the inspection process. In particular, a sampling procedure determines how a sample size is calculated, how inspection characteristics are valuated and if a sample size is dynamically modified. The structure of a sampling procedure includes a sampling type, which specifies how a sample size is calculated, and a valuation mode that includes a valuation rule that governs the acceptance or rejection of a characteristic or sample. The structure also includes an inspection points control indicator that determines the number of inspection points that are created for an inspection lot, an inspection point type, as well as a usage control indicator that ensures a particular sampling procedure is not referenced in a task list. The sampling procedure structure also includes a control chart type that governs the characteristics for which a particular control chart can be used, the variables referenced in the chart and the algorithm used to calculate the chart's control limits. Other control indicators in the sampling procedure are the no stage change control indicator that prevents the use of the dynamic modification procedure to determine the inspection scope or sample size and the multiple samples control indicator for independent or dependent multiple samples.

Q-180:   A. Define sampling procedure in Customizing and C. Assign sampling procedure to inspection characteristic

Sampling procedures, sampling schemes and dynamic modification rules are the basic data needed to create the samples used in the inspection process. In particular, a sampling procedure determines how a sample size is calculated, how inspection characteristics are valuated and if a sample size is dynamically modified. The structure of a sampling procedure includes a sampling type, which specifies how a sample size is calculated, and a valuation mode that includes a valuation rule that governs the acceptance or rejection of a characteristic or sample. The structure also includes an inspection points control indicator that determines the number of inspection points that are created for an inspection lot, an inspection point type, as well as a usage control indicator that ensures a particular sampling procedure is not referenced in a task list. The sampling procedure structure also includes a control chart type that governs the characteristics for which a particular control chart can be used, the variables referenced in the chart and the algorithm used to calculate the chart's control limits. Other control indicators in the sampling procedure are the no stage change control indicator that prevents the use of the dynamic modification procedure to determine the inspection scope or sample size and the multiple samples control indicator for independent or dependent multiple samples. The sampling procedure can be assigned to a task list characteristic if an inspection plan is used for the inspection or the inspection setup for a material master record inspection type if an inspection plan is not used for the inspection.

Q-181: B. Sampling procedure is assigned to inspection characteristic and C. Sampling procedure is defined using the Customizing application

Sampling procedures, sampling schemes and dynamic modification rules are the basic data needed to create the samples used in the inspection process. The manner in which a sampling procedure is selected for use in a quality inspection is dependent on whether a task list or material specification is used to conduct the inspection. If an inspection plan is used, the sampling procedure can be directly assigned to an inspection characteristic in the plan using the inspection planning functions or the Customizing application. If an inspection plan is not used to conduct the inspection, the sampling procedure can be specified in the inspection setup for a material master record inspection type.

Q-182:   A. "Plant maintenance" inspection point type

Sampling procedures, sampling schemes and dynamic modification rules are the basic data needed to create the samples used in the inspection process. In particular, a sampling procedure determines how a sample size is calculated, how inspection characteristics are valuated and if a sample size is dynamically modified. The structure of a sampling procedure includes a sampling type, which specifies how a sample size is calculated, and a valuation mode that includes a valuation rule that governs the acceptance or rejection of a characteristic or sample. The sampling procedure structure also includes a control chart type that governs the characteristics for which a particular control chart can be used, the variables referenced in the chart and the algorithm used to calculate the chart's control limits. Other control indicators in the sampling procedure are the no stage change control indicator that prevents the use of the dynamic modification procedure to determine the inspection scope or sample size and the multiple samples control indicator for independent or dependent multiple samples. The structure also includes an inspection points control indicator that determines the number of inspection points that are created for an inspection lot, an inspection point type, as well as a usage control indicator that ensures a particular sampling procedure is not referenced in a task list. Inspection point types include without inspection points, free inspection points, plant maintenance and sample management. The inspection point types "without inspection points", "free inspection points" and "inspection points for sample management" are used with an inspection plan. In turn, "free inspection points" and "inspection points for sample management" are used with a routing. For a master recipe, the "free inspection points" and "inspection points for sample management" inspection point types are used. In addition, for a maintenance task list, the "inspection points for plant maintenance" inspection point type is used.

Q-183:   A. Dependent multiple samples, B. Independent multiple samples and C. Single samples

Sampling procedures, sampling schemes and dynamic modification rules are the basic data needed to create the samples used in the inspection process. In particular, a sampling procedure determines how a sample size is calculated, how inspection characteristics are valuated and if a sample size is dynamically modified. The structure of a sampling procedure includes a sampling type, such as single samples or dependent or independent multiple samples, which specifies how a sample size is calculated, and a valuation mode that includes a valuation rule that governs the acceptance or rejection of a characteristic or sample. The structure also includes an inspection points control indicator that determines the number of inspection points that are created for an inspection lot, an inspection point type, as well as a usage control indicator that ensures a particular sampling procedure is not referenced in a task list. The sampling procedure structure also includes a control chart type that governs the characteristics for which a particular control chart can be used, the variables referenced in the chart and the algorithm used to calculate the chart's control limits. Other control indicators in the sampling procedure are the no stage change control indicator that prevents the use of the dynamic modification procedure to determine the inspection scope or sample size and the multiple samples control indicator for independent or dependent multiple samples if single samples are not used.

Q-184:   C. Sample management inspection points control indicator

Sampling procedures, sampling schemes and dynamic modification rules are the basic data needed to create the samples used in the inspection process. In particular, a sampling procedure determines how a sample size is calculated, how inspection characteristics are valuated and if a sample size is dynamically modified. The structure of a sampling procedure includes a sampling type, which specifies how a sample size is calculated, and a valuation mode that includes a valuation rule that governs the acceptance or rejection of a characteristic or sample. The structure also includes an inspection points control indicator that determines the number of inspection points that are created for an inspection lot, an inspection point type, as well as a usage control indicator that ensures a particular sampling procedure is not referenced in a task list. The sampling procedure structure also includes a control chart type that governs the characteristics for which

a particular control chart can be used, the variables referenced in the chart and the algorithm used to calculate the chart's control limits. Other control indicators in the sampling procedure are the no stage change control indicator that prevents the use of the dynamic modification procedure to determine the inspection scope or sample size and the multiple samples control indicator for independent or dependent multiple samples if single samples are not used.

Q-185:   B. Independent multiple samples control indicator in the sampling procedure

Sampling procedures, sampling schemes and dynamic modification rules are the basic data needed to create the samples used in the inspection process. In particular, a sampling procedure determines how a sample size is calculated, how inspection characteristics are valuated and if a sample size is dynamically modified. The structure of a sampling procedure includes a sampling type, which specifies how a sample size is calculated, and a valuation mode that includes a valuation rule that governs the acceptance or rejection of a characteristic or sample. The structure also includes an inspection points control indicator that determines the number of inspection points that are created for an inspection lot, an inspection point type, as well as a usage control indicator that ensures a particular sampling procedure is not referenced in a task list. The sampling procedure structure also includes a control chart type that governs the characteristics for which a particular control chart can be used, the variables referenced in the chart and the algorithm used to calculate the chart's control limits. Other control indicators in the

sampling procedure are the no stage change control indicator that prevents the use of the dynamic modification procedure to determine the inspection scope or sample size and the multiple samples control indicator for independent or dependent multiple samples if single samples are not used.

Q-186:   C. Free inspection points inspection point type

Sampling procedures, sampling schemes and dynamic modification rules are the basic data needed to create the samples used in the inspection process. In particular, a sampling procedure determines how a sample size is calculated, how inspection characteristics are valuated and if a sample size is dynamically modified. The structure of a sampling procedure includes a sampling type, which specifies how a sample size is calculated, and a valuation mode that includes a valuation rule that governs the acceptance or rejection of a characteristic or sample. . The sampling procedure structure also includes a control chart type that governs the characteristics for which a particular control chart can be used, the variables referenced in the chart and the algorithm used to calculate the chart's control limits. Other control indicators in the sampling procedure are the no stage change control indicator that prevents the use of the dynamic modification procedure to determine the inspection scope or sample size and the multiple samples control indicator for independent or dependent multiple samples. The structure also includes a usage control indicator that ensures a particular sampling procedure is not referenced in a task list and an inspection points control indicator that determines the number of inspection points that are created for an inspection lot and

334

an inspection point type. Valid inspection point types include without inspection points, free inspection points, plant maintenance and sample management. The inspection point types "without inspection points", "free inspection points" and "inspection points for sample management" are used with an inspection plan. In turn, "free inspection points" and "inspection points for sample management" are used with a routing and the "free inspection points" and "inspection points for sample management" inspection point types are used for a master recipe. In turn, for a maintenance task list, the "inspection points for plant maintenance" inspection point type is used.

Q-187:   A. "No stage change" control indicator in the sampling procedure

Sampling procedures, sampling schemes and dynamic modification rules are the basic data needed to create the samples used in the inspection process. In particular, a sampling procedure determines how a sample size is calculated, how inspection characteristics are valuated and if a sample size is dynamically modified. The structure of a sampling procedure includes a sampling type, which specifies how a sample size is calculated, and a valuation mode that includes a valuation rule that governs the acceptance or rejection of a characteristic or sample. The structure also includes an inspection points control indicator that determines the number of inspection points that are created for an inspection lot, an inspection point type, as well as a usage control indicator that ensures a particular sampling procedure is not referenced in a task list. The sampling procedure structure also includes a control chart type that governs the characteristics for which

a particular control chart can be used, the variables referenced in the chart and the algorithm used to calculate the chart's control limits. Other control indicators in the sampling procedure are the no stage change control indicator that prevents the use of the dynamic modification procedure to determine the inspection scope or sample size and the multiple samples control indicator for independent or dependent multiple samples.

Q-188: C. "Plant maintenance inspection points" inspection point type

Sampling procedures, sampling schemes and dynamic modification rules are the basic data needed to create the samples used in the inspection process. In particular, a sampling procedure determines how a sample size is calculated, how inspection characteristics are valuated and if a sample size is dynamically modified. The structure of a sampling procedure includes a sampling type, which specifies how a sample size is calculated, and a valuation mode that includes a valuation rule that governs the acceptance or rejection of a characteristic or sample. The structure also includes an inspection points control indicator that determines the number of inspection points that are created for an inspection lot, an inspection point type, as well as a usage control indicator that ensures a particular sampling procedure is not referenced in a task list. Inspection point types include without inspection points, free inspection points, plant maintenance and sample management. The sampling procedure structure also includes a control chart type that governs the characteristics for which a particular control chart can be used, the variables referenced in the chart and the algorithm used to calculate the chart's control limits. Other control indicators in the sampling procedure are the no stage change control indicator that prevents the use of the dynamic modification procedure to determine the inspection scope or sample size and the multiple samples control indicator for independent or dependent multiple samples.

Q-189:   A. The sampling plan table is defined on the basis of the inspection lot quantity and an inspection severity excluding the actual quality level

When it's not possible to inspect each item produced by a production process, a sample inspection is used to evaluate the quality of the items in an inspection lot. The sample is picked at random from the lot and, on the basis of the information yielded by the sample, a decision is made regarding the disposition of the lot...namely, the lot is accepted or rejected for its intended use. A sampling procedure can be used to select the entities of the sample, which are subsequently evaluated according to an inspection plan. Instructions for drawing the sample, such as the sample's size and the number of samples to be taken, are documented in a sample drawing procedure that's assigned to the inspection plan. The sampling type, which is defined in the sampling procedure, specifies the method to be used to calculate the sample size. For example, the sampling type may require that a sample size be equal the lot size...namely, 100 percent inspection, a fixed sample size or a size determined by a sampling scheme. If the sampling type requires the use of a sampling scheme that's assigned to the sampling procedure, it will consist of individual sampling tables, each of which includes two or more sampling plans that determine a sample size based on the lot size, inspection severity, inspection severity and acceptable quality level, AQL, or the number of containers in an inspection lot. The quality level and the dynamic modification rule control the inspection severity, which determines the sampling plan in the sampling scheme. The inspection severity is used to adjust the probability of acceptance of an inspection lot, as well as the effort employed to inspect a material. The valuation parameter for which the sampling scheme is created determines the structure of the sampling plan. For instance, the structure of a sampling plan created for an attributive inspection valuation mode will consist of a sample size, acceptance number c, or the maximum number of nonconforming units in a sample that is accepted and a rejection number d, or the least number of nonconforming units in a sample that is rejected. In turn, a sampling plan for a variable inspection will consist of a sample size and k-factor, or acceptability constant that defines the minimum quality score that leads to the acceptance of a sample following a quality inspection. A sampling plan with no valuation parameters will consist only of a sample size.

Q-190: A. Control chart type

Sampling procedures, sampling schemes and dynamic modification rules are the basic data needed to create the samples used in the inspection process. In particular, a sampling procedure determines how a sample size is calculated, how inspection characteristics are valuated and if a sample size is dynamically modified. The structure of a sampling procedure includes a sampling type, which specifies how a sample size is calculated, and a valuation

338

mode that includes a valuation rule that governs the acceptance or rejection of a characteristic or sample. The structure also includes an inspection points control indicator that determines the number of inspection points that are created for an inspection lot, an inspection point type, as well as a usage control indicator that ensures a particular sampling procedure is not referenced in a task list. The sampling procedure structure also includes a control chart type that governs the characteristics for which a particular control chart can be used, the variables referenced in the chart and the algorithm used to calculate the chart's control limits. Other control indicators in the sampling procedure are the no stage change control indicator that prevents the use of the dynamic modification procedure to determine the inspection scope or sample size and the multiple samples control indicator for independent or dependent multiple samples.

Q-191:   B. Free inspection points and C. Inspection points for sample management

Sampling procedures, sampling schemes and dynamic modification rules are the basic data needed to create the samples used in the inspection process. In particular, a sampling procedure determines how a sample size is calculated, how inspection characteristics are valuated and if a sample size is dynamically modified. The structure of a sampling procedure includes a sampling type, which specifies how a sample size is calculated, and a valuation mode that includes a valuation rule that governs the acceptance or rejection of a characteristic or sample. The structure also includes an inspection points control indicator that determines the number of inspection points

that are created for an inspection lot, an inspection point type, as well as a usage control indicator that ensures a particular sampling procedure is not referenced in a task list. Inspection point types include without inspection points, free inspection points, plant maintenance and sample management. The sampling procedure structure also includes a control chart type that governs the characteristics for which a particular control chart can be used, the variables referenced in the chart and the algorithm used to calculate the chart's control limits. Other control indicators in the sampling procedure are the no stage change control indicator that prevents the use of the dynamic modification procedure to determine the inspection scope or sample size and the multiple samples control indicator for independent or dependent multiple samples.

Q-192: A. A collection of sampling plans and D. Specification that enables the determination of a sample size on the basis of inspection lot size, inspection severity or combination of inspection severity and the actual quality level

When it's not possible to inspect each item produced by a production process, a sample inspection is used to evaluate the quality of the items in an inspection lot. The sample is picked at random from the lot and, on the basis of the information yielded by the sample, a decision is made regarding the disposition of the lot...namely, the lot is accepted or rejected for its intended use. A sampling procedure can be used to select the entities of the sample, which are subsequently evaluated according to an inspection plan. Instructions for drawing the sample, such as the sample's size and the number of samples to be taken, are documented in a sample drawing procedure that's assigned to the inspection plan. The sampling type, which is defined in the sampling procedure, specifies the method to be used to calculate the sample size. For example, the sampling type may require that a sample size be equal the lot size…namely, 100 percent inspection, a fixed sample size or a size determined by a sampling scheme. If the sampling type requires the use of a sampling scheme that's assigned to the sampling procedure, it will consist of individual sampling tables, each of which includes two or more sampling plans that determine a sample size based on the lot size, inspection severity, inspection severity and acceptable quality level, AQL, or the number of containers in an inspection lot. The quality level and the dynamic modification rule control the inspection severity, which determines the sampling plan in the sampling scheme. The inspection severity is used to adjust the probability of acceptance of an inspection lot, as well as the effort employed to inspect a material. The valuation parameter for which the sampling scheme is created determines the structure of the sampling plan. For instance, the structure of a sampling plan created for an attributive inspection valuation mode will consist of a sample size, acceptance number c, or the maximum number of nonconforming units in a sample that is accepted and a rejection number d, or the least number of nonconforming units in a sample that is rejected. In turn, a sampling plan for a variable inspection will consist of a sample size and k-factor, or acceptability constant that defines the minimum quality score that leads to the acceptance of a sample following a quality inspection. A sampling plan with no valuation parameters will consist only of a sample size.

Q-193:   A. Special control indicator in sampling procedure

Sampling procedures, sampling schemes and dynamic modification rules are the basic data needed to create the samples used in the inspection process. In particular, a sampling procedure determines how a sample size is calculated, how inspection characteristics are valuated and if a sample size is dynamically modified. The structure of a sampling procedure includes a sampling type, which specifies how a sample size is calculated, and a valuation mode that includes a valuation rule that governs the acceptance or rejection of a characteristic or sample. The structure also includes an inspection points control indicator that determines the number of inspection points that are created for an inspection lot, an inspection point type, as well as a usage control indicator that ensures a particular sampling procedure is not referenced in a task list. The sampling procedure structure also includes a control chart type that governs the characteristics for which a particular control chart can be used, the variables referenced in the chart and the algorithm used to calculate the chart's control limits. Other control indicators in the sampling procedure are the no stage change control indicator that prevents the use of the dynamic modification procedure to determine the inspection scope or sample size and the multiple samples control indicator for independent or dependent multiple samples.

Q-194:   A. Without inspection points

Sampling procedures, sampling schemes and dynamic modification rules are the basic data needed to create the samples used in the inspection process. In particular, a

sampling procedure determines how a sample size is calculated, how inspection characteristics are valuated and if a sample size is dynamically modified. The structure of a sampling procedure includes a sampling type, which specifies how a sample size is calculated, and a valuation mode that includes a valuation rule that governs the acceptance or rejection of a characteristic or sample. . The sampling procedure structure also includes a control chart type that governs the characteristics for which a particular control chart can be used, the variables referenced in the chart and the algorithm used to calculate the chart's control limits. Other control indicators in the sampling procedure are the no stage change control indicator that prevents the use of the dynamic modification procedure to determine the inspection scope or sample size and the multiple samples control indicator for independent or dependent multiple samples. The structure also includes a usage control indicator that ensures a particular sampling procedure is not referenced in a task list and an inspection points control indicator that determines the number of inspection points that are created for an inspection lot and an inspection point type. Valid inspection point types include without inspection points, free inspection points, plant maintenance and sample management. The inspection point types "without inspection points", "free inspection points" and "inspection points for sample management" are used with an inspection plan. In turn, "free inspection points" and "inspection points for sample management" are used with a routing and the "free inspection points" and "inspection points for sample management" inspection point types are used for a master recipe. In turn, for a maintenance task list, the "inspection points for plant maintenance" inspection point type is used.

Q-195:   A. Determine a sample size on the basis of a lot size and inspection severity and C. Determine the number of physical samples per the number of containers in an inspection lot

When it's not possible to inspect each item produced by a production process, a sample inspection is used to evaluate the quality of the items in an inspection lot. The sample is picked at random from the lot and, on the basis of the information yielded by the sample, a decision is made regarding the disposition of the lot...namely, the lot is accepted or rejected for its intended use. A sampling procedure can be used to select the entities of the sample, which are subsequently evaluated according to an inspection plan. Instructions for drawing the sample, such as the sample's size and the number of samples to be taken, are documented in a sample drawing procedure that's assigned to the inspection plan. The sampling type, which is defined in the sampling procedure, specifies the method to be used to calculate the sample size. For example, the sampling type may require that a sample size be equal the lot size...namely, 100 percent inspection, a fixed sample size or a size determined by a sampling scheme. If the sampling type requires the use of a sampling scheme that's assigned to the sampling procedure, it will consist of individual sampling tables, each of which includes two or more sampling plans that determine a sample size based on the lot size, inspection severity, inspection severity and acceptable quality level, AQL, or the number of containers in an inspection lot. The quality level and the dynamic modification rule control the inspection severity, which determines the sampling plan in the sampling scheme. The inspection severity is used to adjust the probability of

acceptance of an inspection lot, as well as the effort employed to inspect a material. The valuation parameter for which the sampling scheme is created determines the structure of the sampling plan. For instance, the structure of a sampling plan created for an attributive inspection valuation mode will consist of a sample size, acceptance number c, or the maximum number of nonconforming units in a sample that is accepted and a rejection number d, or the least number of nonconforming units in a sample that is rejected. In turn, a sampling plan for a variable inspection will consist of a sample size and k-factor, or acceptability constant that defines the minimum quality score that leads to the acceptance of a sample following a quality inspection. A sampling plan with no valuation parameters will consist only of a sample size.

Q-196:   A. Sample size

When it's not possible to inspect each item produced by a production process, a sample inspection is used to evaluate the quality of the items in an inspection lot. The sample is picked at random from the lot and, on the basis of the information yielded by the sample, a decision is made regarding the disposition of the lot…namely, the lot is accepted or rejected for its intended use. A sampling procedure can be used to select the entities of the sample, which are subsequently evaluated according to an inspection plan. Instructions for drawing the sample, such as the sample's size and the number of samples to be taken, are documented in a sample drawing procedure that's assigned to the inspection plan. The sampling type, which is defined in the sampling procedure, specifies the method to be used to calculate the sample size. For example, the sampling type may require that a sample size be equal the lot size…namely, 100 percent inspection, a fixed sample size or a size determined by a sampling scheme. If the sampling type requires the use of a sampling scheme that's assigned to the sampling procedure, it will consist of individual sampling tables, each of which includes two or more sampling plans that determine a sample size based on the lot size, inspection severity, inspection severity and acceptable quality level, AQL, or the number of containers in an inspection lot. The quality level and the dynamic modification rule control the inspection severity, which determines the sampling plan in the sampling scheme. The inspection severity is used to adjust the probability of acceptance of an inspection lot, as well as the effort employed to inspect a material. The valuation parameter for which the sampling scheme is created determines the structure of the sampling plan. For instance, the structure of a sampling plan created for an attributive inspection valuation mode will consist of a sample size, acceptance number c, or the maximum number of nonconforming units in a sample that is accepted and a rejection number d, or the least number of nonconforming units in a sample that is rejected. In turn, a sampling plan for a variable inspection will consist of a sample size k-factor, or acceptability constant that defines the minimum quality score that leads to the acceptance of a sample following a quality inspection. A sampling plan with no valuation parameters will consist only of a sample size.

Q-197:   B. Dependent multiple samples

Sampling procedures, sampling schemes and dynamic modification rules are the basic data needed to create the

samples used in the inspection process. In particular, a sampling procedure determines how a sample size is calculated, how inspection characteristics are valuated and if a sample size is dynamically modified. The structure of a sampling procedure includes a sampling type, which specifies how a sample size is calculated, and a valuation mode that includes a valuation rule that governs the acceptance or rejection of a characteristic or sample. The structure also includes an inspection points control indicator that determines the number of inspection points that are created for an inspection lot, an inspection point type, as well as a usage control indicator that ensures a particular sampling procedure is not referenced in a task list. The sampling procedure structure also includes a control chart type that governs the characteristics for which a particular control chart can be used, the variables referenced in the chart and the algorithm used to calculate the chart's control limits. Other control indicators in the sampling procedure are the no stage change control indicator that prevents the use of the dynamic modification procedure to determine the inspection scope or sample size and the multiple samples control indicator for independent or dependent multiple samples. The processing of double sampling inspections and multiple sampling inspections is enabled by the dependent multiple samples function control indicator that's set in the sampling procedure. A valuation rule, which is defined for the function is defined for the valuation mode in the sampling procedure, valuates a characteristic after the dependent multiple samples are valuated. The use of dependent multiple samples requires a sampling type with a sampling scheme, the attributive inspection valuation mode and the definition of a function

347

module for valuating dependent multiple samples in the dependent multiples samples valuation rule.

Q-198:   A. Variable inspection according to s-method and D. Attributive inspection on the basis of nonconforming units

When it's not possible to inspect each item produced by a production process, a sample inspection is used to evaluate the quality of the items in an inspection lot. The sample is picked at random from the lot and, on the basis of the information yielded by the sample, a decision is made regarding the disposition of the lot...namely, the lot is accepted or rejected for its intended use. A sampling procedure can be used to select the entities of the sample, which are subsequently evaluated according to an inspection plan. Instructions for drawing the sample, such as the sample's size and the number of samples to be taken, are documented in a sample drawing procedure that's assigned to the inspection plan. The sampling type, which is defined in the sampling procedure, specifies the method to be used to calculate the sample size. For example, the sampling type may require that a sample size be equal the lot size...namely, 100 percent inspection, a fixed sample size or a size determined by a sampling scheme. If the sampling type requires the use of a sampling scheme that's assigned to the sampling procedure, it will consist of individual sampling tables, each of which includes two or more sampling plans that determine a sample size based on the lot size, inspection severity, inspection severity and acceptable quality level, AQL, or the number of containers in an inspection lot. The quality level and the dynamic modification rule control the inspection severity, which determines the sampling plan in the sampling scheme. The inspection severity is used to adjust the probability of acceptance of an inspection lot, as well as the effort employed to inspect a material. The valuation parameter for which the sampling scheme is created determines the structure of the sampling plan. For instance, the structure of a sampling plan created for an attributive inspection valuation mode will consist of a sample size, acceptance number c, or the maximum number of nonconforming units in a sample that is accepted and a rejection number d, or the least number of nonconforming units in a sample that is rejected. In turn, a sampling plan for a variable inspection will consist of a sample size and k-factor, or acceptability constant that defines the minimum quality score that leads to the acceptance of a sample following a quality inspection. A sampling plan with no valuation parameters will consist only of a sample size.

Q-199: B. "100%" inspection control indicator is not set for the sampling procedure and C. The "no parameters" valuation mode is set for the sampling procedure

Sampling procedures, sampling schemes and dynamic modification rules are the basic data needed to create the samples used in the inspection process. In particular, a sampling procedure determines how a sample size is calculated, how inspection characteristics are valuated and if a sample size is dynamically modified. The structure of a sampling procedure includes a sampling type, which specifies how a sample size is calculated, and a valuation mode that includes a valuation rule that governs the acceptance or rejection of a characteristic or sample. The structure also includes an inspection points control indicator that determines the number of inspection points that are created for an inspection lot, an inspection point type, as well as a usage control indicator that ensures a particular sampling procedure is not referenced in a task list. The sampling procedure structure also includes a control chart type that governs the characteristics for which a particular control chart can be used, the variables referenced in the chart and the algorithm used to calculate the chart's control limits. Other control indicators in the sampling procedure are the no stage change control indicator that prevents the use of the dynamic modification procedure to determine the inspection scope or sample size and the multiple samples control indicator for independent or dependent multiple samples. The multiple samples control indicator in particular controls a customer's ability to valuate multiple individual samples prior to valuating a characteristic. In this case, the customer selects the independent multiple sampling control indicator and the valuation rule for independent multiple samples in the sampling procedure, and specifies the number of independent multiple samples to be valuated. Also required is that the 100% inspection control indicator is not set for the sampling procedure and the no parameters valuation mode is set for the sampling procedure.

Q-200:   B. Sampling scheme

When it's not possible to inspect each item produced by a production process, a sample inspection is used to evaluate the quality of the items in an inspection lot. The sample is picked at random from the lot and, on the basis of the information yielded by the sample, a decision is made regarding the disposition of the lot…namely, the lot is

accepted or rejected for its intended use. A sampling procedure can be used to select the entities of the sample, which are subsequently evaluated according to an inspection plan. Instructions for drawing the sample, such as the sample's size and the number of samples to be taken, are documented in a sample drawing procedure that's assigned to the inspection plan. The sampling type, which is defined in the sampling procedure, specifies the method to be used to calculate the sample size. For example, the sampling type may require that a sample size be equal the lot size...namely, 100 percent inspection, a fixed sample size or a size determined by a sampling scheme. If the sampling type requires the use of a sampling scheme that's assigned to the sampling procedure, it will consist of individual sampling tables, each of which includes two or more sampling plans that determine a sample size based on the lot size, inspection severity, inspection severity and acceptable quality level, AQL, or the number of containers in an inspection lot. The quality level and the dynamic modification rule control the inspection severity, which determines the sampling plan in the sampling scheme. The inspection severity is used to adjust the probability of acceptance of an inspection lot, as well as the effort employed to inspect a material. The valuation parameter for which the sampling scheme is created determines the structure of the sampling plan. For instance, the structure of a sampling plan created for an attributive inspection valuation mode will consist of a sample size, acceptance number c, or the maximum number of nonconforming units in a sample that is accepted and a rejection number d, or the least number of nonconforming units in a sample that is rejected. In turn, a sampling plan for a variable inspection will consist of a sample size and k-factor, or acceptability constant that defines the minimum quality score that leads to the acceptance of a sample following a quality inspection. A sampling plan with no valuation parameters will consist only of a sample size.

Q-201:   B. Sample size and k-factor

When it's not possible to inspect each item produced by a production process, a sample inspection is used to evaluate the quality of the items in an inspection lot. The sample is picked at random from the lot and, on the basis of the information yielded by the sample, a decision is made regarding the disposition of the lot...namely, the lot is accepted or rejected for its intended use. A sampling procedure can be used to select the entities of the sample, which are subsequently evaluated according to an inspection plan. Instructions for drawing the sample, such as the sample's size and the number of samples to be taken, are documented in a sample drawing procedure that's assigned to the inspection plan. The sampling type, which is defined in the sampling procedure, specifies the method to be used to calculate the sample size. For example, the sampling type may require that a sample size be equal the lot size...namely, 100 percent inspection, a fixed sample size or a size determined by a sampling scheme. If the sampling type requires the use of a sampling scheme that's assigned to the sampling procedure, it will consist of individual sampling tables, each of which includes two or more sampling plans that determine a sample size based on the lot size, inspection severity, inspection severity and acceptable quality level, AQL, or the number of containers in an inspection lot. The quality level and the dynamic modification rule control the inspection severity, which determines the sampling plan in the sampling scheme. The inspection severity is used to adjust the probability of acceptance of an inspection lot, as well as the effort employed to inspect a material. The valuation parameter for which the sampling scheme is created determines the structure of the sampling plan. For instance, the structure of a sampling plan created for an attributive inspection valuation mode will consist of a sample size, acceptance number c, or the maximum number of nonconforming units in a sample that is accepted and a rejection number d, or the least number of nonconforming units in a sample that is rejected. In turn, a sampling plan for a variable inspection will consist of a sample size and k-factor, or acceptability constant that defines the minimum quality score that leads to the acceptance of a sample following a quality inspection. A sampling plan with no valuation parameters consists only of a sample size.

354

www.ingramcontent.com/pod-product-compliance
Lightning Source LLC
Chambersburg PA
CBHW070932050326
40689CB00014B/3173